Framing in Discourse

Framing in Discourse

EDITED BY

DEBORAH TANNEN

Georgetown University

New York   Oxford
Oxford University Press
1993

Oxford University Press

Oxford   New York   Toronto
Delhi   Bombay   Calcutta   Madras   Karachi
Kuala Lumpur   Singapore   Hong Kong   Tokyo
Nairobi   Dar es Salaam   Cape Town
Melbourne   Auckland

and associated companies in
Berlin   Ibadan

Published by Oxford University Press, Inc.
200 Madison Avenue, New York, New York 10016

Library of Congress Cataloging-in-Publication Data
Framing in discourse / edited by Deborah Tannen.
p.   cm.
Includes bibliographical references.
ISBN 0-19-507995-7.
ISBN 0-19-507996-5 (pbk.)
1. Discourse analysis.   2. Speech acts (Linguistics)
I. Tannen, Deborah.
P302.F72   1993
401'.41—dc20   92-25052

2 4 6 8 9 7 5 3 1

Printed in the United States of America
on acid-free paper

To David Wise

Acknowledgment

The work of editing these chapters, writing the introduction, and preparing the manuscript for press was done while I was in residence at the Institute for Advanced Study in Princeton, New Jersey. Work on the copy-edited manuscript, galleys, and page proofs was done while I was a fellow at the Center for Advanced Study in the Behavioral Sciences in Stanford, California. The support of these two scholarly paradises, back to back, is a surfeit of academic blessings for which I will always be grateful. I am also grateful for financial support provided through CASBS by the National Science Foundation SES-9022192.

Contents

2. *Interactive Frames and Knowledge Schemas in Interaction:*
   Examples from a Medical Examination/Interview   57
   Deborah Tannen and Cynthia Wallat

7. *"Samuel?" "Yes, Dear?":*
Teasing and Conversational Rapport   210

Carolyn A. Straehle

8. *"Speaking for Another" in Sociolinguistic Interviews:*
Alignments, Identities, and Frames   231

Deborah Schiffrin

Framing in Discourse

Introduction

DEBORAH TANNEN

Ever since its introduction by Gregory Bateson in "A Theory of Play and Fantasy" ([1954] 1972), the concept of framing has influenced thinking about language in interaction. Bateson demonstrated that no communicative move, verbal or nonverbal, could be understood without reference to a metacommunicative message, or metamessage, about what is going on— that is, what frame of interpretation applies to the move. Observing monkeys playing, he noted that it was only by reference to the metamessage "This is play" that a monkey could understand a hostile move from another monkey as not intended to convey the hostility that it obviously denotes. In other words, metamessages "framed" the hostile moves as play.

Bateson's work was taken up most directly by researchers in communication and psychology, especially those in systems or family therapy (for example, Watzlawick, Beavin, and Jackson 1967). It received some attention from anthropologists as well (see especially Frake 1977). Within sociology, the most important and comprehensive treatment of framing came in Erving Goffman's *Frame Analysis* (1974), which provides a complex and subtly nuanced system of terms, concepts, and examples to elucidate the numerous levels and types of framing that constitute everyday interaction.

Although the influence of Bateson's and Goffman's work has been pervasive, there have been few studies directly applying Bateson's seminal theory or Goffman's elaborate framework in microanalytic linguistic analysis of real discourse produced in face-to-face interaction. In his later work, *Forms of Talk* (1981), Goffman's attention to multiple layers of framing in everyday life focused more and more specifically on the use of language, and Goffman became increasingly interested in the work of linguistic discourse analysis. In the chapter entitled "Footing" he observes that "linguistics provides us with the cues and markers through which such footings become manifest, helping us to find our way to a structural basis for analyzing them"[1] (p. 157). Until now, however, linguists have been slow to justify

I would like to thank Neal Norrick and Deborah Schiffrin for comments on a draft of this introduction. I am grateful to Clifford Geertz and the Institute for Advanced Study in Princeton, New Jersey, for the ideal environment in which to write this introduction.

Goffman's faith in our ability to make framing manifest. I believe that this collection begins to do so.

At the same time that discourse analysis can provide insight into the linguistic means by which frames are created in interaction, the concept of framing provides a fruitful theoretical foundation for the discourse analysis of interaction. In fact, frames theory already lies at the heart of the most comprehensive and coherent theoretical paradigm in interactional socio-linguistics: Gumperz's (1982) theory of conversational inference. Gumperz shows that conversational inference, a process requisite for conversational involvement, is made possible by contextualization cues that signal the speech activity in which participants perceive themselves to be engaged. Gumperz's notion of speech activity is thus a type of frame. Indeed, it is in the work of Gumperz and those influenced by him that one finds the greatest justification for Goffman's belief in the ability of linguistics to elucidate the structural basis for framing. With the possible partial exception of the final chapter by Schiffrin, the articles in this volume derive directly from this research tradition, by way of my training as a student of Gumperz at the University of California, Berkeley. Schiffrin is a more direct descendent of Goffman, with whom she studied at the University of Pennsylvania, though her work also shows the influence of William Labov, as mine also shows the influence of Robin Lakoff and Wallace Chafe.

Genesis of the Volume

Every now and then there is a flowering of intellect and spirit among doctoral students in a graduate program: a critical number of exceptional students appear at a time when the field is experiencing an explosion of interest in a particular subfield, and the department includes faculty members who are full of fire with that excitement. The students and faculty inspire and enlighten each other. This occurred in the graduate program in socio-linguistics at Georgetown University in the mid-80s, when the field of linguistics was experiencing a rise of interest in discourse analysis. The unique placement of Georgetown's Department of Linguistics in relation to the growing field of discourse analysis was the result of two happily coinciding phenomena: the unusual existence of two faculty members working actively in different areas of the same field (Deborah Schiffrin and I)[2] and the opportunity given us to direct meetings that brought leading discourse analysts to the Georgetown University campus. In 1981 I organized the Georgetown University Round Table on Languages and Linguistics "Analyzing Discourse: Text and Talk" (see Tannen 1982 for a collection of the papers delivered at that meeting). Three years later, Deborah Schiffrin organized the 1984 GURT "Meaning, Form, and Use in Context: Linguistic Applications" (see Schiffrin 1984 for papers). The year after that, I directed the 1985 Linguistic Institute "Linguistics and Language in Context: The Interdependence of Theory, Data, and Application" (see Tannen and Alatis 1986, Tannen 1988 for papers from that meeting).

In the fall of 1985, immediately following the Linguistic Institute, I taught a graduate seminar on frame analysis. As a direct outgrowth of that seminar, several of the participants wrote dissertations applying frame analysis to discourse produced in a range of contexts. As the dissertations emerged and were uniformly excellent, I realized that the class members were doing, at last, what Goffman had believed it would be the mission of linguists to do. It was then that I conceived the idea for this volume. Frances Smith and Suwako Watanabe were regular members of the seminar who began their dissertations after the seminar ended. Branca Ribeiro, who was already writing her dissertation at the time, was an auditor. The three chapters by these authors are based on their dissertations, which I directed. Although she did not attend the seminar, Susan Hoyle was a member of the same exceptional group of graduate students. Her chapter is condensed from her dissertation, which was directed by Deborah Schiffrin, whose own work is represented here as well. Schiffrin served as reader on the Ribeiro, Watanabe, and Smith dissertations, and I served as reader on Hoyle's. The chapter by Carolyn Straehle was written at a later time, revised from an independent study that had begun as an outstanding paper written for my graduate course in the discourse analysis of conversation.

This volume, then, reflects the recent burgeoning of work and interest in discourse analysis within linguistics. Together, the chapters demonstrate the importance of framing as a theoretical foundation and methodological approach in the discourse analysis of interaction. They also provide insight into discourse types that have not previously been studied by linguists. All the chapters combine to demonstrate how theories of framing can be translated into nuts-and-bolts discourse analysis. Each makes both theoretical and empirical contributions, enriching our understanding of framing at the same time that it shows how analysis of framing adds to our understanding of conversational interaction.

Overview of Chapters

The volume begins with two of my own articles that lay a theoretical groundwork for the analysis of framing in discourse. Although these chapters have been previously published, they appeared in places not normally seen by linguists: the first in a volume edited by Roy Freedle for his psychologically oriented Discourse Processing series, the second in a special issue of the *Social Psychology Quarterly* edited by sociologist Douglas Maynard. The chapters that follow were all written expressly for this volume, each applying aspects of frames theory to a unique interactional context.

Chapter 1, "What's in a Frame? Surface Evidence for Underlying Expectations," provides a general introduction to research on framing. It begins with a theoretical overview of how the term "frame" and related terms such as "script" and "schema" developed and have been used in a range of disciplines to refer to what I define as "structures of expectation." The disciplines surveyed are linguistics, cognitive psychology, artificial intelligence, social psychology, sociology, and anthropology. I have not attempted to bring the literature review up to date, because it was not intended as a literature review per se but rather as a review of terms and concepts; as it stands, it still fulfills the purpose of introducing the concept of framing, the various terms that have been used to denote the concept, and the ways in which those terms and concepts have been employed in a range of disciplines. The chapter then reports the results of research examining linguistic evidence for the existence of frames underlying narrative performance in a corpus of stories told by Americans and Greeks about a film (which has become known as "the pear film"). First I discuss the levels at which frames operate; then I illustrate sixteen types of linguistic evidence for the presence and character of cognitive frames.

The type of "frames" that are the subject of analysis in Chapter 1 are what I later came to call "schemas": "structures of expectation" associated with situations, objects, people, and so on. Goffman (1981:67) noted that this paper concerns types of framing quite different from the sense in which he and Bateson used the term. Chapter 2, and the remainder of the book, focus primarily on the type of frame that Goffman analyzed: the "alignments" that people "take up to" each other in face-to-face interaction.

Chapter 2, "Interactive Frames and Knowledge Schemas in Interaction: Examples from a Medical Examination/Interview," by me and Cynthia Wallat, suggests a model for integrating these two senses of framing in a single analytic framework. "Knowledge schemas" are the type of framing device discussed in Chapter 1; "interactive frames" are frames in Bateson's and Goffman's sense, that is, what people think they are *doing* when they talk to each other (i.e., are they joking, lecturing, or arguing? Is this a fight or is it play?). The interaction of these two types of frames is illustrated by analysis of a videotaped encounter in which a pediatrician examines a cerebral palsied child in the presence of the child's mother. We show that the frames/schema model allows us to elucidate the complexity of the pediatrician's verbal behavior in the interaction.

In the episode analyzed, the pediatrician balances several competing and conflicting *interactive frames:* within an "examination frame," she conducts a standard pediatric examination according to a prescribed routine; within a "consultation frame," she answers the mother's questions about the child's condition, at times examining the child to discover the answer to the mother's questions; and within a "reporting frame," she announces the findings of the pediatric examination aloud for the residents who may later view the videotape being made. At times, the demands of these frames conflict. For example, the mother's questions in the consultation frame require the doctor to interrupt her examination and put the child "on hold," making her potentially more restless and consequently making the examination more difficult.

At the same time, there are conflicts between the doctor's and the mother's *knowledge schemas*—that is, their expectations about health in general and cerebral palsy in particular. For example, the mother and doctor differ in their interpretations of the child's noisy breathing. Associating "noisy breathing" with "wheezing," the mother fears that the child is having respiratory difficulty. The doctor, in contrast, associates the noisy breathing with cerebral palsy, i.e., as an expected and harmless result of poor muscular control. A conflict in schemas often triggers a shift in frames. Thus, the mother's concern with the child's noisy breathing leads her to interrupt the doctor's examination to exclaim, "That's it! That's how it sounds when she sleeps!" The doctor must then shift from the examination frame to the consulting frame to reassure the mother that the child's noisy breathing is not a sign of danger.

In Chapter 3, "Framing in Psychotic Discourse," Branca Telles Ribeiro uses the frames/schema model to analyze the discourse of a Brazilian woman, Dona Jurema, being interviewed by a psychiatrist, Dr. Edna, at a psychiatric hospital in Rio de Janeiro. On the basis of this interview, Dr. Edna diagnosed Dona Jurema as being in the midst of a psychotic crisis and admitted her to the hospital. Ribeiro demonstrates that frame analysis elucidates the coherence in Dona Jurema's psychotic discourse. There are two frames operating in the interaction: the interview frame, in which Dr. Edna asks the patient questions, and the psychotic crisis frame, in which the patient fails to answer the psychiatrist's questions, speaking instead *to* people who are not present and *as* people who are not present—even, in some cases, not alive—or as herself at a different age or in a different context. Dona Jurema jumps from topic to topic, chants and sings, and assumes different voices and different footings. Ribeiro shows, however, that everything she utters in the frame of her psychotic episode is perfectly coherent within the scenario created—for example, Dona Jurema as a child speaking to her mother, grandmother, or sister. Ribeiro also examines a lower level of framing and its relation to the higher level: the types of moves performed in Dona Jurema's discourse that make up the various interactive frames. Furthermore, she shows that Dona Jurema makes accurate use of knowledge schemas pertinent to each frame, such as the injunction against making noise in a hospital. Ribeiro's study is exemplary of the power of frames theory to illuminate an otherwise seemingly incoherent discourse type. It is also a ground-breaking analysis of psychotic discourse.

In Chapter 4, "Participation Frameworks in Sportscasting Play: Imaginary and Literal Footings," Susan M. Hoyle analyzes discourse produced by her son and his friends while they played dyadic indoor games, such as video basketball and Ping-Pong, and simultaneously reported on the games they were playing by speaking in the role of sportscaster. The primary basis for Hoyle's analysis is spontaneous sportscasting, which the boys initiated on their own, aware that they were being taped but unaware of which aspect of their talk would be the object of interest. In a second part of the study, the boys staged a more elaborate, multivoiced performance, in which they took the roles not only of sportscaster but also of half-time interviewer and interviewee for a hypothetical television audience. These more elaborate instances of sportscasting play were performed in response to Hoyle's specific request that the boys "do sportscasting" for her to tape.

Hoyle integrates the concepts of framing and participation structure to show that the boys balance multiple participation frameworks in their sportscasting play. For example, the "outermost frame" of "play" or "fulfilling a request to do sportscasting" is a rim around the embedded frame of "doing sportscasting." In their spontaneous play, the boys shift between speaking as sportscasters commenting on their play and speaking as themselves, for example, to resolve procedural disputes and manage the game. In the elicited sportscasting, they never speak as themselves, but shift among nonliteral frameworks, for example, to move from announcing the action to acting out a half-time interview with a player. Hoyle demonstrates that the analysis of interaction from the point of view of framing leads to "a greater appreciation of children's discourse abilities" at the same time that analysis of children's framing of their play adds to our understanding of the human capacity to manipulate frames in interaction.

Chapter 5, Frances Lee Smith's "The Pulpit and Woman's Place: Gender and the Framing of the 'Exegetical Self' in Sermon Performances," examines the sermons delivered by students in a preaching lab at a Baptist seminary. Focusing her analysis on the "text exegeter" portions of the sermons—that is, the portion in which the preacher explains, or exegetes, a fixed sacred text, Smith finds that the male and female student preachers she taped tended to take different footings in framing their sermon performances and consequently in presenting themselves as exegeters. Referring not only to Goffman's "footing," as the other contributors do, but also to his concept of the "textual self" as described in his essay "The Lecture" (1981), Smith begins by profiling four discernible "exegetical authority" footings, each projecting a distinct textual self. She finds that the men tended to foreground "their textual-self authority both by putting themselves on record as exegeters of the text and by calling attention to the current participation framework in the exegetical task more often than did the women." In contrast, the women use a variety of framing strategies to downplay their personal authority as text exegeters. For example, one woman referred to the text itself as the source of authority, another framed her sermon as a children's story, and another took the footing of a "low-profile" exegeter.

Smith's contribution is significant for the gender and language topic area, as it shows that the level at which women and men differ is not so much (or not so significantly) the matter of lexical or syntactic choice but the far more complex level of footing, that is, the alignment they take up to the material about which they are speaking and the audience to whom they are addressing their discourse. Smith's analysis is particularly significant in providing an innovative and potentially ground-breaking approach to gender differences. Rather than designing her study as a direct comparison of male and female styles, she focuses her analysis on the footings assumed by the student preachers, the selves projected by these footings, and the linguistic means by which they were created. She begins by developing the categories within which the various footings could be grouped and only then asks where the women and men tend to fall, concluding that women make more use of the linguistic devices that constitute two of the footings. In addition, Smith's chapter makes a significant contribution to the fields of language and religion in general and the language of sermon performance in particular.

In Chapter 6, "Cultural Differences in Framing: American and Japanese Group Discussions," Suwako Watanabe applies frame analysis to issues in cross-cultural communication. Specifically, she addresses the question of why Japanese students in American classrooms find it difficult to participate in small group discussions, a speech activity favored by many American teachers. By comparing American and Japanese small group discussions on similar topics, Watanabe identifies two types of framing: (1) bracketing (delineating the event at its beginning and end), and (2) specific conversational moves such as requesting or joking. Examining the strategies by which participants open and close discussion, present reasons, and structure arguments, she finds that the Japanese students use strategies that grow out of two patterns characteristic of Japanese communication: nonreciprocal language use and avoidance of confrontation. The Americans perceived the group as four individuals bound only by an activity, whereas the Japanese perceived themselves as group members united in a hierarchy. Consequently, the Japanese speakers avoided confrontation by putting forth conclusions that were "inclusive, allowing both supportive and contradictory accounts at the same time." In contrast, the Americans' conclusions were exclusive, leading therefore to some confrontation when individuals' accounts differed.

Watanabe links the level of conversational moves to higher levels of framing. For example, the Japanese gave reasons in the frame of storytelling, whereas the Americans gave reasons in the frame of reporting. Furthermore, in beginning and ending the discussions, the Japanese reflected the hierarchical structure of the group. This observation has interesting implications for the issue of gender. In the Japanese discussion groups, the first to speak was always a woman. Whereas Americans would likely see the first-to-speak position as relatively dominant, Watanabe suggests that in the Japanese framework, speaking is face-threatening to the speaker, so women take this potentially compromising position because they have less face to lose.[3] This chapter, then, demonstrates the usefulness of frames theory for illuminating cross-cultural communication and small group interaction. It also adds to our understanding of differences in Japanese and American discourse strategies.

In Chapter 7, "'Samuel?' 'Yes, Dear?': Teasing and Conversational Rapport," Carolyn A. Straehle examines a particular conversational move, teasing, in a naturally occurring casual conversation among three friends: Samuel, Diana, and the author herself. Straehle aptly observes that teasing is a linguistic analogue to Bateson's playful nip: a move whose obviously hostile meaning is reversed by the frame of play (but is in danger of being perceived as a literally hostile bite). Examining the role of teasing in the relationships among the three participants, she finds, for example, that whereas teasing is pervasive in the interaction, not all participants engage in it equally. Samuel and Diana tease each other incessantly as part of their flirtation and display of mutual affection (they were newly paired), but there is no teasing between Samuel and Carolyn, who is Diana's best friend.

In addition to examining the role of teasing in negotiating relationships, Straehle examines four linguistic cues that frame utterances as teasing: prosody (for example, a high-pitched, whiny voice), laughter (accompanying or immediately following an utterance to signal benign and playful intent), pronouns (a present party is referred to in the third person, as "she," or two parties use the pronoun "we" to exclude a third), and routinized formulae (such as the fixed interchange that provides the chapter's title). Moreover, many of the formats by which Samuel (and, less often, Carolyn) tease Diana are posited on framing her as a child. Teasing is a much noted and little analyzed conversational strategy; Straehle's analysis of its linguistic and interactional components is therefore a significant contribution to an understanding of the act of teasing, as well as to our understanding of framing in conversational interaction.

Chapter 8, Deborah Schiffrin's "'Speaking for Another' in Sociolinguistic Interviews: Alignments, Identities, and Frames," is similar to Straehle's in its focus on a particular interactional move within the context of an interaction in which the author was a participant. Schiffrin analyzes discourse that took place during a sociolinguistic interview she conducted with three members of a lower middle class Jewish community in Philadelphia: a married couple called Zelda and Henry and their neighbor and friend Irene. Schiffrin shows that the previously undescribed conversational move "speaking for another"—that is, voicing something about someone else, in that person's presence, which only that person is in a position to know—accomplishes a frame shift by realigning participants. Just as Straehle shows that conversational participants align themselves to each other and create their relationship by teasing, Schiffrin shows that by speaking for someone else who is present and by allowing oneself to be spoken for, the participants in this conversational interview negotiate their relationships to each other as well as their gender identities. Thus, global or macro level relationships are created as well as evidenced by local or micro level moves that align, or frame, participants in relation to each other.

In Schiffrin's analysis, Henry and Zelda both speak for Irene, their neighbor and friend, who is significantly younger than they, but they frame themselves differently in doing so. Zelda's realignments are supportive and integrative: by speaking for her, she protects Irene from Henry's potential criticism. Henry's realignments are judgmental, challenging, and divisive: they align him with the interviewer in opposition to Irene, negatively evaluate her behavior, and prompt her to reveal potentially compromising infor-mation, although he does, like Zelda, take a protective stance toward her.

Schiffrin goes on to examine types of framing found in the sociolinguistic interview and shows that the interview itself provides a frame for the realignments and identity displays she previously discussed. Although speaking for another occurs both within and outside the interview frame, it occurs only during question/answer exchanges. On the broadest level, by speaking for Irene, Zelda and Henry display and reinforce the closeness of their relationship with her and also transform the interview frame. Schiffrin's tripartite conclusion demonstrates that (1) sequential coherence in discourse results from the availability of a range of interpretive frames; (2) speaking for another is a ritualization of the submersion of the self in interaction which constitutes the interactive process itself; and (3) an understanding of how participants construct and shift gender identities and mutual alignments is crucial for the analysis of variation in sociolinguistic interviews.

Each chapter, then, applies aspects of frames theory to a unique interactional context to which frame analysis has not previously been applied. The volume thus demonstrates how frame analysis provides a framework for linguistic discourse analysis.

Organization of the Volume[4]

With the exception of the first chapter, which provides an introduction to frames theory, the chapters are arranged in descending order of the level of framing they primarily address. Chapters 2 through 4 use frame analysis to account for the nature of the events they examine. Chapter 2, by Tannen and Wallat, introduces a frames/schema model to elucidate the nature of the pediatrician's task in the examination/interview. Chapter 3, by Ribeiro, logically follows Tannen and Wallat both because it is concerned with a medical encounter and because it applies Tannen and Wallat's frames/schema model. More importantly, however, it uses frame analysis to characterize the nature of psychotic discourse. In Chapter 4, the study of boys' sportscasting play, the frame shifts that Hoyle describes actually give the event its character as sportscasting. Chapter 5, Smith's analysis of sermon performance, is liminal in terms of the level of framing it addresses. The concept of 'exegetical self' is an essential element of preaching but not in itself constitutive of it.

The remaining chapters link macro and micro levels of framing. The two types of framing identified by Watanabe in her study of American and Japanese discussion groups in Chapter 6 operate on the event and discourse levels, respectively. The first type, bracketing, by which participants open and close discussion, operates on the event level; conversational moves of the second type, such as presenting reasons and constructing arguments, operate on the local or discourse level. The last two chapters, by Straehle and

Schiffrin, focus on particular conversational moves within a larger event, and the role of these moves in the negotiation of relationships among participants. Thus they address framing at both more local and also more global levels than the other chapters. Within the casual conversation among friends that Straehle analyzes in Chapter 7, talk framed as teasing (a local level framing type) functions to establish a flirtatious intimacy between two speakers (framing at the global, relationship level). Analogously, Schiffrin shows in Chapter 8 that within the context of a diffuse sociolinguistic interview (an interview which in many ways resembles a casual conversation among acquaintances and friends), "speaking for another" frames Irene, the younger neighbor, as somewhat childlike in relation to Zelda and Henry. The book, therefore, builds toward an appreciation of the role of framing in the most significant and pervasive realm of human interaction: the negotiation of interpersonal relations and personal identity.

Notes

1. In fact, Goffman makes this remark in reference to the work that appears as Chapter 2 in this volume.

2. Geertz (1983:158–159), in an illuminating ethnography of American academic ways of thinking, notes the odd career path by which academics tend to be trained at one of a few centers and then be consigned for life to some outlying college or university. I would add that academic departments tend to hire one person in each field or subfield, setting each scholar in intellectual isolation in the home institution, driven to seek collegial interchange outside the university at professional meetings.

3. This hypothesis is reminiscent of Fishman's (1978) observation that women in casual conversations at home with their husbands do the grunt work of keeping the conversation going.

4. A note on transcription conventions is in order because of minor differences in conventions employed in each chapter. Since, with the exception of Schiffrin, all the authors use transcription conventions based on Tannen (1984), there is uniformity in the gross characteristics, but each author uses a few idiosyncratic conventions adapted to the needs of her own study. This may be irritating to a reader who reads the volume through from beginning to end. Yet I have refrained from making the conventions uniform, since that would entail forcibly altering all but one author's transcript excerpts to make them conform to a single system, probably my own. Aside from the hegemonic implications of such a move, I am keenly aware of how central my transcription system is to my own analysis. Recent research (for example, Ochs 1979, Preston 1982, 1985, Edwards 1990) makes abundantly clear that transcription systems are not neutral and interchangeable but rather represent interpretation in themselves. Readers' indulgence is asked, therefore, in the matter of small differences in conventions from one chapter to the next. To prevent confusion, each chapter is followed by its own key to transcription conventions used in that chapter.

References

Bateson, Gregory. 1954. A theory of play and fantasy. Steps to an ecology of mind, 177–93. New York: Ballantine.

Edwards, Jane. 1992. Transcription of discourse. Oxford International Encyclopedia of Linguistics 1:367–70. Oxford and New York: Oxford University Press.

Fishman, Pamela M. 1978. Interaction: The work women do. Social Problems 25:397–406.

Geertz, Clifford. 1983. Local knowledge: Further essays in interpretive anthropology. New York: Basic Books.

Goffman, Erving. 1974. Frame analysis. New York: Harper & Row.

Goffman, Erving. 1981. A reply to Denzin and Keller. Contemporary Sociology 10:60–68.

Goffman, Erving. 1981. Forms of talk. Philadelphia: University of Pennsylvania Press.

Gumperz, John J. 1982. Discourse strategies. Cambridge: Cambridge University Press.

Ochs, Elinor. 1979. Transcription as theory. Developmental pragmatics, ed. by Elinor Ochs and Bambi Schieffelin, 43–72. New York: Academic Press.

Preston, Dennis R. 1982. 'Ritin Fowklower Daun 'Rong: Folklorists' failures in phonology. Journal of American Folklore 95:304–26.

Preston, Dennis R. 1985. The Li'l Abner syndrome: Written representations of speech. American Speech 60:328–36.

Schiffrin, Deborah (ed.). 1984. Meaning, form and use in context: Linguistic applications. Georgetown University Round Table on Languages and Linguistics 1984. Washington, DC: Georgetown University Press.

Tannen, Deborah (ed.). 1982. Analyzing discourse: Text and talk. Georgetown University Round Table on Languages and Linguistics 1981. Washington, DC: Georgetown University Press.

Tannen, Deborah. 1984. Conversational style: Analyzing talk among friends. Norwood, NJ: Ablex.

Tannen, Deborah (ed.). 1988. Linguistics in context: Connecting observation and understanding. Lectures from the 1985 LSA/TESOL and NEH Institutes. Norwood, NJ: Ablex.

Tannen, Deborah, and James E. Alatis. 1986. Languages and linguistics: The interdependence of theory, data and application. Washington, DC: Georgetown University Press.

Watzlawick, Paul, Janet Helmick Beavin, and Don D. Jackson. 1967. The pragmatics of human communication. New York: Norton.

1

What's in a Frame?
Surface Evidence for
Underlying Expectations

DEBORAH TANNEN

Georgetown University

Introduction

I have been struck lately by the recurrence of a single theme in a wide variety of contexts: the power of expectation. For example, the self-fulfilling prophecy has been proven to operate in education as well as in individual psychology. I happened to leaf through a how-to-succeed book; its thesis was that the way to succeed is to expect to do so. Two months ago at a conference for teachers of English as a second language, the keynote speaker explained that effective reading is a process of anticipating what the author is going to say and expecting it as one reads. Moreover, there are general platitudes heard every day, as for example the observation that what is wrong with marriage today is that partners expect too much of each other and of marriage.

The emphasis on expectation seems to corroborate a nearly self-evident truth: in order to function in the world, people cannot treat each new person, object, or event as unique and separate. The only way we can make

Research for this study was supported in part by NIMH Grant 25592 to Wallace Chafe. In addition, I am grateful to the University of California, Berkeley, for a travel grant which contributed to the cost of my airfare to Greece, and to the staff and students of the Hellenic American Union in Athens. Cleo Helidonis conducted the interviews in Greek and transcribed them. I wish most of all to thank Wallace Chafe for his encouragement and guidance. In addition, I want to thank Louis Gomez for directing me to and talking to me about the relevant constructive memory research, and David Levy for doing the same with artificial intelligence research. This chapter originally appeared in *New Directions in Discourse Processing*, edited by Roy Freedle. Norwood, NJ: Ablex, 1979, pp. 137–181.

sense of the world is to see the connections between things, and between present things and things we have experienced before or heard about. These vital connections are learned as we grow up and live in a given culture. As soon as we measure a new perception against what we know of the world from prior experience, we are dealing with expectations.

The notion of expectations is at the root of a wave of theories and studies in a broad range of fields, including linguistics. It is this notion, I believe, which underlies talk about frames, scripts, and schemata in the fields of linguistics, artificial intelligence, cognitive psychology, social psychology, sociology, and anthropology at least (and I would not be surprised if similar terms were used in other disciplines I do not happen to know about). In this chapter I will illustrate a way of showing the effects of these "structures of expectation" on verbalization in the telling of oral narratives. Before I proceed, however, it will be useful to give a brief sketch of the various ways in which these terms have been used in the fields I have mentioned.

Because of the infinite confusion possible as a result of the great number of authors and contexts we will need to discuss, I will categorize the main theorists first according to the disciplines they work in, and then according to their choice of terms.

In the field of psychology we need to consider the work of Bartlett (1932), Rumelhart (1975), and Abelson (1975, 1976). Rumelhart is a cognitive psychologist and Abelson a social psychologist, but both have become increasingly associated with the field of artificial intelligence. In the latter field, Abelson works closely with Schank (Schank & Abelson 1975). The second major researcher in this field is Minsky (1974). Linguists we will consider are Chafe (1977a,b) and Fillmore (1975, 1976). In anthropology, Bateson (1972) (his work was originally published in 1955) and Frake (1977) must be noted, as well as Hymes (1974), who may more precisely be called an ethnographer of speaking (to use the term he himself coined). In sociology the theorist is Goffman (1974).

Let us now consider the above scholars in groups according to the terms they prefer to use. The term "schema" traces back to Bartlett (1932) in his pioneering book, *Remembering* (Bartlett himself borrows the term from Sir Henry Head). This term has been picked up by Chafe as well as Rumelhart, and by others, as for example Bobrow and Norman (1975), who are also in the field of artificial intelligence. The term "script" is associated with the work of Abelson and Schank. The term "frame" is associated most often with the anthropological/sociological orientation of Hymes, Goffman, and Frake, and with the artificial intelligence research of Minsky. Their use of the term stems from Bateson. "Frame" is also used by Fillmore, who notes that he came to it by a different route, that of the structuralist notion of syntagmatic frame.

To complicate matters further, a number of these writers use more than one term (Fillmore: scene-and-frame; Chafe: schema, frame, and categorization), or express dissatisfaction with the term they use (Bartlett writes that he would really prefer "active developing patterns" or "organized setting"; Fillmore says he would prefer "module").

To uncomplicate matters, however, all these complex terms and approaches amount to the simple concept of what R. N. Ross (1975) calls "structures of expectations," that is, that, on the basis of one's experience of the world in a given culture (or combination of cultures), one organizes knowledge about the world and uses this knowledge to predict interpretations and relationships regarding new information, events, and experiences. Bartlett (1932), the earliest of the theorists discussed here and the first psychologist to use the term "schema," in effect said it all: "The past operates as an organized mass rather than as a group of elements each of which retains its specific character" (p. 197).

Bartlett's concern, as his title indicates, is "Remembering"; he relies heavily on Head's notion of "schema" (quoting extensively from a book entitled *Studies in neurology*) (Head 1920) in order to support his theory that memory is constructive rather than consisting of the storage of all previously perceived stimuli. Bartlett contends that an individual "has an overmastering tendency simply to get a general impression of the whole; and, on the basis of this, he constructs the probable detail" (p. 206). One more aspect of Bartlett's work that is particularly significant, in his estimation as well as mine, is the "whole notion, that the organized mass results of past changes of position and posture are actively *doing* something all the time; are, so to speak, carried along with us, complete, though developing, from moment to moment" (p. 201). This is the aspect of schemata which he felt was lost in that term, and it is for this reason that he preferred the term "active, developing patterns." Bartlett's apprehensions about the term "schema" were obviously justified, for in most of his work, the notion of constant change has been lost. For example, Charniak (1975), an artificial intelligence (AI) investigator who follows Minsky, states, "I take a frame to be a static data structure about one stereotyped topic . . . " (p. 42).

Perhaps the most direct descendent of Bartlett is Chafe (who, although he does not specifically emphasize the dynamic nature of schemata, does not imply a necessarily static notion of them either, perhaps because as a linguist he is not so much subject to the computer metaphor). In fact, as Bartlett investigated the nature of memory by reading passages to groups of subjects and having them recall them at later intervals, so Chafe (1977a,b) has been studying the recall of events by showing a film to groups of subjects and having them retell what they saw at later intervals (in fact, these data are the basis of the present paper).

As a linguist, however, Chafe (1977a) is interested in verbalization. He posits the question: after witnessing or experiencing an event, "What kinds of processes must this person apply to convert his knowledge, predominantly nonverbal to begin with, into a verbal output?" (p. 41). The first element in this process, he hypothesizes, is the determination of a schema, which refers to the identification of the event; the second is the determination of a frame, which refers to the sentence-level expression about particular individuals and their roles in the event; finally, a category is chosen to name objects or actions which play parts in the event. For all these choices, one must "match the internal representation of particular events and individuals with internally represented prototypes" (p. 42).

Since we are encountering the term "prototype" here, it is as good a time as any to note that this is another currently popular term which is inextricably intertwined with the notion of expectations. As Fillmore (1975) notes, the "prototype idea can be seen in the color term studies of B. Berlin and P. Kay (1969) and in the 'natural category' researches of E. Rosch (1973)" (p. 123). Fillmore lists a number of other related concepts as well from a variety of disciplines. The prototype, like the frame, refers to an expectation about the world, based on prior experience, against which new experiences are measured and interpreted.

Returning to our discussion of the uses of the term "schema," we may note the work of Rumelhart (1975), who devises a schema for stories in the interest of developing an automatic "story parser" for artificial intelligence consumption. Rumelhart acknowledges his debt to Schank as well as Propp (1958).

To give one final example of how the notion of schemata has been used in AI, we refer to Bobrow and Norman (1975), who "propose that memory structures [in a computer] be comprised of a set of active schemata, each capable of evaluating information passed to it and capable of passing information and requests to other schemata" (p. 148). Their association of schemata with automatic processes seems to reflect faithfully the function of expectations: "Any time there is a mismatch between data and process or expectations and occurrences, conscious processes are brought in" (p. 148). This reflects, then, the way in which a person's perception of the world proceeds automatically so long as expectations are met, while s/he is stopped short, forced to question things, only when they are not.

Abelson's interest in scripts spans three fields: ideology, story understanding (that is, for the purpose of computer simulation), and social behavior (talk at UC Berkeley, March 1977). Abelson's broad interests render his work on scripts particularly interesting. He became interested in scripts, he explains, in connection with the predictability he discerned in Goldwater's belief system! Among the most interesting of the perspectives Abelson (1976) investigates are the relationships of scripts, attitudes, and behavior: "In our view, attitude toward an object consists in the ensemble of scripts concerning that object" (p. 16). He notes, therefore, that it is interesting to talk about scripts when there is a clash between how people behave and how you might expect them to behave. An understanding of their scripts, then, explains the link between attitudes and behavior.

In the area of story understanding, Abelson has worked alongside Schank. They note that their notion of script is like Minsky's notion of frames, "except that it is specialized to deal with event sequences" (Schank & Abelson 1975). In fact, for Schank and Abelson, *script* is only one form of knowledge structure; it is their aim to define others as well. Schank &

Abelson (1977) differentiate among scripts, plans, goals, and themes, which, they note, are explained in descending order of clarity. It should be noted, perhaps, that earlier papers make other distinctions. In Abelson (1975), there are script, theme ("a conceptual structure which accounts for a number of related scripts"), and dreme ("a conception of the possibility that one or more themes are subject to change") (p. 275). In Abelson (1976), "The basic ingredient of scripts we label a *vignette*" (p. 2). Finally, Schank and Abelson (1975) distinguish two kinds of scripts: situational and planning scripts. Planning scripts are said to "describe the set of choices that a person has when he sets out to accomplish a goal" (p. 154), and therefore seem identical to what they now define as a separate knowledge structure called a plan. The situational script seems to be what they now simply call "script," that is, a familiar, causally connected sequence of intentional (goal-oriented) events (Abelson talk, UC Berkeley, March 1977).

Schank and Abelson's (1975) notion of script is best characterized by their example of the restaurant script. They illustrate the existence of scripts in knowledge structures by presenting the following sort of story:

> John went into the restaurant. He ordered a hamburger and a coke. He asked the waitress for the check and left.

One might ask how the story can refer to "*the*" waitress and "*the*" check "just as if these objects had been previously mentioned." The fact that they can is evidence of the existence of a script which "has implicitly introduced them by virtue of its own introduction" (p. 4).

It remains now for us to determine the notion of *frame*. As mentioned above, this term has probably the widest distribution, occurring in the work of Bateson and Frake in anthropology, Hymes and Goffman in sociology, Minsky in artificial intelligence, and Fillmore in linguistics.

Bateson introduced the notion of *frame* in 1955 to explain how individuals exchange signals that allow them to agree upon the level of abstraction at which any message is intended. Even animals can be seen to use frames to interpret each other's behavior, by signaling, for example, "This is play." Bateson (1972) insists that "frame" is a psychological concept, but to characterize it, he uses "the physical analogy of the picture frame and the more abstract . . . analogy of the mathematical set" (p. 186).

In his work on the ethnography of speaking, which seeks to analyze language as it is used by people in specific cultures, Hymes (1974) includes frames as one of the "means of speaking." In order to interpret utterances in accordance with the way in which they were intended, a hearer must know what "frame" s/he is operating in, that is, whether the activity being engaged in is joking, imitating, chatting, lecturing, or performing a play, to name just a few possibilities familiar to our culture. This notion of frames as a culturally determined, familiar activity is consonant with the term as used by Goffman (1974) and Frake (1977).

Frake traces the cognitive anthropological use of "frame" to structural linguistics and credits his field with having broadened the concept from its linguistic application to isolated sentences to a sequence of conversational exchange. Frake goes on to complain, however, of the very misconception that Bartlett cautioned against and which we have noted in the work of the artificial intelligence theorists, that is, the idea that people have in their heads fully formed "cognitive ideolects" which can be described and which add up to "culture." In other words, he is opposing a static notion of frames in favor of an interactive model. He notes that anthropologists had come to refer to "eliciting frames," as if they were there and had merely to be tapped. Frake suggests instead, and this is an approach basic to the work of John Gumperz and other ethnographers of speaking, that the key aspect of frames is what the people are *doing* when they speak. He discusses the notion of *event* which seems to correspond to what Gumperz (1977) calls an *activity* as the unit of study: an identifiable interactional happening that has meaning for the participants. Thus the anthropological/sociological view stresses *frame* as a relational concept rather than a sequence of events; it refers to the dynamic relationship between people, much like Bartlett's (1932) "organized mass" of past experience which is "actively *doing* something all the time" (p. 201, italics his). Frake (1977) ends his paper with the extended metaphor of people as mapmakers whose "culture does not provide a cognitive map, but rather a set of principles for mapmaking and navigation," resulting in "a whole chart case of rough, improvised, continually revised sketch maps" (pp. 6–7). This metaphorical chart case seems awfully like a set of overlapping, intertwining, and developing scripts.

In contrast with the anthropological/sociological characterization of frames as an interactional unit with social meaning, Minsky's (1974) is a static concept, rooted in the computer model of artificial intelligence. Acknowledging his debt to Schank and Abelson, Bartlett, Piaget, and others, Minsky propounds the notion of frame as an all-inclusive term for "a datastructure for representing a stereotyped situation" (p. 212). For Minsky, this term denotes such event sequences as a birthday party (corresponding to Schank and Abelson's restaurant script), but also ordered expectations about objects and setting (for example, a certain kind of living room). Minsky distinguishes at least four levels of frames: surface syntactic frames ("mainly verb and noun structures"), surface semantic frames (seemingly corresponding to Fillmore's notion of case frame), thematic frames ("scenarios"), and narrative frames (apparently comparable to Schank and Abelson's scripts). Although Minsky's explication of the frame theory, which appeared in 1974 as a memo from the MIT Artificial Intelligence Lab, does not constitute much theoretical innovation beyond the work of Bartlett and others we have seen who followed him, it represents a particularly coherent, complete, and readable formulation of the theory, and perhaps for this reason it has had resounding impact on the field of AI as well as on many other disciplines.

Fillmore, too, has chosen the term "frame," and it is perhaps fitting to end with his treatment of this material, for his short paper (1975) brings all these ideas into focus in connection with linguistics. He begins with a listing of theories of Prototype and Frame from a variety of disciplines. Fillmore uses nearly all the terms we have discussed somewhere in his paper (except "scripts"). His thesis is that a frame-and-scene analysis of language can elucidate hitherto fuzzy areas of linguistics. He uses "the word *frame* for any system of linguistic choices . . . that can get associated with prototypical instances of scenes" and the word *scene* for "any kind of coherent segment of human beliefs, actions, experiences or imaginings" (p. 124). Furthermore, "people associate certain *scenes* with certain linguistic *frames*" (p. 2). Fillmore then shows how this approach to meaning is useful in three areas: (1) analysis of discourse, (2) acquisition of word meaning, and (3) the boundary problem for linguistic categories.

These, then, have been the major theories making use of notions of frames, schemata, and scripts. They may all be seen, in some sense, to be derived from Bartlett. It may be useful, before proceeding to our data, to consider one more research tradition which also can be seen to derive from Bartlett, and to be related to the concept of structures of expectation, even though it does not employ the specific terms we have been investigating. This is the work of the constructive memory theorists in cognitive psychology.

Research in this tradition has demonstrated the effect of context on memory performance tasks. The first of these were Pompi and Lachman (1967), who showed the superior performance on memory tasks of subjects who had read a passage in coherent order over those who had read a scrambled version of it. Even more striking, however, is the research of Bransford and his co-workers (Bransford & Franks 1971; Bransford & Johnson 1973). They showed that subjects were unable to recall well a passage which contained only pronouns and described a series of actions. When the same passage was read, however, under the title which identified the sequence of actions as, for example, someone washing clothes, subjects were able to recall it well. In the terms we have been considering, we might say that the title identified the sequence of events as a familiar script, or that it fit the activity into a known frame.

Similar evidence lies in the research of Anderson and Ortony (1975). They presented subjects with sentences like "The woman was waiting outside the theater." After reading a list of such sentences to subjects, they tried to elicit the sentences by using one-word cues. It was found that context-associated words which did not actually appear in the sentences were better cues than context-free words which actually were in the sentence. In other words, in the sentence given, "actress" was a better cue than "woman," even though the word "woman" actually was in the target sentence while "actress" was not. This is reminiscent of the Schank and Abelson restaurant script hypothesis, which pointed to the fact that a waitress could be treated as given when no waitress had been mentioned.

What unifies all these branches of research is the realization that people approach the world not as naive, blank-slate receptacles who take in stimuli as they exist in some independent and objective way, but rather as experienced and sophisticated veterans of perception who have stored their prior experiences as "an organized mass," and who see events and objects in the world in relation to each other and in relation to their prior experience. This prior experience or organized knowledge then takes the form of expectations about the world, and in the vast majority of cases, the world, being a systematic place, confirms these expectations, saving the individual the trouble of figuring things out anew all the time.

At the same time that expectations make it possible to perceive and interpret objects and events in the world, they shape those perceptions to the model of the world provided by them. As Bartlett put it, one forms a general impression (we might say, one labels something as part of a certain scene, frame, or script) and furnishes the details which one builds from prior knowledge (that is, from the script). Thus, structures of expectation make interpretation possible, but in the process they also reflect back on perception of the world to justify that interpretation.

All these theories have referred to frames and other structures of expectation, but they have shown no way of discovering what those structures consist of, for they have been mainly concerned with language comprehension. In this chapter, I would like to consider how expectations affect language production, and, in the process, show a way of discovering what constitutes them—that is, to show how we can know what's in a frame.

Data for the Present Study

In connection with a project directed by Wallace Chafe, a movie was shown to small groups of young women who then told another woman (who they were told had not seen the film) what they had seen in the movie. The film was a six-minute short, of our own production, which included sound but no dialogue. It showed a man picking pears from a tree, then descending and dumping them into one of three baskets on the ground. A boy comes by on a bicycle and steals a basket of pears. As he's riding away, he passes a girl on a bike, his hat flies off his head, and the bike overturns. Three boys appear and help him gather his pears. They find his hat and return it to him, and he gives them pears. The boys then pass the farmer who has just come down from the tree and discovered that his basket of pears is missing. He watches them walk by eating pears.

This film was shown and this procedure followed in ten different countries. I oversaw the administration of the experiment in Athens, Greece, and have studied the Greek narratives.[1] In describing the events and people in the movie, subjects organized and altered the actual content of the movie in many ways. The ways in which they did this are evidence of the effect of their structures of expectation about objects and events in the film. The comparison of narratives told by Greek and American subjects makes it possible to see that these structures are often culturally determined, as one would expect.

On the basis of this hypothesis, I have isolated sixteen general types of evidence which represent the imposition of the speakers' expectations on the content of the film. These are not absolute categories, and certainly this is not a definitive list, yet they cover a broad range of linguistic phenomena, and they represent a way in which structures of expectation can be characterized.

Labov (1972) discusses a series of surface linguistic phenomena in oral narratives which he calls "evaluative." They are "the means used by the narrator to indicate the point of the narrative," or to answer in advance the question, "So what?" Since the point of a narrative is directly related to the expectations of people in the culture in which it is told, it is not surprising that Labov's evaluative elements are closely related to my notion of evidence of expectations. I will note these similarities as they arise in the following discussion.

Levels of Frames

Any speech event represents the overlapping and intertwining of many relations concerning the context as well as the content of communication. In the case of the oral narratives under study here, the larger context is the one in which the speaker is the subject of an experiment, and the context in which that experiment is being carried out is an interview mode, in which the speaker knows that her voice is being tape-recorded. Clearly, the speaker's expectations about being the subject of an experiment in an academic setting, and her feelings about having her voice recorded, affect her narrative performance.

The content of the story, furthermore, is the narration of events in a film, so the speaker's expectations about films as well as her expectations of herself as a film viewer also come into play. Finally, the events, objects, and people depicted in the film trigger expectations about similar events, objects, and people in the real world and their interrelationships. All these levels of knowledge structures coexist and must operate in conjunction with each other to determine how the events in the film will be perceived and then verbalized. In the following discussion, I will consider these various levels of expectation structures in turn, in order of scope (that is, from the overriding context, subject of experiment, to the relatively narrow object level) and in each case I will demonstrate how the expectations are revealed in surface evidence of the types I have been looking at. In cases in which there are significant differences between Greek and American responses, that will be noted. After expectations have been seen to operate on these various levels, I will list the sixteen types of evidence used in the preceding discussion and explain and exemplify each. In a final section, I will discuss the elements of one specific set of expectations, that is, parts of the narratives relating to the occurrence of a theft.

Subject of Experiment

The broadest level of context operating in the film narratives relates to the situation in which the speakers find themselves. As subjects of an experiment, they are telling a story to a person they have never met before.[2] They do not know the purpose of the experiment, so they do not know what elements in their story will be of interest to the hearer. This is clearly an unnatural context for storytelling. The fact that it is an experiment situation may well affect every aspect of the telling, although it is also likely that the speakers have told stories and told plots of films so often that they lapse into a habitual narrative mode. It is, nonetheless, a context in which the speakers are subjects of the experiment, and they reveal expectations about that situation in their talk.

On the average, the American narratives are longer and more detailed than the Greek ones. It is possible that this is a function of the Americans' assumptions about the experiment situation. That is, not knowing the purpose of the experiment, they may feel that the more details they give, the more likely they will include what is wanted. Moreover, they may have an instinctive feeling that it is a memory test. A number of American subjects overtly express their discomfort about how much detail to include (some repeatedly), while a few Greeks ask at the beginning but do not return to the issue. For example, S34 says

> S34 (45)   ... and then-- UM ... just .. how .. I mean how picky do you want.[3]

Another American subject expresses regret that she does not remember more details:

> S49 (55)   ... That's all I remember. You should have caught me ... ten minutes ago when I remembered ... Who pašśed the ... the man before the kid on the bicycle, I don't remember.

The use of a *negative statement* is one of the clearest and most frequent indications that an expectation is not being met. As Labov (1972) puts it, "What reason would the narrator have for telling us that something did not happen since he is in the business of telling us what did happen?" He explains, "it expresses the defeat of an expectation that something would happen" (pp. 380–81). I have demonstrated this in a natural narrative (Tannen 1977) elsewhere, and numerous examples will be seen in this paper as well. In the above example, the negative statement "I don't remember" indicates the speaker's expectation that she should have remembered the characters in the film in order to tell about them.

The fact that the speaker is wondering about the purpose of the experiment shows up in another narrative in this way:

> S39 (169)   ... If this is for gestures, this is a great movie for gestures.

The non-syntactic anaphora (Gensler 1977), "this," refers to the experiment, indicating that this "frame" has been in the speaker's mind even though she has not mentioned it overtly. Moreover, twelve Americans begin their narratives with "Okay," and three others with "All right" or "Sure," implying that they are agreeing to fulfill a request.[4] Two American subjects and one Greek indicate that they have kept this frame in mind, for they end their narratives by asking "Okay?" (Greek: *endaxi?*), which seems to be asking, "Is that what you wanted?"

Even though the storytelling is occurring in an experiment situation, it is an interaction between two people, both women, of roughly the same age and class. Thus it is inevitable that the speakers' habitual conversational expectations come into play. This can be seen in the following example. S37's storytelling mode is automatically triggered, but it conflicts with the interview conventions which require that the subject answer questions rather than the interviewer, and that the subject, moreover, conform to the rules established by the addressee. S37 has just made a statement which is a *judgment* about the sounds in the film. Since a judgment is clearly a comparison of the events of the film to her own expectations, she wants to check out her judgment with the addressee, who she knows has heard about the film from other speakers as well.

> S37 (24)   ... has anybody told you that before? Or r you're not supposed to tell me that.

S37 acknowledges the constraint of the interview situation by her negative statement, "you're not supposed to tell me that." Two more sorts of evidence of expectations can be seen here: the appearance of the *modal*, "be supposed to," lexically measures the addressee's actions against expected norms (Labov discusses modals as "evaluative" as well). Finally, the false start is a frequent occurrence in oral narratives which indicates the operation of expectations. The false start in this example, "r," is minimal, but it seems that the aborted "r" was intended to begin the phrasing, "Are you allowed to tell me?" The speaker's decision to switch to a negative statement seems to be evidence that she recalled the interview situation and its attendant constraints.

Storytelling Frame

For some subjects, awareness of the experiment situation seems less overriding than for others. For example, S4 gives the following reason for including details in her narrative.

> S4 (52)   ... I'm gĭving you ăll these details. I don't know if you want
> them. ... UM-- ... the ... reason I'm giving you all the details is
> cause I don't know what the point of the movie was. ... Okay?
> So maybe yŏu can see something that I didn't. ... Okay?
> /laugh/

S4 apparently feels that when telling about a movie, she should know and communicate what "the point" was. Her inability to do this creates enough discomfort for her to mention it as a reason for telling details. She seems to feel, moreover, that it is odd for her to tell details without fitting them into some structure or "point." Her statement about the interviewer's ability to make sense of the details (note again the modal, "can") indicates that she is operating on a cooperative model in which she assumes her purpose is to communicate to her hearer. This is somewhat different from the expectation of a purpose of furnishing data for an identified researcher.

A similar expectation about the reasonableness of the hearer shows up in S39's narrative.

> S39 (124)   don't say yes, because you don't you've never seen that /??/ All right. Okay.

All subjects had been told that the person they were telling their story to had not seen the film. Therefore, S39 expects the hearer to act like an ignorant addressee. Similarly, S47 asks:

> S47 (20)   ... AH-- would you like to know what ... the goat looked like? [*thiyə*]? I hate to take away the suspe⁻-nse or anything.

This statement reveals the expectation that limits the amount one ought to tell about a film to someone who has not seen the film and intends to, since part of film-viewing involves not knowing any more than the film itself has shown you, or "suspense." Thus S47 is approaching the telling task from a "film-telling" frame rather than from an "interview-for-experiment" frame, such as the one which causes S34 to ask, "how picky do you want?"

There are a number of ways in which subjects reveal that they have expectations about how to tell a story. For example, it is clear that they feel they should tell only important elements. However, since they are not sure what they are telling the story for, they cannot always judge whether elements are important. This discomfort is verbalized, making that expectation overt.

> S4 (15)   .. he's wearing like an apron with huge pockets. .. But I don't think you see the apron at first. I don't know if that's important or not.
>
> S4 (152)   ... Who looks like a Mexican-American if that's important?
>
> S34 (79)   ... And I don't know if this-- ... really is important, it's not important it's just something I noticed,

The word "just" frequently functions to underplay a statement to block criticism on the basis that it is not more, therefore revealing the assumption that others might expect more. This function of "just" is discussed at length elsewhere (Tannen 1977). In the above example, S34 says that the point she has made is "just something I noticed"; the "just" follows a negative, as it often does: "it's not important." Both these traces reveal the expectation that anything worth mentioning in the narrative is important.

A number of subjects reveal the expectation that events be related in the story in the temporal order in which they occurred.[5]

> S4 (33)   ... Let's see is it while he's up in the ladder? or .. or before. ... UM-- ... anyway,

The "anyway" is a common type of evidence that an expectation is violated.[6] In this case it functions as an admission of defeat, at the same time that it marks the fact that an attempt was made to get the temporal order right. This speaker uses "anyway" in the same way later and expresses the same expectation when she gives an excuse for putting something out of its temporal order. Like many other subjects, she mentions later in her story that a rooster was heard in the beginning of the film. Then she explains,

> S4 (67)   Anyway. ... I just remembered that. ... Anyway,

She seems to be saying, "I'm breaking the rules of storytelling a bit, but be indulgent. I tried." Another subject shows a similar concern with getting the temporal order of events right.

> S39 (105)   ... Came dow .. oh no, that didn't happen yet. ... So-- ... the sequence is funny ... if you don't really ... remember.

Moreover, the strength of this constraint is evidenced in the striking accuracy in all our narratives, both Greek and American, with regard to temporal sequence.

What's in a Film?

The narratives in this sample constitute a special kind of storytelling; they are about events in a film. At least one subject commented about how it felt to be talking about a film in this setting.

> S39 (22)   ... so ... it's very funny to make this telling.

We may assume that others felt "funny" about it as well, even if they did not say so, since when we tell each other about films we have seen, we usually do so for internally generated reasons. Still, talking about films is a common practice in American and Greek society, and in these narratives, expectations about being subjects of an experiment clearly interplay with expectations about telling about movies.

The narratives of the American women contain more evidence of expectations about films as films than the Greek narratives. For example, nine Americans mention that the film contains no dialogue. As usual, the negative statement indicates that its affirmative was expected. Another way in which this film clearly did not adhere to subjects' expectations about films is with regard to its sound effects. Six American speakers mention the sounds in the film. For two of them, the sound track of the film is the theme which unifies their narratives, about which they adduce details, and which they return to repeatedly. Another subject, in fact, telling about the film a year after she first saw it, recalled this as the most salient feature of the film, even though she had not mentioned the sound at all the first time she told about it.

Three Americans devote a considerable amount of attention to this aspect of the film. One introduces it this way:

S37 (20)   but there .. is ... a lot of sound effects. ... Which are nŏt ...
            totally UM-- ... consistent.

The "but" is another important kind of evidence of expectations. It marks
the contrast with the expectation established by the preceding statement
about there being no dialogue in the film.[7] Two other Americans say:

S44 (13)   and the soŭnd is just ... is ... is really intensified /well/ ...
            from what .. it .. usually .. would be, I think.
S46 (22)   ... And what I noticed ... first off ... was that all the noises in
            the movie, ... were UM-- ... out of proportion.

The fact that these three subjects were particularly uncomfortable about the
violation of this expectation about film sound tracks is marked in a number
of ways. First of all, they continue to devote large portions of their narratives
to discussing it. Second, their statements are broken up by numerous
pauses. Finally, and most obviously, judgment is implied in their choice of
adjectives: "not consistent," "intensified," "out of proportion." Other subjects, however, mention this aspect of the film without implying judgment.

S4 (65)   ... And the movie had a sound track. ... It's important.
S12 (2)   The movie seemed very ... sound oriented.

S4, still concerned with making it clear that she is adhering to the expectation that what she tells be important, notes that the sound track is "important" because it is unusual. Otherwise, one would assume that a movie has a
sound track, and it would not be reportable. (Schank and Abelson would
say that it is known by virtue of its inclusion in the "film script.")
    American subjects reveal other expectations about verisimilitude in
films. For example, one speaker comments on the quality of the color:

S24 (9)   ... Something that I noticed about the /movie/ particularly
            unique was that the colors .. were ... just ... vêry strânge. ...
            Like ... the green was a ... inordinately bright green, ... for the
            pears, .. and ... these colors just seemed a little ... kind of bold,
            almost to the point of ... being artificial.

S24 assumes that the colors are not supposed to be "artificial," and she is
making a judgment about the fact that they were. This is, again, a significant
verbal act, and her raised amplitude reveals her emotional investment in the
process ("very strange"), as well as the hedges ("just," "a little ... kind of,"
"almost to the point of ... being"). Another subject makes a similar judgment about the costumes.

S39 (45)   ... And the pĕople looked very funny, because they were
            suppŏ²-sed, ... to be-- ... far--mer--ish, ... and really just had
            ... clothes like a person with like ... store levis, and ... a n²˙ew
            red bandana around his neck and a ... things like

S39 expects the film to be realistic in its effects and considers it noteworthy that the characters' clothing seemed inauthentic to her. She is maintaining a "film-viewer" point of view, reporting the costumes as artifacts of the film, rather than simply describing them as clothes worn by people involved in the events she is reporting, as all the others who talk about clothing in fact do. Increased pitch and amplitude as well as elongated sounds and pauses also contribute to the denial-of-expectation implication of her statement; they connote surprise.

Films are expected to be internally consistent with regard to concrete details. Thus S34 was very troubled because she thought she detected a contradiction; she recalled seeing two baskets on the ground before the boy stole one, and then she recalled seeing two remaining. In fact, she made an error. There were actually three baskets in the first place. However, her sense that the film was inconsistent was so disturbing to her that she spent a great deal of time talking about it in her initial narrative, and when she was asked to retell the narrative six weeks later, she again devoted a large portion of her story to discussing this detail.

Another expectation about films revealed in our narratives is related to its pace. Two subjects comment, with reference to a scene in which a man is picking pears,

> S34 (29)   .. There's nothing ... doesn't seem to be very hurried. ... In the movie. It's fairly ... slow,
> S50 (21)   ... A--nd ... he's ... it ... the .. cǎmera spends a lot of time watching him ... pick these pears,

Again, they comment on the pace as an artifact of the film, not as a comment on the way the man is behaving, indicating that the speakers are in a film-description frame.

A final observation about film expectations entails that any character introduced in the film must play a role in the plot. Three Americans comment about a man who passes by with a goat, to the effect that he does not figure in the action. S24, for example, says that the man and goat

> S24 (28)   ... and just kind of walk off. They don't really seem to have too much to do, ... with .. what's going .. on.

Again, the word "just" (in fact the almost formulaically common qualification-plus-hedge "just kind of") marks the expectation that more was expected. The implied judgment in the second part of the statement is again signaled by the clutch of hedges ("really," "seem," "too much") which soften the impact of the negative statement. Similarly, in another scene, a girl on a bicycle passes the boy on his bicycle. Two Americans indicate that the appearance of the girl had less significance than they expected of a character introduced into the film. In one case this is shown by the statement,

> S39 (135)   ... That was all that .. you saw of her in the movie.

In another it takes the form of a report of the viewer's thoughts:

>S6 (78)   ... a--nd UH-- ... you wonder how she's going to figure in on
>this.

Film-Viewer Frame

This last example is an indication of another level of frame, closely related to that of the "film frame" we have been discussing. The speaker, S6, reports the events of the movie from her own point of view and therefore is characterizing herself as a film viewer. She reveals her expectations of herself and how she interacts with the film. In the above example, she shows herself anticipating the events of the film before they occur, trying to "psych out" the strategy of the plot. This speaker does this a number of times in her narrative. Another instance is:

>S6 (69)   .. and you think "Aha. ... UH ... Are we gonna go back to the
>man over there" but no.

Thus the interplay between her expectations and the events of the film are part of her narrative content. Her experience as a viewer is part of her story which therefore becomes a story not only of the movie but of her viewing of it as well.

This can be seen in another subject's conclusion of a particularly short and straightforward narrative:

>S8 (59)   And ... yŏu're left with this dilemma, ... what does this guy
>[laugh] you know what does this guy really think.

S8, like nearly all our subjects, assumes that the pear picker's thoughts are significant. She expresses this in terms of the expectation that the film should make clear the character's attitude toward the events of the film, so that uncertainty about that attitude becomes a "dilemma" for her as a viewer.

A similar point of view can be seen in S34:

>S34 (24)   I don't know what ... I wasn't sure at first if they were apples,
>or if they were pears, but ... UM ... he's picking pears,

If the task is to describe what happened in the film, and if the speaker's conclusion is unquestionably that the man was picking pears, why does she report her initial uncertainty as to whether they were apples or pears? Her inclusion of this internal process of interpretation reflects her telling not only the story of the film, but the story of her experience watching it.

There are other examples of the "film-viewer frame." Perhaps one more aspect of it will suffice to indicate its function in the narratives. When a speaker reports her interpretation of the film, she necessarily characterizes herself as a film viewer. Therefore, for example, a speaker who reveals her expectation that an event in the film will have significance by saying that she thought the goat would eat the pears, follows this up with,

> S39 (69)   That's .. I don't know whether you're supposed to think that or not.

Her *false start,* the *negative statement* about her own knowledge, and the *modal* all indicate her insecurity about the image she has presented of herself as a film viewer. The expectation is revealed that an adept viewer correctly interprets the actions of a film.

Strikingly, preoccupation with the film as a film and oneself as a film viewer is absent from the Greek narratives. No Greek speaker criticizes the film or comments on it as a film in any way. The Greek narratives include no comment about the sound track, and no discussion of the speakers' anticipation of what would happen. In fact, fully half of the Greek subjects tell their entire narratives without ever making reference to the film as a film. Rather, they tell about the events directly. This is particularly noticeable in the beginning and end of their narrations, where there is the greatest likelihood in English narratives for the film to be mentioned as a film. For example, a typical beginning of a Greek narrative is:

> G1 (1)   ... e ... *to proto praghma pou eidha,* .. *itan ena pra--sino kataprasino topio,*
> ... e ... the first thing that I saw, .. was a gree--n verygreen landscape,[8]

This narrative ends:

> G1 (77)   *esti ... menei aporimenos o--*
> thus ... (he) remains wondering the--

This is in contrast to such openings as "The film opened with . . ." or "The first scene showed. . . ." While ten of the twenty Greek subjects make no reference at all to the fact that the events they are telling about occurred in a film, all twenty Americans make some allusion to it somewhere in their narratives, and most make much more than passing reference, as has been seen.

Of the ten Greek subjects who make some reference to the fact that they are talking about a film, only three actually mention the word "film" directly. Two of these mention it only once, in the first line of their narratives, and the third mentions it in both the first and the last lines. The other seven Greeks refer to it indirectly, generally through the verb *edheichne* or *dheichnei,* "(it) showed" or "it shows," in which the deleted subject is "the film."

This unmistakable difference between the points of view or frames of the Greek and American subjects seems to indicate that Americans are media-wise, or media-conscious, so their expectations about films and film viewing are more developed and more salient to them. This tendency, however, to view the film as a film (or, put another way, to be conscious of the frame "film watching") may be related to another striking difference between Greek and American narratives: the tendency of Greeks to interpret and make judgments about the events and people portrayed. While a number of Americans develop their narratives into extensions of the theme that the film had a strange soundtrack, a number of Greeks develop their narratives into extensions of some theme about the significance of the events in it. Thus, the Greeks are also seeing the film as a film, but they are interested in its "message" rather than its execution.

In order to illustrate this characteristic of the Greek narratives, I will translate the entire narrative of one speaker, eliminating pauses and other details of transcription so that the events can be followed easily. Although this is an extreme case, it dramatizes a tendency which is present to some extent in nearly all the Greek narratives. First of all, it is full of *interpretations* and *judgments*. Second, it is interesting to note which of the events of the film this speaker chooses to include in her story, and which she *omits*.

> G12 From what I understood, it was an episode, it happened in Mexico. I suppose, the people seemed Mexican to me, and it showed the how a person was gathering pears, and it insisted that which he did, he was living. The in other words that he cultivated the earth, that he gathered these the harvest, was something special for him ... it was worth something. He lived that which he did, he liked it. And it showed a scene-- it must have been the agricultural life of that region, someone who passed with a goat, a child a child with a bicycle, who saw the basket, with the pears, and took it, and then as he was passing, he met in the middle of the field, another girl with a bicycle, and as he looked at her, he didn't pay attention a little, and fell from him fell from him the basket with the pears, and there again were three other friends of his, who immediately helped him and this was anyway something that showed how children love each other, they have solidarity, they helped him to gather them, and and as he forgot his hat, there was a beautiful scene where he gave them the pears and returned it back again. In other words generally I think it was a scene from the agricultural life of the region it showed. That's it.

A vast array of interpretive devices are operating here to support G12's main idea: an all's-right-with-the-world, romantic view of the meaning of the film. She discusses at length the pear picker's attitude toward his work, as if it were known to her, yet it is clearly her own interpretation, as is her comment that the interaction between the boy and the three others who help him shows "how children love each other." These interpretations seem to be motivated by her own expectations about farmers and children. Similarly, her use of the adjective "beautiful" to describe the scene in which one boy gives the others some pears constitutes a judgment about the events. A process I have called *interpretive naming* can be seen in her reference to the three boys as "friends of his," without overtly marking that this is an interpretation, which it clearly is. Finally, to support her interpretation, G12 omits parts of the film that would suggest a less rosy picture of the world. For example, she is the only one who actually omits to mention that the boy fell off his bicycle. She also omits the entire last scene in which the three boys pass by the tree where the man has discovered that his pears are missing. Moreover, she underplays the fact of the theft. Thus, the use of *interpretation* shapes this entire narrative in a way that it never does for our American subjects' narratives.

Such free use of interpretation first of all reveals a different attitude toward the activity of film viewing and/or of being the subject of an experiment. It also yields an especially clear insight into the speaker's expectations. G12's idiosyncratic interpretation of the pear-picking film indicates her pastoral view of or expectations about farmers and children, which are part of a larger expectation about the romantic message of the film.

The tendency to approach the film for its "message" can be seen in other Greek narratives as well. For example, G6 ends by saying,

G6 (50)   ... *allo an /dhinei/ tora-- ... o kathenas alles erminies.*
           ... other if /gives/ now-- ... each (one) other interpretations.
           [it's something else again if each person gives different inter-
           pretations]

Another subject indicates her expectation that she should be able to interpret the film by a negative statement which she in fact *repeats*.

G9 (107)   ... *tora to topio vevaia itan orai--o. ... alla dhen xero na to
           exighiso.*
           ... now the landscape certainly was lovely. ... but (I) don't
           know (how) to explain it.

After saying a few more sentences about the landscape, she says again, "but I don't know how to-- how to explain it."

Furthermore, while G12 was an extreme example of interpretive narration, other Greeks showed similar tendencies. For example, G11 says (again I will simply write the English translation to facilitate reading):

G11   ... (there) was a perso--n ... a person of the earth. ... one of those
       who labor. ... a farmer, ... (he) was gathering-- ... (he) had
       worked-- the whole year, ... and (he) wanted to take his fruits. ...
       (he) was going up, (he) was going down, (he) was sweating,
       (he) was looking at .. EH with a devo--tion you know the pear ...
       (he) was taking it (he) was putting it in the basket, ... (it) was
       falling down from him (he) was going down (he) was grasping it
       (he) was putting it back in the basket [sigh] ... very devoutly.

That the man was a farmer is *interpretive naming:* that he worked all year is an *inference* which contributes to the romantic interpretation of the farmer's relationship to his fruit. The speaker used the *katharevousa* word for "fruit," *karpous,* which is a more literary word, suggesting the notion "fruits of his labor" rather than simply "fruit" in the sense of "pears." She also *generalizes* the actions which occur once in the film and reports them as if they were done repeatedly, contributing to the interpretation of the farmer as a hard-working person. Even the speaker's intonation and her slow rate of speech conspire to create this effect. This personal view of the pear picker surfaces at the end as well, where G11 reports his reaction to discovering that a basket is missing, from his point of view:

G11 (117)   .. *to allo ghemato pou einai?*
                   .. the other full (one) where is (it)?

Finally, she infers his emotions at that point and repeats her inference, switching to his point of view without marking the switch overtly.

G11 (119)   ... *TSK alla ... moirolatrika to pire dhen boro-- na kano tipota tora pia. ... EH-- vlepei tous .. treis bobires pou troghane to-- ... achladhi, .. tous koitaze moirolatrika-- alla dhen boro na kano tipota allo*
                 ... TSK but ... fatefully (he) took it (I) can't-- do anything now anymore. ... EH-- (he) sees the .. three kids who were eating the-- ... pear, .. (he) was looking at them fatefully-- but (I) can't do anything else

"He took it fatefully" means something like "He was philosophical about it." The speaker, however, seems to be characterizing her own view of life, or her expectation about farmers, rather than reporting what was actually dramatized in the movie.

Another Greek subject also interprets the pear picker's actions at the end, although her interpretation is somewhat different. She also makes her identification with the man more immediate by assuming his point of view:

G16 (80)   ... *dhen-- UH-- anti na tou pi-- na t na tou pi paidhia-- einai ap ta achladhia ta opoia-- pithanon na echete pari eseis, ... ta vlepei, kai-- ... ta koitaei etsi me ... choris na tous pi tipota, evg evghenika as poume tous ferthike, ... UH koitaxe, kai-- eidhe as poume oti-- troghan ta achladhia, kai-- sa na efcharistithike /??/ kai dhen eipe tipota oti einai dhika mou ta achladhia afta,*
                 ... (he) didn't-- UH-- instead of telling them-- of of telling them children-- (they) are from the pears which-- possibly you have taken, ... (he) sees them, and-- ... (he) looks at them thus with ... without telling them anything, ki kindly let's say (he) treated them, ... UH (he) looked, and-- (he) saw let's say that-- (they) were eating the pears, and-- as if (he) was glad /??/ and (he) didn't say anything that these pears are mine,

G16 thus has interpreted that the man picking pears is glad to see the boys enjoying his pears, and that he treats them "kindly." The fact that she

believes she should evaluate the film's message is seen, finally, in her following and last comment:

> G16 (93)   ... *ghenikos echei stoicheia etsi anthropias /alla/ synedhiazmena*
> *kai me-- ... me ti ... tha borouse perissotero na eiche as poume*
> *stin archi--*
> ... generally (it) has elements thus of humanism /but/ com-
> bined also with-- ... with what ... (it) could have had more
> let's say in the beginning--

Thus G16 makes it explicit that her inferences about the pear picker's attitude contribute to an interpretation of the message of the film. Her complaint about "what it could have had more," that is, "the more meaning it
could have had" in the beginning, seems to refer to her dissatisfaction with
the film's moral viewpoint at first. This may be related to her rather complex
and clearly emotionally tinged complaint that the boy who had fallen off his
bicycle should have thanked the three boys who helped him by giving them
pears right away, instead of doing so only when they returned his hat to him,
after he had been on his way already. In addition, it may refer to her interpretation of the same motions and expression of the pear picker in the
opening scene which led G12 to interpret that he revered his pears. G16
said,

> G16 (3)   ... *TSK kai-- ta mazevei-- etsi me-- ... me poli-- ... e-- sa na ta*
> *thelei dhika tou. me poli etsi-- /s/ idhioktisia dh dheichnei mesa.*
> ... TSK and-- (he) gathers them-- thus with-- ... with a lot--
> ... EH-- as if (he) wants them (to be) his own. with a lot
> thus-- (of) /s/ proprietariness (it, he) sh shows inside.

With an equally free stroke, G16 interprets the pear picker's motions as
indicating possessiveness. These interpretations come from the same slow
motions which led Americans to comment on the pace of the film.

Another example of the kind of interpretation found in the Greek but
not the American narratives is G2's comment about the three boys' appearance:

> G2 (46)   ... *TSK ... en to metaxi pros ironia ... e pros ironia tis tychis*
> ... TSK ... in the meantime by irony ... EH by irony of luck

Like her judgment about the boy's failure to thank his helpers (a comment
made by a number of other Greeks as well), her comment about luck's irony
indicates she is regarding the events of the film as intrinsically significant
rather than as events to remember for a memory task.

Finally, a number of Greek subjects show a pronounced inclination to
philosophize about the film and its meaning after they have told it. G16
goes on after the interviewer has indicated satisfaction:

> G16   It has such elements as, of course, and the young man who took
> the basket, I believe that he shouldn't have taken it, he took it at

first, but then with the young men's deed who called to him and didn't ask, he gave them pears. And in the beginning the gentleman who was gathering pears took great care of them, this shows that man to be, that is, there are many contrasts in the film. Although in the beginning you believe that the child will give (them) pears, he goes away. But then after they give him the hat he changes his mind and gives them again. And the gentleman who was harvesting in the beginning and you thought that he was collecting them for himself and it shows a man but when he sees the children going away each holding a pear and sees that they are his and doesn't call them you see a conflict and you think it wasn't as I thought. It has many conflicts in it and--

Just as this speaker goes on and on about the conflicts in the film, another one continues interminably about the pessimism of the film because it had a lot of falls in it!

It is clear then that the way in which the subjects talk about the film is shaped by their notion of what constitutes appropriate comment about a film. Americans tended to operate from a film-viewer frame and criticize the film as a technical product; Greeks tended to operate from a film-interpreter frame and expected the film to have a "message" which they proceeded to explain.[9]

Expectations about Events

We have seen many ways in which speakers reveal expectations about the context and activity in which they are taking part. In addition, the way they describe the events in the film indicates their expectations about specific events portrayed in it.

Personal Encounters

When a man with a goat walks by the tree where the man is picking pears, S6 typically reports,

S6 (20)   And the man up in the tree doesn't even notice,

Similarly, when the boy comes by and takes a basket of pears, she says,

S6 (65)   and the man up in the tree doesn't even ... doesn't notice anything.

The negative statement, as has been seen repeatedly, indicates that an expected action failed to take place. The use of *even* intensifies this effect; it implies that "at least" this was expected and indicates surprise that it did not occur. In this case, the expectation is that when two people cross paths in a setting in which they are the only people present, they will notice and probably acknowledge each other. This shows up in another narrative this way:

> S34 (43)   .. And there doesn't seem there's no communication be-
> tween the two of them, ... or anything,

Comments like these are frequent in both Greek and American narratives. They are even more frequent with regard to the passing of the boy on his bike than about the man passing with the goat. In the case of the boy coming by, the expectations about interactions dovetail with expectations about the theft. That is, in addition to an expectation that the man and the boy would interact, there is an assumption that in order for the boy to steal the pears, he must not be noticed by the man. Thus, mentions of the fact that the man did not notice the boy both mark a denial of expectation based on an interaction frame and also make explicit an element of a theft frame. For example, one subject says,

> S44 (54)   and the man doesn't know that the little boy is there.
>   (60)   ... And like .. so the man didn't hear the little boy, .. you
>   know ... being there, ... and-- he-- .. ended up .. UM-- ...
>   swiping .: one of his baskets of pears,

By juxtaposition, it is clear that the theft of the pears is seen as a consequence of the man's inattention. S6, the American who habitually verbalizes her expectations about the movie and plays them off against what actually happens, puts it this way:

> S6 (30)   ... At least .. it seems to me that .. you know he would notice
>   this boy

The same idea is operating more subtly in the following statement:

> S50 (67)   ... But he's very brazen. I mean there's [o] .. they're only
>   about three feet apart.

The use of the *evaluative adjective* "brazen" and the word "only" both allude to the expectation that the man would notice the boy. These are two kinds of evidence of expectations. The second statement is, in effect, an explanation of the first. In fact, *adjectives* nearly always represent an interpretive or evaluative process on the part of the speaker at least in these narratives and probably in any storytelling event.

Confrontation

A related expectation about encounters between people which also overlaps with the theft frame can be seen in the way speakers describe the last scene in the film, in which the three boys pass the man who has just discovered that his pears are missing. S53 says,

> S53 (66)   ... and he just kind of looks at them and ... doesn't do
>   anything.

There are a number of indications that the speaker expected a confrontation of some sort between the man and the passing boys. Once again, the word "just," and indeed the combination "just kind of," implies that more was expected. The increased pitch on "looks at them" also indicates surprise. Furthermore, the negative statement, "doesn't do anything," as has been seen so often, indicates that its affirmative was expected: he should have done something when the boys passed eating pears.

Another subject reveals the same expectation in this way:

S49 (49)   for sŏme reason he didn't stop them or ask them where they got the pears.

Again, the negative statement indicates what S49 expected the man to do. Also, an increase in pitch and amplitude indicates surprise that this did not happen. Another example of the same expectation is in S50's account:

S50 (171)   and I thought maybe that there was going to be a big dramatic moment, where ... he's going to accuse the little boys who'd actually been like .. good Samaritans, of stealing the pears. ... But he just sort of watches them, .. as they walk by, and they don't pay any attention to them ... to him, he's .. they're just eating their pears,

There are numerous other similar examples in both the Greek and American narratives, all showing roughly the same pattern of evidence that a confrontation was expected when the boys passed the man. This is a good example of how structures of expectation overlap, for there are at least three contexts operating in this scene. For one thing, there is the situation of people passing each other in the country, and in this way this scene is similar to the ones already discussed in which the man passes with a goat and the boy passes on a bicycle. Second, the expectation of confrontation arises since the man has had his pears stolen, and the boys pass holding pears. Finally, this is a movie, and there is an expectation of a "climax" at the end of a film, as well as the expectation that something startling should happen somewhere in the film. This is what the subject seems to have in mind when she says "a big dramatic moment."

Accident Frame

A scene in the film that lends itself to interpretation is one in which the boy falls off his bicycle. Two sets of expectations come into play here: those about accidents and additionally and contrapuntally those about causality. There are noticeable differences between Greek and American narratives with regard to this scene.

The scene in which the boy falls off his bicycle is intentionally ambiguous. In the film, the following events are seen in the following order:

1. The boy is riding his bike.
2. A girl is riding her bike.

3. The boy and girl pass each other on their bikes.
4. The boy's hat flies off his head.
5. The boy turns his head backward.
6. A bicycle wheel is seen hitting a rock.
7. The boy is on the ground under his fallen bike.

The conclusion that the boy has fallen off his bicycle is drawn by everyone seeing this film. This is interpretive in some sense, since the boy is not actually seen falling off, but it is the only rational conclusion to be drawn from the juxtaposition of events in which the boy is riding his bike and is then seen on the ground under it. However, the reason for the boy's fall can be interpreted in a number of ways.

Some interpretation about the causality of the fall is made by all subjects in our sample. Theoretically, they could have simply reported that the boy fell without explaining why, but in fact no one does this. In keeping with the interpretive penchant of Greeks already noted, six Greek speakers explain the boy's fall from his bicycle by reference to events that did not actually appear in the film. In fact, they make *incorrect statements* in their explanations; the hypothesis, then, is that their interpretations came from their own expectations about what might cause a boy to fall off his bicycle.

Four Greeks say that the boy fell because the bicycles collided, and two others say that he fell during the "meeting" of the two bikes, implying but not stating that the bikes collided. No American makes such a statement. In general, the Greek explanations for why the boy fell are more varied than the American explanations. There is striking unanimity among Americans that the boy fell because his bike hit a rock. Fifteen say that he turned and hit a rock, while four say simply that he hit a rock. Only one makes an incorrect statement, saying that he fell because he was tipping his hat to the girl. By contrast, two Greeks say he fell because he was looking at the girl; four say he tripped on a rock; eight say he turned and then hit a rock; one says he was rushing; six, as we have seen, attribute the fall to a collision. Such explanations as "rushing" and "collision" clearly come from an accident frame, that is, the expectation that a bicycle accident might be caused in this way. The "tipping hat" explanation comes from the coincidence of an accident frame (not paying attention causes accident) and a greeting frame (boy meets girl and tips hat). Two Greeks but no Americans opt for the boy-meets-girl frame by itself as a cause (he fell because he was looking at the girl).

A pattern of interpretive omission can be seen here as well for the Greek subjects. Table 1.1 shows who and what were mentioned in the narratives. Thus, American subjects mentioned all three objects or two of them. Even if they did not include the girl in their explanation for the fall, yet they noted that she had appeared in the film. Greeks, however, more often than not, failed to mention all three objects which were portrayed in the fall sequence. It may be that their tendency to interpret events led them to a commitment to one interpretation of causality, and as a result to ignore objects or people that did not contribute to their interpretation. A total of nine Greek subjects

Table 1.1 Number of Subjects
Mentioning Person and/or Objects

	Americans	*Greeks*
Girl only	0	7
Rock only	0	2
Girl and hat	0	1
Girl, rock, hat	13	4
Girl and rock	7	6

(nearly half) mention only the person or object to which they are attributing causality.

While no Americans actually make the incorrect statement that the bikes collided, they are aware of this expectation. Two subjects make this overt:

S6 (84)   and you think "U?." You know "Are they going to collide,

S24 (58)   and you wonder if there's going to be a collision. ... But .. instead they just .. kind of .. brush .. by each other

S24 exhibits the by now familiar set of cues marking denial of expectation: the use of "but," "just kind of," and the negative implied in "instead." "You wonder" is a variant of a negative for it states something that did not happen.

Another aspect of the accident frame has to do with the boys' emotions. Such elements as the characters' emotions and thoughts are necessarily interpretive, for the film does not represent these directly. S6 reports,

S6 (109)   .. He's kind of crushed, and I don't know ... you know ... I think his ego was hurt.

The hedges are a clue to the fact that she is stating something that is different in kind from a report of events directly witnessed.

Reaction to Theft

In the end of the film, the man discovers that a basket of pears is missing. Americans, even more than Greeks, tell what his emotions were when he made this discovery. Sixteen Americans and eleven Greeks mention the man's reactions, either by describing his actions or inferring his emotions.

Ten Americans and three Greeks report the man's actions; eight of these Americans and two of these Greeks mention that he counts the baskets (one Greek, by *generalization,* says that he "counts and counts again," generalizing the gesture of counting which was portrayed once in the film and thereby creating an effect of great perplexity on the part of the man). Most of the subjects in both groups who report the man's feelings say that he was puzzled or wondering (seven Americans, five Greeks). There is a difference,

however, in what the others say. Two Americans say that he was angry or
upset, while three Greeks say that he was surprised. That is, the deviant
responses go in different directions; the Americans opt for a more intense
negative reaction, and the Greeks go for a less negative one.

Then the three boys pass eating pears. Seventeen Americans and twelve
Greeks report the man's reaction in some way. An equal number, roughly,
say that he was puzzled or something similar (eight Americans and nine
Greeks). One American and one Greek say that the man does not do anything (revealing the expectation that he would). Four Americans say that the
man "just looks" at the boys, indicating by the "just" that they expected him
to do more. Five Greeks say that he "doesn't say anything to them," implying that they expected him to say something.

These interpretive adjectives about the man's reaction when the boys
pass with pears can only come from the expectations of the speakers about
how he should react, for the film does not show feelings.

Expectations about Objects

It has been seen that expectations can reflect assumptions about broad
context and actions. In addition, we have expectations about specific activities and even objects. For example, the film shows a man in a tree picking
pears. The film was shot in Briones Park, where there happened to be a
single pear tree. Three Americans, in the beginning of their narratives, state
that the film was set in an orchard. They *generalize*, it seems, on the basis of
their expectations that a pear tree would be in an orchard. In one case, we
can practically see the inferential process by which one tree becomes an
orchard:

> S37 (3–6)   ... the-- landscape is like U--H a f-- ... sort of peasant
>   landscape but it isn't really farmland, it's like an orchard.
>   ... It's a small orchard,

From the approximation "like an orchard" comes the conclusion "it is an
orchard." In a fourth narrative, the speaker reveals the same expectation by
her *negative statement*.

> S24 (6)   it wasn't a pear orchard, ... or anything like that.

As usual, her statement of what it was not is evidence of an expectation that
it should have been. This expectation operates for Americans but not for
Greeks.

A similar pattern can be seen in mentions of the road in the film. Four
Americans refer to it as a "dirt road," and a fifth calls it a "gravel path."
Again, a negative statement and the use of "just sort of" are familiar signals:

> S50 (72)   this road that's ... UH it's not paved, it's just sort of a dirt
>   road,

Thus we have evidence that Americans expect roads to be paved. By contrast, only one Greek refers to the road as "*chomatodhromos*," "a dirt road." It seems reasonable to attribute this difference to the greater likelihood of a road's being unpaved in Greece. This pattern of evidence indicates again how the use of adjectives tends to be evaluative (in Labov's sense), that is, to reveal some expectations.

Evidence of Expectations

I have thus far shown that structures of expectation are constantly mediating between a person and her/his perceptions, and between those perceptions and the telling about them. These expectations operate on all levels, from the broad level of context and activity (interview, subject of experiment) to ideas about episodes and actions, to objects and people. The kinds of evidence that have been seen to reveal the existence of these expectations (or scripts or frames or schemata) will now be listed and exemplified briefly. The types of evidence I have looked at, listed roughly in order of the degree to which they depart from the material in the film, are[10]: (1) omission, (2) repetition, (3) false starts, (4) backtrack, (5) hedges and other qualifying words or expressions, (6) negatives, (7) contrastive connectives, (8) modals, (9) inexact statements, (10) generalization, (11) inference, (12) evaluative language, (13) interpretation, (14) moral judgment, (15) incorrect statements, (16) addition.

1. Omission

A narrator cannot recount every detail. Some things are necessarily omitted. However, omissions can indicate expectations, especially when contrasted with what is included by other speakers. This was seen in the narrative of G12, who omitted events that would have contradicted her optimistic interpretation. One more example can be seen in the way in which reference is made to the man who passes with a goat. All Americans who mention this man refer to him as a man with a goat. In contrast, three of the fourteen Greeks who mention this man omit to mention that he had a goat with him. The conclusion suggested is that it is less remarkable, less unexpected, for Greeks that a passing man should be leading a goat. In Schank and Abelson's terms, the goat is in the Greeks' script for a passing country person. For Americans, however, the goat is unexpected and therefore reportable. We may say that the Greeks omitted to mention the goat and thereby revealed something about their expectations.

2. Repetition

Repetition is another element that does not violate the reality of the events in the film but is nonetheless a departure from straight narrative syntax.

Labov (1972) has shown that repetition can be an effective device in making "the point" of a story.

There are at least three different types of repetition: false starts (which will be discussed under that heading), linking (which seems to be a time-filler), and repetition of complete statements. The third type, which we will be concerned with, can take the form of (a) identical or changed wording and (b) immediate or later restatement.

An immediate repetition, like a linking repetition, can be a stalling mechanism, especially when it is uttered at a slowed pace, with elongations of syllables and pauses, and with clause final intonation at the end:

G18 (106)   *kai ta paidhakia synechisane to dhromo. ... synechisane-- ... to dhromo,*
             and the children continued the road. ... (they) continued-- ... the road,

When a repetition comes after some intervening commentary, however, it generally underlines a key phrase or idea which constitutes a kind of evidence of frame:

G11 (119)   *... TSK alla ... moirolatrika to pire*
     (124)   *tous koitaze moirolatrika--*
     (119)   *... TSK but ... fatefully (he) took it*
     (124)   (he) looked at them fatefully--

This reemphasis indicates the speaker's main interpretation of the film, which, as has been seen, comes from her own expectations about the pear picker's point of view. Repetition, then, is closely related to the phenomenon of reportability which is a direct function of unexpectedness.

3. False Starts

There are a number of types of false starts; the most significant in terms of discovering frames is a type I have dubbed "contentful." That is an instance of a statement being made or begun and then immediately repudiated or changed. For example, G11 said of the boy,

G11 (113)   *synantise ... ochi dhen synantise tipota allo,*
             (he) met ... no (he) didn't meet anything else,

The speaker began to say, incorrectly, that the boy met someone else, revealing her expectation that the story would continue with another meeting.

An expectation about conversational coherence can be seen in a false start in which "and" is switched to "but."

G14 (20)   *... kai-- alla-- meta to-- /s/ kaloskeftike,*
            ... and-- but-- then (he) thought better of it--,

The fact that G14 began by saying "and" indicates the expectation that the following statement would be consonant with the preceding one, a basic assumption about narrative connections.

4. Backtrack

A backtrack represents a break in temporal or causal sequentiality, a disturbance in the narrative flow. A temporal backtrack returns to an event that occurred earlier than the one just stated. A causal backtrack is an interruption for the purpose of filling in background information.

An example of a temporal backtrack can be seen when a Greek subject introduces her narrative, tells of the pear picker, and then says,

> G9 (9)   ... /a/ *stin archi archi omos EH-- lalisan kati-- koko--ri.*
> ... /a/ in the beginning beginning however EH-- crowed some-- roo--ster.

The co-occurrence of a false start, elongations of sounds, and a filler (EH--) with a backtrack is frequent. A mistake has been made, and the backtrack constitutes a correction. Therefore there are numerous traces of the speaker's discomfort. In the above example, the backtrack reflects the realization of a violation of the expectation that the narrative adhere to temporal constraints, at the same time that it reflects the speaker's subject-of-experiment expectation that she tell as much as she can recall.

A causal backtrack supplies information that was not included at first (we might say it was assumed as part of the script) but is later considered needed.

> G18 (57)   *kai-- epese-- m-- meta to paidhi opos pighaine brosta dhen eidhe kala, ... kai tou epese-- m-- TSK tou pesane ta frouta kato.*
> and-- (he) fell-- m-- then the child as (he) was going forward didn't see well, ... and (from) him fell-- m-- TSK (from) him fell the fruit down.

G18 apparently began to say that the child fell, but then she felt that it was appropriate to explain why he fell, and finally she decided that the important fact was that the fruit fell to the ground. The backtrack shows her awareness of the expectation that causality be explained. The beginning of her utterance, "and-- (he) fell--" constitutes a false start, but in this case it is the content of the replacing statement rather than the content of the repudiated statement which is of interest.

5. Hedges and Hedgelike Words or Phrases

There are numerous words and phrases that may be classed as hedges or hedgelike. By qualifying or modifying a word or statement, hedges measure the word or idea against what is expected. They caution: "not so much as you might have expected." To consider all hedges would be a mammoth study in itself. They include such expressions as "really," "anyway," "just," "obviously," "even," "kind of." Examples discussed in the preceding text are such words as "anyway" and "just."

Let us look at one other example. Following are the sentences from one narrative that contain the word "even."

S6 (20)   And the man up in the tree doesn't even notice.
   (65)   and the man up in the tree doesn't even ... doesn't notice anything.
  (142)   He doesn't .. he doesn't even notice that the pears are stolen yet.

(20) refers to the pear picker's not noticing the goatman go by. (65) refers to his not noticing the boy make off with the pears. In all three cases, there seems to be an element of surprise that the man did not notice what was happening. "Even" implies that this would be the least one might expect. The frame, then, calls for people to notice what is happening around them. "Even" intensifies the effect of the negative statement. As with "just kind of," "doesn't even" seems to be almost formulaic, as is seen in (65), where it contains a false start as well.

6. Negatives

Numerous examples of negatives have been discussed. In general, a negative statement is made only when its affirmative was expected.

One of the most consistently reappearing negative statements refers to the fact that the man picking pears is not watching the boy who steals a basket from him. Ten American subjects make some negative statement about this, such as was seen in the previous example from S6 (65). As stated above, this reflects an interaction frame. However, it is stated by so many speakers because it is also a necessary part of the theft frame: that is, there is a scenario for a theft that includes the thief's not being noticed by the victim. The theft frame will be investigated in detail in the last section of this chapter.

7. Contrastive Connectives

I have shown (Tannen 1977) that an oral narrative uses the word "but" to mark the denial of an expectation not only of the preceding clause (Lakoff 1971) but of an entire preceding set of statements or of narrative coherence in general. Thus in Greek, the word *alla* ("but") is often used to introduce a new scene in the narratives, in accordance with the expectation that things continue as they are unless otherwise marked. There is also an expectation that when people turn to leave, they continue on their way: a leaving frame. Thus when in the film the three boys interrupt their departure and turn back because they found the bicycle boy's hat on the ground, the fact that they found his hat is introduced by the word *alla* in the narratives of eight Greek subjects. Thus it has been seen that the word "but" often introduces a negative statement or, as in the following example, follows a negative.

G18 (46)   ... *kathondas ... kai-- mallista dhen kathise sti thesi tou, ... alla kathise-- m-- ... brosta brosta sto podhilato.*
... sitting ... and-- indeed (he) didn't sit in his seat, ... but (he) sat-- m-- way up front on the bicycle.

A bike-riding frame leads one to assume that a boy sits on the seat of his bike. This subject pointed out a departure from the frame: the boy did not sit on the seat. No one else made this observation, perhaps because the same frame led them to make an inference. I, for example, assumed that although the film showed the boy standing on the pedals and leaning forward as he mounted the bike, that he would immediately sit down on the seat when he got out of camera range. My own expectations about bike riding led me to assume that.

8. Modals

Modals are relatively infrequent in narratives since they make statements which are not directly narrative. "Must," "should," and Greek *prepei* reflect the speaker's judgment according to her own standards and experience. "May," "can," and Greek *borei* measure what happened against what is possible. The most frequent modal construction in the present data is the type that marks inferences of the form "must have been."

G13 (3)   ... *tha prepei na epine krasi ghiati itan poli kokkinos,*
... (he) must have drunk a lot of wine because (he) was very red,

The use of *prepei* ("must have") overtly marks the fact that G13 is making an inference. It has already been seen that inferences represent evidence of structures of expectation.

Two other instances of modals reflect the judgment that the boy should have given the three helpers pears earlier than he did. Two others indicate interpretation of the future, which can only be based on expectations (that is, that the farmer will fill the third basket with pears). Finally, "can" is used twice to describe ability, which must be an inference since it cannot be observed from the outside.

G14 (17)   ... *borouse na to sikosi aneta aftos o mikros.*
... this little boy could lift it easily.

The mention of the boy's ability indicates that G14 did not expect him to be able to lift a whole basket of pears.

9. Inexact Statements

Inexact statements are not like interpretations and inferences, for they relate what was in fact shown in the film, but they do not report events precisely as they occurred. Rather, they are fuzzy or slightly altered.

The greatest number of inexact statements about a single episode are about the fall as, for example, when the boy is said to have fallen during his meeting with the girl.

Another common type of inexact statement represents a kind of collapsing of events into a significant kernel. For example, in the film the boy gives three pears to one of the three boys who helped him, and that boy then distributes one pear to each of his friends. Some subjects explain this in just this way. However, some others say something like,

> G2 (45)   *tous edhose ta tria achladhia*
>   (he) gave them the three pears

That is, the events are collapsed to convey the significant outcome: the three boys ended up with the pears. The mechanics of their distribution is not seen as significant, since the entire event is grouped under the heading of a giving frame. The frame, by its definition, operates as a selection process, determining which details are significant.

Finally, by the same process, the "name of the frame" can influence the categorization of actions within it, causing them to be represented inexactly. For example, since the film about the pears has no dialogue, when the boys wish to get the attention of the other boy who is walking away with his bike in order to return his hat to him, one of the threesome is seen to whistle, and the sound of a whistle is heard. Yet one subject reports,

> G14 (59)   ... *kai-- tou-- fonaxe enas-- o allos*
>   ... and-- (to) him-- called a-- the other [and the other one
>   called to him]

Thus the action of "whistling" becomes "calling." The word "called" is used automatically to describe the action of getting the boy's attention because an attention-getting frame is thought of as "calling." Put another way, it may be said that calling is the prototypical way of getting someone's attention.

10. Generalization

Closely related to inexact statements is the process of generalization or multiplication by which one object or action is reported as more than one. This may reflect the nature of art, in this case the movie, in which a single instance is understood to represent multiple instances. It is furthermore intriguing to speculate that the phenomenon supports Bartlett's hypothesis of constructive memory, by which memory is seen as a process of storing individual images and recalling them as representative of numerous instances, based on structures of expectation.

Generalization has been seen in the tendency for the lone pear tree to be recalled as being in an orchard and for activities depicted once in the film to be recalled as repeated actions. For example, the man in the tree is shown climbing down the ladder. The single descent is taken to represent repeated descents:

G14 (8)   ... *kai katevaine kathe toso,*
             ... and (he) was coming down every now and then,

Another subject makes the same generalization and creates the effect of repeated actions through her intonation combined with the past continuous tense:

G11 (8)   ... *anevaine, katevaine, ydhrone,*
             ... (he) was going up, (he) was coming down, (he) was sweating,

The knowledge that fruit picking necessitates numerous trips up and down clearly triggered this generalization.

11. Inferences

Inferences are statements which could not be known simply from observation of the film, as for example when subjects report characters' thoughts, feelings, and motivations. Thus when G10 said that the man on the ladder "was afraid of falling," she was saying more about her own expectations of what a man on a ladder would feel than about what the film showed.

Inferences about why the boy fell off his bicycle have been discussed at length. That the boy loses his hat and turns his head back is a fact, but that he turns to look at the girl is an inference. While six Greek subjects make this inference, two Greeks and three Americans say that he turned to look at his hat, and two Greeks and four Americans say that he looked, without saying at what. One subject makes both inferences:

S24 (62)   he's .. UM ... kind of looking back ... at her .. and the hat,

In general, speakers state inferences as categorically as they state things they actually saw. In other words they believe they saw what they expect to have been the case, based on what they saw combined with what they know of the world.

12. Evaluative Language

I have so far distinguished three types of evaluative language: (a) adjectives, (b) adverbs, and (c) adverbs whose domain is an entire episode.

Adjectives are used to describe setting, people, and objects. As Labov noted, they occur rather infrequently in narrative. When they do occur, however, the fact that the speaker chose that quality to comment upon is significant, and more often than not, the quality expressed reveals some comparison with what might have been expected. For example, a Greek woman calls the pear picker *psilos* ("tall") while no American does. This may well reflect some framelike notion of how tall a person ordinarily is. Similarly, a Greek subject calls the setting,

G1 (2)   *ena pra--sino kataprasino topio*
         a gree--n verygreen landscape

The second adjective, "verygreen," seems to reflect an impression that the landscape is greener than might be expected (it is, in comparison to Greek landscapes). In general, the assignment of values like "tall," "big," and "very" anything are the result of some evaluative process on the part of the speaker. First, these qualities are not absolute in the sense that a man can be called a man or a tree a tree, and second, the fact that they are singled out for mention must be accounted for.

Adverbs describe the way in which something was done, and such description reflects a distinctly evaluative process. For example, one Greek subject says that the three boys at the end walk past the pear picker in this way:

G8 (61)   *kai troghane amerimna ta achladhia min xerontas oti itan klemmena.*
          and (they) were eating carelessly the pears not knowing that (they) were stolen.

The comment that the boys were eating the pears "carelessly" (or "indifferently") indicates some contrast with another way they might have been behaving: in particular, that those who are in possession of stolen goods would be nervous. The inclusion of the adverb measures the boys' behavior against expected behavior for people in their position.

Adverbs such as "suddenly" or "luckily" are often used to introduce new episodes. They indicate the speaker's attitude toward the event about to be reported and how it relates to those that have already been told. For example, in Greek, *etyche*, which corresponds to English "(he) happened to," is used a number of times. This word is related to the word *tychi*, "luck," so that its meaning is something like, "as luck would have it."

G3 (42)   *etyche ekeini tin ora na katevainei o-- erghatis apo ti-- skala,*
          (at) that time the-- worker happened to come down from the ladder,

Etyche comments on the unexpectedness of the event, that is, for the victim to cross paths with the possessors of the goods stolen from him.

13. Interpretation

Interpretation is similar to evaluation and inference, but it is a bit further removed from the events depicted in the film. It has already been seen that in our sample, Greek subjects exhibited more inclination to interpret events than Americans.

Interpretive naming is the process by which a noun is used for a character or object which represents more information than the film presented. This was seen when the three boys were called "friends" of the other boy. In a more frequent example, if a speaker calls the man who is picking pears simply "a man," she is not imposing any more information about him than that which is obvious to anyone. However, if she calls him a "farmer" or "worker," she is imposing her knowledge of the world and expectations about picking activities and the people who engage in fruit picking.

A final example of interpretation can be seen in the exchange of pears scene, in which the boy with the bicycle gives three pears to one of the other boys after that boy has returned his hat to him. Generally, Americans tend to report the exchange without comment while Greeks tend to interpret the giving of pears as a gesture of thanks. This interpretation depends upon expectations based on a helping frame. One Greek does not mention the exchange as such but indexes it for its significance alone, saying simply that the boy "thanked" the threesome. Thus interpretation can substitute for events.

14. Moral Judgment

Moral judgments are the first of the last three types of evidence which come entirely from the speaker's frames or knowledge of the world and are imposed on the events of the film. A number of Greek subjects, for example, comment that the boy should have given some pears to the three boys who helped him earlier than he did. One American does this as well:

S6 (122)   ... UM-- ... I thought why didn't he think of it before.

A moral judgment is often emotionally charged, sometimes accompanied by much verbal fussing, as can be seen in G16's account:

G16 (40)   *kai-- tote to paidhi, .. katalavainei stin /a/ eno eprepe kanoni-ka-- otan to voithisan na dhos na-- ton voithisan na ta-- dhos ta achladhia pa na ta vali sti thesi tous, eprepe kanonika ... na dhosi na prosferi EH-- na-- ... se ol se osa paidhia itane na prosferi-- ligha achladhia, kai dhen prosfere. ... alla otan eidhe na tou xanapighan ton fonaxan ghia na-- tou pane to kapello, ... tote sa na katalave oti-- eprepe na prosferi stin archi, ... kai prosfere meta ap afti ti cheironomia pou to xanafonaxan ghia to-- na tou dhosoun to kapello tou. ... kai-- archizei kai moirazei apo ena achladhi sto kathe paidhi.*
            and-- then the child, .. realizes in the /beg/ while (he) should have ordinarily-- when (they) helped him to give to-- (they) helped him to give the-- them the pears (he) goes to put them in their place, (he) should have ordinarily

> ... given offered EH-- to-- ... to al to as many children as
> there were to offer-- a few pears, and (he) didn't offer. ...
> but when (he) saw them bring him back (they) called to--
> give him the hat, ... then as if (he) realized that-- (he)
> should have offered in the beginning, ... and (he) offered
> after this gesture that (they) called him back for the-- in
> order to give him his hat. ... and-- (he) starts to distribute
> one pear each to each child.

The passage is confusing because of the plethora of interruptions, back-tracks, false starts, hesitations, elongations of sounds, and repetitions. All of these evidence the speaker's strong feelings about her moral judgment.

A moral judgment can be much more subtle, as for example when an American commented that the pears the boy gave to the three helpers "weren't the best of the bunch," implying a negative judgment about his character.

15. Incorrect Statement

Incorrect statements represent false recollections. For example, one Greek subject refers to the boy among the threesome who is the most prominent in the action as the tallest. In fact he is not the tallest. Her incorrect recall seems to reflect her preconception about "leaders" (the very idea that this boy is the "leader" is an interpretation which is made overt by at least one other Greek subject who calls him *archighos*).

A number of incorrect statements were seen in connection with the boy falling off his bicycle (p. 38). Another expectation shows through the incorrect statement by a number of subjects that the boy remounts his bike after the accident. This recollection can only come from the speakers' expectations, for in the film the boy walks off with the bike. One subject even extends the image of the three boys helping:

G20 (42)   *to voithisane na anevi-- pali sto podhilato,*
             (they) helped him to get up-- again on the bicycle,

Sometimes the speaker is aware that there is something wrong with her recall; sometimes she corrects herself, and sometimes she opts for the incorrect version.

G1 (46)   *... UH ... kai n'anevi pali sto po .. ochi ... nai.*
            ... UH ... and to get up again on the bi .. no ... yes.

Two other strikingly similar accounts illustrate that the incorrect statement is simply a more extreme manifestation of the operation of expectations which in other cases result in negative statements.

G9 (79)   *... EH-- kai anevike to aghoraki pano s ochi dhen anevike sto
            podhilato,*

... EH-- and the littleboy got up on no (he) didn't get up on
the bicycle,
G18 (89)   *kai anevike to paidhi epano sto ochi dhen anevike sto podhilato,*
and the child got up on the no (he) didn't get up on the
bicycle.

16. Addition

The most extreme evidence of a speaker's expectations lies in the process of
addition: the mention of a character or episode that was not in the film at all.
For example, one Greek subject introduced the three boys this way:

G21 (83)   *... e--keini tin ora, edheixe-- ... TSK mia ghynaika, ... itan
dhyo ghynaike ... mia ghynaika me tria paidhia,*
... (at) tha--t time, (it) showed-- ... TSK a woman, (there)
were two wome, ... a woman with three children,

There was no woman in the film. The appearance of the woman, therefore,
evidences an expectation on the part of G21 that children in the road would
be accompanied by a woman—or two!

In some cases, as with incorrect statements, the speaker questions her
recollection, but she may still opt for the incorrect one:

G18 (11)   *... EH-- sto dhromo omos, ... E--M ... pou pighaine, synantise ...
ochi dhe synantise tipota allo, ... nai. epighe ekei, kai--m-- ...
TSK itan aftos o-- meta pighe ena koritsaki, ... sto dhromo pou
pairnousan ta dhyo podhilata, synantise ena allo koritsaki,*
... EH-- on the way however, ... E--M ... where he was
going, (he) met ... no (he) didn't meet anything else, ... yes
(he) went there, and-- m-- ... TSK (it) was this-- then a
littlegirl was going, ... on the road where the two bicycles
were passing, (he) met another littlegirl,

As with previous examples, there are numerous verbal cues that the speaker
is unsure of what she is saying. Yet once she commits herself to the assertion
that the boy met another girl, she repeats it, as if to reassure herself.
Through the process of generalization, that is, of reduplicating what was a
single instance, G18 builds upon what she did see to add something she did
not, on the basis of her expectations of what would have been likely, had the
film contained more. In fact, as will be seen in the final section, she goes on
to say that the second girl was going to steal pears.

What's in a Theft?

In the discussion so far I have indicated a number of levels of expectations,
ranging from interactional context to objects, and I have shown various
kinds of linguistic evidence for these expectations, ranging from omissions

Table 1.2   Number of Mentions of Actions
Relating to Theft by Greeks and Americans

Action	*Greeks*	*Americans*
Thief enters	19	20
Thief stops	4	12
Victim not paying attention	6	10
Thief sees victim's inattention	10	8
Thief decides to take goods	3	14
Thief takes goods	19	16
Thief puts goods on vehicle	14	12
Thief leaves	15	17
Victim returns to scene	16	18
Victim discovers theft	14	19
Victim reacts	11	18

and additions to false starts and raised pitch. Another way to approach frames or sets of expectations may be to look at which elements in a set of actions are chosen for mention by a large number of speakers. In order to see how this operates for one set of events, I noted all mentions of all activities relating to the theft. In all, thirty different actions were mentioned by at least one speaker. Of these, only eleven actions were mentioned by more than ten speakers in either group (Greeks or Americans). A list of these eleven (see Table 1.2), then, constitute a profile of the most salient parts of a theft frame. The number of subjects who mentioned each action gives an indication of the relative salience of each action. Only sixteen Americans directly state that the boy takes the pears. The four others say this indirectly by stating he decided to take them and leaving it at that.

Other Effects of Theft Theme

The fact that the film centers around a theft has effects on how other events in it are told; in a way, the theft theme diffuses. For example, after telling that a man passed (the goatman), one Greek subject said,

G16 (9)   *dhen vazei dhen-- ... ... thelei tipota na k pari apo afta.*
          (he) doesn't put (he) doesn't-- ... ... want to st take from them.

The negative statement, as usual, prompts the question why she would tell what the man did NOT want. She even begins, apparently, to say "he doesn't want to *steal* any," as she utters the false start "k," probably from *klepsi*, "steal." It seems likely that she had in mind the subsequent act by the boy. Similarly, the Greek speaker who added a second girl passing on the road after the accident scene, inferred from her own false recall that this girl also wanted to take some pears.

G18 (120)   *synantise ena allo koritsaki, .. to opoio pighaine-- ekei fainetai*
            na pari kai afto-- ...frouta.
            (he) met another littlegirl, ...who was going-- there (it)
            seems to take fruit too.

More subtly, another Greek describes the boy leaving the place where the
farmer was up in the tree "quickly" (*ghrighora*). Again, the adverb attributes
a quality to the boy's action which is furnished by the speaker's expectations
about how a person leaves the scene of mischief.

Conclusion

I have shown that the notions of script, frame, and schema can be understood as structures of expectation based on past experience, and that these
structures can be seen in the surface linguistic form of the sentences of a
narrative. Furthermore, the structures of expectation which help us process
and comprehend stories serve to filter and shape perception. That is why
close analysis of the kinds of linguistic evidence I have suggested can reveal
the expectations or frames which create them.

Appendix: Transcription Conventions

Transcription conventions were developed by linguists working on
"the pear project" under the direction of Wallace Chafe: Rob Bernardo,
Patricia Clancy, Pamela Downing, John DuBois, and me.

... is a measurable pause, more than 0.1 second. Precise measurements have
   been made and are available.
.. is a slight break in timing.
. indicates sentence-final intonation.
, indicates clause-final intonation ("more to come")
-- indicates length of the preceding phoneme or syllable.
Syllables with ˘ were spoken with heightened pitch.
Syllables with ˆ were spoken with heightened loudness.
/ / enclose transcriptions which are not certain.
[ ] enclose phonemic transcriptions or nonverbal utterances such as laughter.
ʔ is a glottal stop: an abrupt cutting off of breath.

Notes

1. No attempt was made, in gathering our narratives, to find "equivalent" or
"comparable" subject populations from the point of view of socioeconomic status or
other external variable besides age and sex. Our interest was in exploring *different*
approaches to verbalization of events in the same film. While it is tempting to
hypothesize that the differences are culturally based, this need not be the case to
demonstrate that there are consistent differences in the way these two groups of
subjects approached the verbalization task. It may be noted briefly, however, that the

twenty American subjects were students at the University of California, Berkeley, while the twenty Greek subjects were attending evening classes in the English language at the Hellenic American Union in Athens. Seven were university students, two were university graduates, six were high school students, and four were employed high school graduates. The American subjects were slightly older, ranging in age from 18 to 30 with a median of 23, while the Greeks ranged in age from 16 to 26 with a median of 19. Virtually all the American subjects had been raised in cities, and most of the Greeks had been born and raised in Athens, except for one from Istanbul and four from Greek towns. It might be noted, however, that a typical Athenian has closer ties with rural life than do American city-dwellers, as Athenians often make "excursions" to the villages and most have relatives living in the countryside whom they visit regularly.

2. The interviewer was of the same sex and similar age, to minimize the discomfort caused by this situation.

3. The number following *S* (in this case S34) refers to the subject number. The number in parentheses refers to a "chunk" number, in accordance with a process of chunking utterances developed in the Chafe project. Other conventions of transcription are in the Appendix.

4. Nine Greek subjects began by saying *Nai,* "Yes." The others simply launched into their narratives. This coincides with my findings (Tannen 1976) that *nai,* commonly translated "yes," in fact is often used more like the English "okay" or "yeah" than the English "yes."

5. We know from the work of A. L. Becker that this is not so for members of Balinese or Javanese society.

6. "Anyway" was investigated in an elicitation-of-interpretations format. Results are discussed in Tannen (1976) under the subheading taken from one respondent's apt characterization, "Sour Grapes Anyway."

7. "But" as a denial if expectation signal is discussed in Lakoff (1971); its function in discourse is discussed in Tannen (1977).

8. Greek transliteration will reflect Greek spelling as closely as possible. Translation will reflect syntax in the original whenever possible without making the meaning incomprehensible. The G# represents the subject number for Greek subjects.

9. It is tempting to hypothesize that this reflects a more general tendency of Greeks to philosophize—an observation which coincides with my impressions during several years' residence in Greece.

10. It is clear that paralinguistic and prosodic features such as raised pitch and amplitude and drawn out vowels also function as evidence of expectations, and I have considered them in my discussion. However, I have not studied these in depth and therefore limit this list to strictly linguistic features.

References

Abelson, Robert P. 1975. Representing mundane reality in plans. Representation and understanding, ed. by Daniel G. Bobrow & Allan M. Collins, 273–309. New York: Academic Press.

Abelson, R. P. Script processing in attitude formation and decision-making. Cognition and social behavior, ed. by John S. Carroll & John W. Payne. Hillsdale, N.J.: Lawrence Erlbaum.

Anderson, R. C., and Andrew Ortony. 1975. On putting apples into a bottle: A problem in polysemy. Cognitive Psychology, 7:167–180.

Bartlett, Frederic C. 1932. Remembering: A study in experimental and social psychology. Cambridge: Cambridge University Press.

Bateson, Gregory. 1972. A theory of play and fantasy. Reprinted in Steps to an ecology of mind, 117–193. New York: Ballantine Books.

Bobrow, Daniel G., and Donald A. Norman. 1975. Some principles of memory schemata. Representation and understanding, ed. by Daniel G. Bobrow and Allan M. Collins, 131–149. New York: Academic Press.

Bransford, J. D., and J. J. Franks. 1971. The abstraction of linguistic ideas. Cognitive Psychology, 2:331–350.

Bransford, J. D., and M. K. Johnson. 1973. Consideration of some problems in comprehension. Visual information processing, ed. by William G. Chase, New York: Academic Press.

Chafe, Wallace. 1977. Creativity in verbalization and its implications for the nature of stored knowledge. Discourse production and comprehension, ed. by Roy O. Freedle, 41–55. Norwood, NJ: Ablex.

Chafe, Wallace. 1977. The recall and verbalization of past experience. Current issues in linguistic theory, ed. by R. W. Cole, 215–46. Indiana University Press, 1977.

Charniak, Eugene. 1975. Organization and inference in a frame-like system of common sense knowledge. Theoretical issues in natural language processing: An interdisciplinary workshop in computational linguistics, psychology, linguistics, and artificial intelligence, ed. by Roger Schank & Bonnie L. Nash-Weber, 42–51. Arlington, VA: n.p.

Fillmore, Charles J. 1975. An alternative to checklist theories of meaning. In Proceedings of the first annual meeting of the Berkeley Linguistics Society, Institute of Human Learning, 123–131. University of California, Berkeley.

Fillmore, Charles J. 1976. The need for a frame semantics within linguistics. Statistical methods in linguistics, 5–29. Stockholm: Skriptor, 1976.

Frake, Charles O. 1977. Plying frames can be dangerous: Some reflections on methodology in cognitive anthropology. The Quarterly Newsletter of the Institute for Comparative Human Development. The Rockefeller University, 1:1–7.

Gensler, Orin. 1977. Non-syntactic anaphora and frame semantics. Proceedings of the third annual meeting of the Berkeley Linguistics Society, 321–34. Institute of Human Learning, University of California, Berkeley.

Goffman, Erving. 1974. Frame analysis. New York: Harper & Row.

Gumperz, John. 1977. Sociocultural knowledge in conversational inference. Linguistics and anthropology: Georgetown University Round Table on Languages and Linguistics 1977, ed. by Muriel Saville-Troike, 191–211. Washington, DC: Georgetown University Press.

Head, Sir Henry. 1920. Studies in neurology. Oxford: Oxford University Press.

Hymes, Dell. 1974. Ways of speaking. Explorations in the ethnography of speaking, ed. by Richard Bauman & Joel Sherzer, 433–51. Cambridge: Cambridge University Press.

Labov, William. 1972. The transformation of experience in narrative syntax. Language in the inner city, 354–396. Philadelphia: University of Pennsylvania Press.

Lakoff, Robin. 1971. If's, and's and but's about conjunction. Studies in linguistic semantics, ed. by Charles J. Fillmore & D. Terence Langendoen. New York: Holt, Rinehart & Winston, 1971.

Minsky, Marvin. 1975. A framework for representing knowledge. The psychology of computer vision, ed. by Patrick H. Winston, 211–277. New York: McGraw Hill.

Pompi, K. F., and Lachman, R. 1967. Surrogate processes in short-term retention of connected discourse. Journal of Experimental Psychology, 75:145–157.

Propp, Vladimir. 1958. Morphology of the folktale, 2nd ed. Austin: University of Texas Press.

Ross, Robert N. 1975. Ellipsis and the structure of expectation. San Jose State Occasional Papers in Linguistics, 1:183–191.

Rumelhart, David E. 1975. Notes on a schema for stories. Representation and understanding, ed. by Daniel G. Bobrow and Allan M. Collins, 211–236. New York: Academic Press.

Schank, Roger C., and Abelson, Robert P. 1975. Scripts, plans and knowledge. Advance papers of the Fourth International Joint Conference on Artificial Intelligence, Tbilisi, Georgia, USSR, 151–157. Cambridge, MA: Artificial Intelligence Lab.

Schank, Roger C., and Abelson, Robert P. 1977. Scripts, plans, goals, and understanding: An inquiry into human knowledge structures. Hillsdale, NJ: Lawrence Erlbaum Associates.

Tannen, Deborah. 1976. An indirect/direct view of misunderstandings. Master's thesis. Linguistics Department: University of California, Berkeley.

Tannen, Deborah. 1978. The effect of expectations on conversation. Discourse Processes 1:203–209.

2

Interactive Frames and Knowledge Schemas in Interaction: Examples from a Medical Examination/Interview

DEBORAH TANNEN

Georgetown University

CYNTHIA WALLAT

Florida State University

Introduction

Goffman (1981a) introduces the term "footing" as "another way of talking about a change in our frame for events," "a change in the alignment we take

This chapter originally appeared in *Social Psychology Quarterly* (50:2.205–16, 1987). It is a final synthesis of a long-term project analyzing videotapes made at Georgetown University's Child Development Center. We are grateful to the Center administrators and staff who gave us permission to use the tapes, and to the pediatrician, the mother, and the parent coordinator for permission to use the tapes and for taking the time to view and discuss them with us. We thank Dell Hymes for his observations on how our work blends social psychological and sociolinguistic concerns. Tannen is grateful to Lambros Comitas and the Department of Philosophy and the Social Sciences of Teachers College Columbia University for providing affiliation during her sabbatical leave which made possible the revision of the manuscript. We thank Douglas Maynard for incisive editorial suggestions. Preliminary findings of parts of these analyses were presented in Tannen and Wallat (1982, 1983, and 1986). Literature review and analysis is the work of both authors. Theoretical discussion of frames and schemas, and the final write-up, are the work of Tannen; a significantly shorter discussion appears in Tannen (1985).

up to ourselves and the others present as expressed in the way we manage the production or reception of an utterance" (p. 128). He describes the ability to shift footing within an interaction as "the capacity of a dexterous speaker to jump back and forth, keeping different circles in play" (p. 156). Goffman asserts that "linguistics provides us with the cues and markers through which such footings become manifest, helping us to find our way to a structural basis for analyzing them" (p. 157). Using linguistic "cues and markers" as a "structural basis for analyzing" talk in a pediatric interaction, we show that a mismatch of knowledge schemas can trigger frame switches which constitute a significant burden on the pediatrician when she conducts her examination of a child in the mother's presence. Combining the perspectives of a social psychologist (Wallat) and a linguist (Tannen), we thus examine the specifics of talk in interaction in a particular setting to provide a basis for understanding talk in terms of shifting frames.

Like many of our colleagues, we make use of videotape to analyze interaction which is evanescent in nature. In his description of the theoretical and methodological complexity of making informed use of filmed records in social psychological research, Kendon (1979) cautions that microanalytic analysis must be based on a theoretical perspective involving "context analysis." He sees context analysis as a conceptual framework which presumes that participants are not isolated senders and receivers of messages. When people are in each other's presence, all their verbal and nonverbal behaviors are potential sources of communication, and their actions and meanings can be understood only in relation to the immediate context, including what preceded and may follow it. Thus, interaction can be understood only in context: a specific context. We have chosen the pediatric setting as an exemplary context of interaction. Understanding how communication works in this context provides a model which can be applied in other contexts as well.

In examining talk in a pediatric setting, we are interested in the duality of what emerges in interaction: the stability of what occurs as a consequence of the social context, and the variability of particular interactions which results from the emergent nature of discourse. On one hand, meanings emerge which are not given in advance; on the other, meanings which are shaped by the doctor's or patient's prior assumptions (as we will argue, their knowledge schemas) may be resistant to change by the interlocutor's talk.

As Cicourel (1975) cautioned over a decade ago, when social scientists create a data base for addressing the issues involved in integrating structure and process in the study of participants in medical settings, their textual material should "reflect the complexities of the different modalities and emergent contextual knowledge inherent in social interaction" (p. 34). One important way that Cicourel, and after him Richard Frankel (1989), sought to observe such complexities has been to compare discourse produced in spoken and written modalities. We have adopted this practice and have also developed a method of analyzing videotapes of participants in more than one setting.

Our analysis is based on videotapes of interaction involving a cerebral palsied child, her family, and a group of health care professionals at a university medical facility. (More detailed background to the study is provided below.) We began by focusing on the pediatric examination/interview. In preliminary analysis, we applied the notion of frames (Tannen and Wallat 1982, 1983). Comparing interaction involving different combinations from the same pool of participants in five different settings, as well as spoken and written modalities, we investigated the negotiation, elaboration and condensation of information (Tannen and Wallat 1986). In this paper we develop and expand our discussion of frames; briefly recap our earlier analysis of frames in the pediatric interview/examination; and then further develop and illustrate their operation by reference to new examples. We then develop and expand our notion of knowledge schemas, using new examples as well as further analysis of an example presented for other purposes in an earlier study (Tannen and Wallat 1986). Based on our refinement of the terms "frames" and "schemas," we show how the two interact and affect communication. Finally, we consider the implications of our study both for medical practice and for analysis of human interaction.

Frames and Schemas

The term "frame," and related terms such as "script," "schema," "prototype," "speech activity," "template," and "module," have been variously used in linguistics, artificial intelligence, anthropology and psychology. Tannen (this volume) reviews this literature and suggests that all these concepts reflect the notion of structures of expectation. Yet that early treatment of a variety of concepts of frames and schemas in the disciplines of linguistics, cognitive psychology and artificial intelligence said little about the type of frames that Goffman (1974) so exhaustively analyzed, as he himself observed (Goffman 1981b). The present paper broadens the discussion of frames to encompass and integrate the anthropological/sociological sense of the term.

The various uses of "frame" and related terms fall into two categories. One is interactive "frames of interpretation" which characterize the work of anthropologists and sociologists. We refer to these as "frames," following Bateson (1972), who introduced the term, as well as most of those who have built on his work, including scholars in the fields of anthropology (Frake 1977), sociology (Goffman 1974) and linguistic anthropology (Gumperz 1982, Hymes 1974). The other category is knowledge structures, which we refer to as "schemas," but which have been variously labeled in work in artificial intelligence (Minsky 1975, Schank and Abelson 1977), cognitive psychology (Rumelhart 1975), and linguistic semantics (Chafe 1977; Fillmore 1975, 1976).

Interactive Frames

The interactive notion of frame refers to a definition of what is going on in interaction, without which no utterance (or movement or gesture) could be interpreted. To use Bateson's classic example, a monkey needs to know whether a bite from another monkey is intended within the frame of play or the frame of fighting. People are continually confronted with the same interpretive task. In order to comprehend any utterance, a listener (and a speaker) must know within which frame it is intended: for example, is this joking? Is it fighting? Something intended as a joke but interpreted as an insult (it could of course be both) can trigger a fight.

Goffman (1974) sketched the theoretical foundations of frame analysis in the work of William James, Alfred Schutz and Harold Garfinkel to investigate the socially constructed nature of reality. Building on their work, as well as that of linguistic philosophers John Austin and Ludwig Wittgenstein, Goffman developed a complex system of terms and concepts to illustrate how people use multiple frameworks to make sense of events even as they construct those events. Exploring in more detail the linguistic basis of such frameworks, Goffman (1981a) introduced the term "footing" to describe how, at the same time that participants frame events, they negotiate the interpersonal relationships, or "alignments," that constitute those events.

The interactive notion of frame, then, refers to a sense of what activity is being engaged in, how speakers mean what they say. As Ortega y Gasset (1959, p. 3), a student of Heidegger, puts it, "Before understanding any concrete statement, it is necessary to perceive clearly 'what it is all about' in this statement and 'what game is being played.'"[1] Since this sense is gleaned from the way participants behave in interaction, frames emerge in and are constituted by verbal and nonverbal interaction.

Knowledge Schemas

We use the term "knowledge schema" to refer to participants' expectations about people, objects, events and settings in the world, as distinguished from alignments being negotiated in a particular interaction. Linguistic semanticists have been interested in this phenomenon, as they have observed that even the literal meaning of an utterance can be understood only by reference to a pattern of prior knowledge. This is fundamental to the writing of Heidegger (for example, 1962, p. 199), as in his often quoted argument (p. 196) that the word "hammer" can have no meaning to someone who has never seen a hammer used. To borrow an example from Fillmore (1976), the difference between the phrases "on land" and "on the ground" can be understood only by reference to an expected sequence of actions associated with travel on water and in the air, respectively. Moreover, the only way anyone can understand any discourse is by filling in unstated information which is known from prior experience in the world. This became clear to researchers in artificial intelligence as soon as they tried to get computers to understand even the simplest discourse—hence, for example, the need for Schank and Abelson's (1977) restaurant script to account for the use of the definite article "the" in a minimal discourse such as, "John went into a restaurant; he asked the waitress for a menu."

Researchers in the area of medical sociology and anthropology such as Kleinman (1980) and Mishler (1984) have observed the problem of doctors' and patients' divergent knowledge schemas, although they may not have used this terminology. Cicourel (1983), for example, describes the effects of differing "structures of belief" in a gynecological case. The contribution of our analysis is to show the distinction and interaction between knowledge schemas and interactive frames.

At an earlier stage of this study, we referred to an interactive notion of frame as "dynamic" and the knowledge structure notion of schema as "static," but we now realize that all types of structures of expectations are dynamic, as Bartlett (1932), whose work underlies much of present day schema theory, pointed out, and as others (for example, Frake 1977) have emphasized. That is, expectations about objects, people, settings, ways to interact, and anything else in the world are continually checked against experience and revised.

The Interaction of Frames and Schemas

We demonstrate here a particular relationship between interactive frames and knowledge schemas by which a mismatch in schemas triggers a shifting of frames. Before proceeding to demonstrate this by reference to detailed analysis of pediatric interaction, we will illustrate briefly with reference to an example of a trivial, fleeting and mundane interchange that was part of a telephone conversation.

One author (Tannen) was talking to a friend on the telephone, when he suddenly yelled, "YOU STOP THAT!" She knew from the way he uttered this command that it was addressed to a dog and not her. She remarked on the fact that when he addressed the dog, he spoke in something approximating a southern accent. The friend explained that this was because the dog had learned to respond to commands in that accent, and, to give another example, he illustrated the way he plays with the dog: "I say, 'GO GIT THAT BALL!'" Hearing this, the dog began running about the room looking for something to fetch. The dog recognized the frame "play" in the tone of the command; he could not, however, understand the words that identified an outer frame, *"referring* to playing with the dog," and mistook the reference for a literal invitation to play.

This example illustrates, as well, that people (and dogs) identify frames in interaction by association with linguistic and paralinguistic cues—the way words are uttered—in addition to what they say. That is, the way the speaker uttered "You stop that!" was associated with the frame "disciplining a pet" rather than "chatting with a friend." Tannen drew on her familiarity with the use of linguistic cues to signal frames when she identified her friend's interjection "You stop that!" as addressed to a dog, not her. But she also drew on the knowledge that her friend was taking care of someone's dog. This was part of her knowledge schema about her friend. Had her schema included the information that he had a small child and was allergic to dogs, she might have interpreted the same linguistic cues as signaling the related frame, "disciplining a misbehaving child." Furthermore, her expectations about how any speaker might express orders or emotions, i.e., frame such expressions, were brought to bear in this instance in conjunction with her expectations about how this particular friend is likely to speak to her, to a dog and to a child; that is, a schema for this friend's personal style. Thus frames and schemas interacted in her comprehension of the specific utterance.

The remainder of this paper illustrates frames and schemas in a videotaped interaction in a medical setting: the examination of a child by a pediatrician in the presence of the mother. It demonstrates that an understanding of interactive frames accounts for conflicting demands on the pediatrician. In addition to communicative demands arising from multiple interactive frames, much of the talk in the pediatric encounter can be understood as resulting from differing knowledge schemas of the mother and the pediatrician. This will be illustrated with reference to their schemas for health and cerebral palsy. Finally, it is the mismatch in knowledge structure schemas that prompts the mother to ask questions which require the doctor to switch frames.

Background of the Study

The videotapes on which our analysis is based were obtained from the Child Development Center of the Georgetown University Medical School, following our presentation of a proposal to the Center's Interdisciplinary Research Committee. The videotapes had been made as raw material for a demonstration tape giving an overview of the Center's services, and therefore documented all the encounters involving a single family and Center staff, which took place over three weeks.

The primary goal of the Center is to provide interdisciplinary training to future professionals in serving developmentally disabled children and their families. Staff members work in interdisciplinary teams which include an audiologist, speech pathologist, pediatrician, social worker, nutritionist, dentist, nurses and an occupational, an educational, and a physical therapist. Each professional meets with the child and, in some cases, other family members; then all meet to pool the results of their evaluations, which are presented to the parents in a group meeting.

The parents of Jody, the 8-year-old cerebral palsied child in this study, were referred to the Center by the parents of another child. Their chief concern was Jody's public school placement in a class for mentally retarded children. Their objective, which was met, was to have a Center representative meet with the supervisor of special education in their district and have Jody placed in a class for the orthopedically rather than mentally handicapped.

In addition to the spastic cerebral palsy (paralysis resulting from damage to the brain before or during birth), Jody was diagnosed as having a seizure disorder; a potentially lethal arteriovenous malformation in her brain (this was subsequently, and happily, rediagnosed as a less dangerous malformation involving veins only, rather than both arteries and veins); facial hemangiomas (red spots composed of blood-filled capillaries); and slight scoliosis (curvature of the spine).

We began our analysis by focusing on the pediatrician's examination/interview, which took place with the mother present. As part of our analysis, we met, separately, with the doctor and the mother, first talking with them and then reviewing segments of the tape. The mother expressed the opinion that this doctor "was great," in explicit contrast with others who "cut you off and make you feel stupid" and deliver devastating information (for example, "she'd be a vegetable") in an offhand manner.

Interactive Frames in the Pediatric Examination

The goal of this paper is to show that examining Jody in her mother's presence constituted a significant burden on the pediatrician, which can be attributed to a conflict in framing resulting from mismatched schemas. To demonstrate this interaction between frames and schemas, we will first show what framing is and how it works, beginning with the crucial linguistic component of register.

Linguistic Registers

A key element in framing is the use of identifiable linguistic registers. Register, as Ferguson (1985) defines it, is simply "variation conditioned by use": conventionalized lexical, syntactic and prosodic choices deemed appropriate for the setting and audience. Early analysis of the videotape of the pediatrician examining Jody indicated that the pediatrician used three distinct registers in addressing each of three audiences (Tannen and Wallat 1982). We will briefly recap the findings of that study.

In addressing the child, the pediatrician uses "motherese": a teasing register characterized by exaggerated shifts in pitch, marked prosody (long pauses followed by bursts of vocalization), and drawn out vowel sounds, accompanied by smiling. For example, while examining Jody's ears with an ophthalmoscope (ear light), the pediatrician pretends to be looking for various creatures, and Jody responds with delighted laughter: (See Appendix for transcription conventions.)

Doctor: Let me look in your ear. Do you have a monkey in your ear?
Child: [laughing] No::::.
Doctor: No:::? ... Let's see. ... I .. see ...... a birdie!
Child: ⌈[laughing] No:::.
Doctor: ⌊[smiling] No.

In stark contrast to this intonationally exaggerated register, the pediatrician uses a markedly flat intonation to give a running account of the findings of her examination, addressed to no present party, but designed for the benefit of pediatric residents who might later view the videotape in the teaching facility. We call this "reporting register." For example, looking in Jody's throat, the doctor says, with only slight stumbling:

> Doctor: Her canals are are fine, they're open, um her tympanic membrane was thin, and light,

Finally, in addressing the mother, the pediatrician uses conventional conversational register, as for example:

> Doctor: As you know, the important thing is that she does have difficulty with the use of her muscles.

Register Shifting

Throughout the examination the doctor moves among these registers. Sometimes she shifts from one to another in very short spaces of time, as in the following example in which she moves smoothly from teasing the child while examining her throat, to reporting her findings, to explaining to the mother what she is looking for and how this relates to the mother's expressed concern with the child's breathing at night.

[Teasing register]

> Doctor: Let's see. Can you open up like this, Jody. Look.
>   [Doctor opens her own mouth]
> Child: Aaaaaaaaaaaaah.
> Doctor: ⌐ Good. That's good.
> Child: ⌊ Aaaaaaaaaaah.

[Reporting register]

> Doctor: /Seeing/ for the palate, she has a high arched palate →
> Child: ⌊Aaaaaaaaaaaaaaaaaaaaaaaaah
> Doctor: but there's no cleft,
>   [maneuvers to grasp child's jaw]

[Conversational register]

>   ... what we'd want to look for is to see how she ...
>   mmoves her palate. ... Which may be some of the
>   difficulty with breathing that we're talking about.

The pediatrician's shifts from one register to another are sometimes abrupt (for example, when she turns to the child and begins teasing) and sometimes gradual (for example, her reporting register in "high arched palate" begins to fade into conversational register with "but there's no cleft," and comes to rest firmly in conversational register with "what we'd want to look for . . ."). In the following example, she shifts from entertaining Jody to reporting findings and back to managing Jody in a teasing tone:

[Teasing register]

Doctor: That's my light.
Child: /This goes up there./
Doctor: It goes up there. That's right.

[Reporting register]

> Now while we're examining her head we're feeling for
> lymph nodes in her neck ... or for any masses ...
> okay ... also you palpate the midline for thyroid,
> for goiter ... if there's any.

[Teasing register]

> Now let us look in your mouth. Okay? With my light.
> Can you open up real big? ... Oh, bigger. ... Oh
> bigger. ... Bigger.

Frame Shifting

Although register shifting is one way of accomplishing frame shifts, it is not the only way. Frames are more complex than register. Whereas each audience is associated with an identifiable register, the pediatrician shifts footings with each audience. In other words, she not only talks differently to the mother, the child and the future video audience, but she also deals with each of these audiences in different ways, depending upon the frame in which she is operating.

The three most important frames in this interaction are the social encounter, examination of the child and a related outer frame of its videotaping, and consultation with the mother. Each of the three frames entails addressing each of the three audiences in different ways. For example, the social encounter requires that the doctor entertain the child, establish rapport with the mother and ignore the video camera and crew. The examination frame requires that she ignore the mother, make sure the video crew is ready and then ignore them, examine the child, and explain what she is doing for the future video audience of pediatric residents. The consultation frame requires that she talk to the mother and ignore the crew and the child—or, rather, keep the child "on hold," to use Goffman's term, while she answers the mother's questions. These frames are balanced nonverbally as well as verbally. Thus the pediatrician keeps one arm outstretched to rest her hand on the child while she turns away to talk to the mother, palpably keeping the child "on hold."

Juggling Frames

Often these frames must be served simultaneously, such as when the pediatrician entertains the child and examines her at the same time, as seen in the example where she looks in her ear and teases Jody that she is looking for a monkey. The pediatrician's reporting register reveals what she was actually looking at (Jody's ear canals and tympanic membrane). But balancing frames is an extra cognitive burden, as seen when the doctor accidentally mixes the vocabulary of her diagnostic report into her teasing while examining Jody's stomach:

[Teasing register]

Doctor: Okay. All right. Now let me /?/ let me see what I
           can find in there. Is there peanut butter and jelly?
           Wait a minute.┐
Child: └No┐
Doctor: └No peanut butter and jelly in there?
Child: No.

[Conversational register]

Doctor: Bend your legs up a little bit. ... That's right.

[Teasing register]

           Okay? Okay. Any peanut butter and jelly in here? ┐
Child: └No┐
Doctor: └No.
           No. There's nothing in there. Is your spleen
           palpable over there?┐
Child: └No.

The pediatrician says the last line, "Is your spleen palpable over there?" in the same teasing register she was using for peanut butter and jelly, and Jody responds with the same delighted giggling "No" with which she responded to the teasing questions about peanut butter and jelly. The power of the paralinguistic cues with which the doctor signals the frame "teasing" is greater than that of the words spoken, which in this case leak out of the examination frame into the teasing register.

    In other words, for the pediatrician, each interactive frame, that is, each identifiable activity that she is engaged in within the interaction, entails her establishing a distinct footing with respect to the other participants.

The Interactive Production of Frames

Our analysis focuses on the pediatrician's speech because our goal is to show that the mismatch of schemas triggers the frame switches which make this interaction burdensome for her. Similar analyses could be performed for any participant in any interaction. Furthermore, all participants in any interaction collaborate in the negotiation of all frames operative within that interaction. Thus, the mother and child collaborate in the negotiation of frames which are seen in the pediatrician's speech and behavior.

For example, consider the examination frame as evidence in the pediatrician's running report of her procedures and findings for the benefit of the video audience. Although the mother interrupts with questions at many points in the examination, she does not do so when the pediatrician is reporting her findings in what we have called reporting register.[2] Her silence contributes to the maintenance of this frame. Furthermore, on the three of seventeen occasions of reporting register when the mother does offer a contribution, she does so in keeping with the physician's style: Her utterances have a comparable clipped style.

The Homonymy of Behaviors

Activities which appear the same on the surface can have very different meanings and consequences for the participants if they are understood as associated with different frames. For example, the pediatrician examines various parts of the child's body in accordance with what she describes at the start as a "standard pediatric evaluation." At times she asks the mother for information relevant to the child's condition, still adhering to the sequence of foci of attention prescribed by the pediatric evaluation. At one point, the mother asks about a skin condition behind the child's right ear, causing the doctor to examine that part of Jody's body. What on the surface appears to be the same activity—examining the child—is really very different. In the first case the doctor is adhering to a preset sequence of procedures in the examination, and in the second she is interrupting that sequence to focus on something else, following which she will have to recover her place in the standard sequence.

Conflicting Frames

Each frame entails ways of behaving that potentially conflict with the demands of other frames. For example, consulting with the mother entails not only interrupting the examination sequence but also taking extra time to answer her questions, and this means that the child will get more restless and more difficult to manage as the examination proceeds. Reporting findings to the video audience may upset the mother, necessitating more explanation in the consultation frame. Perhaps that is the reason the pediatrician frequently explains to the mother what she is doing and finding and why.

Another example will illustrate that the demands associated with the consultation frame can conflict with those of the examination frame, and that these frames and associated demands are seen in linguistic evidence, in this case by contrasting the pediatrician's discourse to the mother in the examination setting with her report to the staff of the Child Development Center about the same problem. Having recently learned that Jody has an arteriovenous malformation in her brain, the mother asks the doctor during the examination how dangerous this condition is. The doctor responds in a way that balances the demands of several frames:

Mother: I often worry about the danger involved too.→
Doctor: └Yes.
         cause she's well I mean like right now,
         ... uh ... in her present condition.→
Doctor: └mhm
Mother: I've often wondered about how dangerous
         they they are to her right now.
Doctor: We:ll ... um ... the only danger would be from bleeding.
         ... Fróm them. If there was any rupture, or anything
         like that. Which CAN happen. ... um ... that would
         be the danger.
Mother: └mhm
Doctor: ... Fór that. But they're ...... mm ... nót
         going to be something that will get worse
         as time goes on.
Mother: Oh I see.
Doctor: But they're just thére. Okay?

The mother's question invoked the consultation frame, requiring the doctor to give the mother the information based on her medical knowledge, plus take into account the effect on the mother of the information that the child's life is in danger. However, the considerable time that would normally be required for such a task is limited because of the conflicting demands of the examination frame: the child is "on hold" for the exam to proceed. (Notice that it is the admirable sensitivity of this doctor that makes her aware of the needs of both frames. According to this mother, many doctors have informed her in matter-of-fact tones of potentially devastating information about her child's condition, without showing any sign of awareness that such information will have emotional impact on the parent. In our terms, such doctors acknowledge only one frame—examination—in order to avoid the demands of conflicting frames—consultation and social encounter. Observing the burden on this pediatrician, who successfully balances the demands of multiple frames, makes it easy to understand why others might avoid this.)

The pediatrician blunts the effect of the information she imparts by using circumlocutions and repetitions; pausing and hesitating; and minimizing the significant danger of the arteriovenous malformation by using the word "only" ("only danger"), by using the conditional tense ("that would be the danger"), and by stressing what sounds positive, that they're not going to get worse. She further creates a reassuring effect by smiling, nodding and using a soothing tone of voice. In reviewing the videotape with us several years after the taping, the pediatrician was surprised to see that she had expressed the prognosis in this way, and furthermore that the mother seemed to be reassured by what was in fact distressing information.

The reason she did so, we suggest, is that she was responding to the immediate and conflicting demands of the two frames she was operating in: consulting with the mother in the context of the examination.

Evidence that this doctor indeed felt great concern for the seriousness of the child's condition is seen in her report to the staff regarding the same issue:

Doctor: ... uh: I'm not sure how much counseling has been dóne, ... wíth these parents, ... around .. the issue ... of the a-v malformation. Mother asked me questions, ... about the operability, inoperability of it, ... u:m ... which I was not able to answer. She was told it was inoperable, and I had to say well yes some of them are and some of them aren't. ... And I think that this is a ... a ... an important point. Because I don't know whether ... the possibility of sudden death, intracranial hemorrhage, if any of this has ever been discússed with these parents.

Here the pediatrician speaks faster, with fluency and without hesitation or circumlocution. Her tone of voice conveys a sense of urgency and grave concern. Whereas the construction used with the mother, "only danger," seemed to minimize the danger, the listing construction used with the staff ("sudden death, intracranial hemorrhage"), which actually refers to a single possible event, gives the impression that even more dangers are present than those listed.

Thus the demands on the pediatrician associated with consultation with the mother; those associated with examining the child and reporting her findings to the video audience; and those associated with managing the interaction as a social encounter are potentially in conflict and result in competing demands on the doctor's cognitive and social capacities.

Knowledge Schemas in the Pediatric Interaction

Just as ways of talking (that is, of expressing and establishing footing) at any point in interaction reflect the operation of multiple frames, similarly, what individuals choose to say in an interaction grows out of multiple knowledge schemas regarding the issues under discussion, the participants, the setting, and so on. We have seen that conflicts can arise when participants are oriented toward different interactive frames, or have different expectations associated with frames. Topics that the mother introduces in the consultation frame sometimes interfere with the doctor's conducting the examination, and time the doctor spends examining Jody in areas in which she has had no problems does not help the mother in terms of what prompted her to take Jody to the Child Development Center: a concern that she was regressing rather than improving in skills. Similarly, when participants have different schemas, the result can be confusion and talking at cross-purposes, and, frequently, the triggering of switches in interactive frames. We will demonstrate this with examples from the pediatrician's and mother's discussions of a number of issues related to the child's health and her cerebral palsy.

Mismatched Schemas

Before examining Jody, the pediatrician conducts a medical interview in which she fills out a form by asking the mother a series of questions about Jody's health history and current health condition. After receiving negative answers to a series of questions concerning such potential conditions as bowel problems, bronchitis, pneumonia and ear infections, the pediatrician summarizes her perception of the information the mother has just given her. However, the mother does not concur with this paraphrase:

Doctor: Okay. And so her general overall health has been good.
Mother: ...... [sighs] Not really .... uh: ... back
           ... uh ... after she had her last seizure, ... uh ...
           uh ... it was pretty cold during this .. that time ...
           a:nd uh ... it seemed that she just didn't have much
           energy⌐
Doctor: └mm
Mother: ... and she uh ... her uh ...... motor abilities at
           the time didn't seem ... very good. ... She kept
           bumping into walls, ... and falling, and ... uh

The mother's schema for health is a comprehensive one, including the child's total physical well-being. The child's motor abilities have not been good; therefore her health has not been good. In contrast, the pediatrician does not consider motor abilities to be included in a schema of health. Moreover, the pediatrician has a schema for cerebral palsy (cp): she knows what a child with cp can be expected to do or not do, i.e., what is "normal" for a child with cp. In contrast, as emerged in discussion during a staff meeting, the mother has little experience with other cp children, so she can only compare Jody's condition and development to those of non-cp children.

Throughout our tapes of interaction between Jody's mother and the pediatrician, questions are asked and much talk is generated because of unreconciled differences between the mother's and doctor's knowledge schemas regarding health and cerebral palsy, resulting from the doctor's experience and training and the mother's differing experience and personal involvement.

Mismatches based on the cp schema account for numerous interruptions of the examination frame by the mother invoking the consultation frame. For example, as briefly mentioned earlier, the mother interrupts the doctor's examination to ask about a skin eruption behind the child's ear. The mother goes on to ask whether there is a connection between the cerebral palsy and the skin condition because both afflict Jody's right side. The doctor explains that there is no connection. The mother's schema for cp does not include the knowledge that it would not cause drying and breaking of skin. Rather, for her, the skin condition and the cp become linked in a "right-sided weakness" schema.

Similar knowledge schema mismatches account for extensive demands on the pediatrician to switch from the examination to the consultation frame. When Jody sleeps, her breathing sounds noisy, as if she were gasping for air. The mother is very concerned that the child might not be getting enough oxygen. When the doctor finishes examining the child's throat and moves on to examine her ears, the mother takes the opportunity to interrupt and state her concern. The doctor halts the examination, turns to the mother and switches to the consultation frame, explaining that the muscle weakness entailed in cp also affects the muscles used in breathing; therefore Jody's breathing sounds "coarse" or "floppy." However, this does not mean that she is having trouble breathing.

Doctor: Jody? ... I want to look in your ears. ... Jody?
Mother: This problem that she hás, ... is not ...
          interfering with her breathing, is it?
Child: /Hello/ [spoken into ophthalmoscope]
Doctor: No.
Mother: It just appears that way?
Doctor: Yes. It's very ... it's ... really ... it's like
          flóppy you know and that's why it sounds the way it is.
Mother: She worries me at night.
Doctor: Yes
Mother: Because uh ... when she's asleep I keep checking on
          hér so she doesn't⌐
Doctor: ⌊As you know the important⌐
Mother: ⌊I keep
          thinking she's not breathing properly. [spoken while chuckling]
Doctor: As you know, the impórtant thing is that she dóes
          have difficulty with the use of her muscles.⌐
Mother: ⌊mhm
Doctor: So she has difficulty with the use of her muscles, ...
          as far as the muscles of her chest, that are used with
          breathing. Y'know as well as the drooling, the muscles
          with swallowing, and all that ⌐so all her muscles
Mother: ⌊Is there some exercise
          /to strengthen or help that/.

The mother's schemas for health and cerebral palsy do not give her the expectation that the child's breathing should sound noisy. Rather, for her, noisy breathing is "wheezing," which fits into a schema for ill health: Noisy breathing is associated with difficulty breathing. In fact, the parents, in the initial medical interview at the Child Development Center, characterize

Jody as having difficulty breathing, and this is entered into the written record of the interview.

These schemas are not easily altered. The pediatrician's assurance that Jody is not having trouble breathing goes on for some time, yet the mother brings it up again when the doctor is listening to Jody's chest through a stethoscope. Again the doctor shifts from the examination frame to the consultation frame to reassure her at length that the child is not having trouble breathing, that these sounds are "normal" for a child with cerebral palsy.

Doctor: Now I want you to listen, Jody. We're going to listen
            to you breathe. Can you? Look at me. Can you go like
            this? [inhales] Good. Oh you know how to do all this.
            You've been to a lot of doctors. [Jody inhales] Good.
            Good. Once ... good. Okay. Once more. Oh you have a
            lot of extra noise on this side. Go ahead. Do it once
            more. ⌈Once more.
Mother: ⌊That's the particular noise she makes when
            she sleeps. [chuckle]
Doctor: Once more. Yeah I hear all that. One more. One more.
            [laughs] Once more. Okay. That's good. She has very
            coarse breath sounds um ... and you can hear a lot of
            the noises you hear when she breathes you can hear when
            you listen. But there's nothing that's⌉
Mother: ⌊That's the kind
            of noise I hear when she's sleeping at night.
Doctor: ⌊ Yes.⌋
            Yes. There's nothing really as far as a pneumonia is
            concerned or as far as any um anything here. There's
            no wheezing um which would suggest a tightness or a
            constriction of the thing. There's no wheezing at all.
            What it is is mainly very coarse due to the ...
            the wide open kind of flopping.

Nonetheless, during the session in which the staff report their findings to the parents, when the pediatrician makes her report, the mother again voices her concern that the child is having trouble breathing and refers to the sound of Jody's breathing as "wheezing." At this point the doctor adamantly reasserts that there is no wheezing. What for the mother is a general descriptive term for the sound of noisy breathing is for the doctor a technical term denoting a condition by which the throat passages are constricted.

As we have argued elsewhere (Tannen and Wallat 1986), an understanding of the mother's schemas accounts for the resilience of her concern about the child's breathing, despite the doctor's repeated and lengthy reassurances. Our point here is that the mismatch in schemas—that is, the mother's association of noisy breathing with difficulty breathing and the doctor's dissociation of these two conditions and her emphasis on the medical definition of "wheezing" (irrelevant to the mother)—creates a mismatch in expectations about what counts as adequate reassurance. This mismatch causes the mother to ask questions which require the doctor to shift frames from examination to consultation.

Summary and Conclusion

We have used the term "frame" to refer to the anthropological/sociological notion of a frame, as developed by Bateson and Goffman, and as Gumperz (1982) uses the term "speech activity." It refers to participants' sense of what is being done, and reflects Goffman's notion of footing: the alignment participants take up to themselves and others in the situation. We use the term "schema" to refer to patterns of knowledge such as those discussed in cognitive psychology and artificial intelligence. These are patterns of expectations and assumptions about the world, its inhabitants and objects.

We have shown how frames and schemas together account for interaction in a pediatric interview/examination, and how linguistic cues, or ways of talking, evidence and signal the shifting frames and schemas. An understanding of frames accounts for the exceedingly complex, indeed burdensome nature of the pediatrician's task in examining a child in the mother's presence. An understanding of schemas accounts for many of the doctor's lengthy explanations, as well as the mother's apparent discomfort and hedging when her schemas lead her to contradict those of the doctor. Moreover, and most significantly, it is the mismatch of schemas that frequently occasions the mother's recurrent questions which, in their turn, require the doctor to interrupt the examination frame and switch to a consultation frame.

The usefulness of such an analysis for those concerned with medical interaction is significant. On a global level, this approach begins to answer the call by physicians (for example, Brody 1980 and Lipp 1980) for deeper understanding of the use of language in order to improve services in their profession. On a local level, the pediatrician, on hearing our analysis, was pleased to see a theoretical basis for what she had instinctively sensed. Indeed, she had developed the method in her private practice of having parents observe examinations, paper in hand, from behind a one-way mirror, rather than examining children in the parents' presence.

The significance of the study, however, goes beyond the disciplinary limits of medical settings. There is every reason to believe that frames and schemas operate in similar ways in all face-to-face interaction, although the particular frames and schemas will necessarily differ in different settings. We may also expect, and must further investigate, individual and social differences both in frames and schemas and in the linguistic as well as nonverbal cues and markers by which they are identified and created.

Appendix: Transcription Conventions

┌Brackets linking two lines show overlap:
└Two voices heard at once
Reversed-flap brackets show latching┐
                                    └No pause
between lines
/words/ in slashes reflect uncertain transcription
/?/ indicates inaudible words
? indicates rising intonation, not grammatical question
. indicates falling intonation, not grammatical sentence
: following vowels indicates elongation of sound
.. Two dots indicate brief pause, less than half second
... three dots indicate pause of at least half second; more dots indicate longer
   pauses
→ Arrow at left highlights key line in example
Arrow at right means talk continues without interruption→
on succeeding lines of text
´ Accent mark indicates primary stress
CAPS indicate emphatic stress

Notes

1. Thanks to A. L. Becker for the reference to Ortega y Gasset. For a discussion of framing based on numerous examples from everyday life, see chapter 5, "Framing and Reframing," in Tannen (1986).

2. The notion of "reporting register" accounts for a similar phenomenon described by Cicourel (1975) in an analysis of a medical interview.

References

Bartlett, Frederic C. 1932. Remembering. Cambridge: Cambridge University Press.

Bateson, Gregory. 1972. Steps to an ecology of mind. New York: Ballantine.

Brody, David S. 1980. Feedback from patients as a means of teaching non-technological aspects of medical care. Journal of Medical Education 55:34–41.

Chafe, Wallace. 1977. Creativity in verbalization and its implications for the nature of stored knowledge. Discourse production and comprehension, ed. by Roy Freedle, 41–55. Norwood, NJ: Ablex.

Cicourel, Aaron V. 1975. Discourse and text: Cognitive and linguistic processes in studies of social structure. Versus 12:33–84.

Cicourel, Aaron V. 1983. Language and the structure of belief in medical communication. The social organization of doctor-patient communication, ed. by Sue Fisher and Alexandra Dundas Todd, 221–39. Washington, DC: Center for Applied Linguistics.

Ferguson, Charles A. 1985. Editor's introduction. Special language registers. Special issue of Discourse Processes 8:391–94.

Fillmore, Charles J. 1975. An alternative to checklist theories of meaning. Proceedings of the First Annual Meeting of the Berkeley Linguistics Society, 123–32. Berkeley, CA: Linguistics Department, University of California, Berkeley.

Fillmore, Charles J. 1976. The need for a frame semantics within linguistics. Statistical Methods in Linguistics, 5–29. Stockholm: Skriptor.

Frake, Charles O. 1977. Plying frames can be dangerous: Some reflections on methodology in cognitive anthropology. The Quarterly Newsletter of the Institute for Comparative Human Cognition 1:1–7.

Frankel, Richard M. 1989. "I was wondering—could Raid affect the brain permanently d'y'know?": Some observations on the intersection of speaking and writing in calls to a poison control center. Western Journal of Speech Communication 53:195–226.

Goffman, Erving. 1974. Frame analysis. New York: Harper & Row.

Goffman, Erving. 1981a. Forms of talk. Philadelphia: University of Pennsylvania Press.

Goffman, Erving. 1981b. Reply to review of frame analysis by Norma Denzin. Contemporary Sociology 10:60–68.

Gumperz, John. 1982. Discourse strategies. Cambridge: Cambridge University Press.

Heidegger, Martin. 1962. Being and time. New York: Harper & Row.

Hymes, Dell. 1974. Ways of speaking. Explorations in the ethnography of speaking, ed. by Richard Bauman and Joel Sherzer, 433–51. Cambridge: Cambridge University Press.

Kendon, Adam. 1979. Some theoretical and methodological aspects of the use of film in the study of social interaction. Emerging strategies in social psychological research, ed. by Gerald P. Ginsburg, 67–92. New York: Wiley.

Kleinman, Arthur. 1980. Patients and healers in the context of culture: An exploration of the borderland between anthropology, medicine, and psychiatry. Berkeley, CA: University of California Press.

Lipp, Martin R. 1980. The bitter pill: Doctors, patients, and failed expectations. New York: Harper & Row.

Minsky, Marvin. 1975. A framework for representing knowledge. The psychology of computer vision, ed. by P. H. Winston, 211–77. New York: McGraw Hill.

Mishler, Elliot. 1984. The discourse of medicine: Dialectics of medical interviews. Norwood, NJ: Ablex.

Ortega y Gasset, Jose. 1959. The difficulty of reading. Diogenes 28:1–17.

Rumelhart, David E. 1975. Notes on a schema for stories. Representation and understanding, ed. by Daniel G. Bobrow and Allan Collins, 211–36. New York: Academic Press.

Schank, Roger C. and Robert P. Abelson. 1977. Scripts, plans, goals, and understanding: An inquiry into human knowledge structures. Hillsdale, NJ: Erlbaum.

Tannen, Deborah. 1979. What's in a frame? Surface evidence for underlying expectations. New directions in discourse processing, ed. by Roy Freedle, 137–81. Norwood, NJ: Ablex.

Tannen, Deborah. 1985. Frames and schemas in interaction. Quaderni di Semantica's round table discussion on frame/script semantics, ed. Victor Raskin. Quaderni di Semantica 6:326–35.

Tannen, Deborah. 1986. That's not what I meant!: How conversational style makes or breaks your relations with others. New York: William Morrow. Paperback: Ballantine.

Tannen, Deborah and Cynthia Wallat. 1982. A sociolinguistic analysis of multiple demands on the pediatrician in doctor/mother/patient interaction. Linguistics and the professions, ed. by Robert Di Pietro, 39–50. Norwood, NJ: Ablex.

Tannen, Deborah. 1983. Doctor/mother/child communication: Linguistic analysis of pediatric interaction. The social organization of doctor-patient communication, ed. by Sue Fisher and Alexandra Dundas Todd, 203–19. Washington, DC: The Center for Applied Linguistics.

Tannen, Deborah. 1986. Medical professionals and parents: A linguistic analysis of communication across contexts. Language in Society 15:295–312.

3

Framing in Psychotic Discourse

BRANCA TELLES RIBEIRO

Overview

"Thought disorder" is a diagnostic label associated with those psychiatric cases where the patient's speech is so confusing to the examining clinician that the patient is considered to be unable to think properly (Rochester & Martin 1979). Of course, what is implicit in this assumption is the link between thought and speech, and psychologists, psycholinguists and linguists have been addressing this issue for the past 20 years. "Thought disorders" or "talk disorders," however, may have a coherence of their own. As one analyzes the discourse of a psychotic patient, it becomes clear that her speech may be segmented into several frames. Within each frame, the speaker signals a different metamessage which indicates the type of interaction that she believes is taking place at that moment. And interactive frames bring about particular schemas (Tannen 1985, 1986, Tannen & Wallat this volume) which represent the speaker's prior experiences and expectations about people, objects, and situations. In this paper, I will show the ways in which a thought-disordered patient achieves coherence within successive

This chapter is adapted from my dissertation, "Coherence in Psychotic Discourse: Frame and Topic" (Georgetown University 1988), which has been revised as *Coherence in Psychotic Discourse* (NY: Oxford University Press, 1993). I gratefully acknowledge Deborah Tannen for her encouragement and comments on earlier drafts. My warm thanks to Susan Hoyle and Carolyn Kinney for their helpful suggestions and constructive criticisms. This research results from the support of the Conselho Nacional de Pesquisa (CNPq), who sponsored my doctoral studies in the United States. I am grateful to Drs. Eustaquio Portella and Jeremias Ferraz-Lima for providing me with the videotaped material. I am also thankful to the doctor who conducted the interview for her availability and interest in my work. And even though I have never met the patient, I remain indebted to her.

frames of talk, despite the incoherent responses that she provides in a psychiatric interview.

Background: Discourse Coherence

There are several approaches to the study of coherence in discourse. One can talk about coherence in terms of our cultural assumptions about what a text is and how it can be said to be meaningful (Becker 1979:216); in terms of participants sharing stylistic strategies (Tannen 1984:152); in terms of the concepts of connectivity and register which define a text (Halliday & Hasan 1976:23); in terms of local coherence, that is, coherence between adjacent units in discourse (Schiffrin 1985, 1987); or in terms of the communicative function of utterances and their relationship to actions (Labov 1972; Labov & Fanshel 1977).

In discussing language and coherence, Becker (1982:127) points out:

> The problem is not only that there is language, but that it is so complex. Using language involves doing several things at once, any one of which can go wrong. That is, in using language I am making sounds (or inscribing them), shaping structures, interacting with people, remembering and evoking prior text, and referring to the world—all at once.

Any one of these things can go wrong, since, as Becker adds, "it is at best an unstable integration" (1982:128). When the integration is disrupted, an unsuccessful language and interactional experience results.

In this paper I focus on one type of coherence, the examination of which is particularly appropriate for the data that I analyze: a psychiatric interview. I look at how the participants convey superordinate messages—metamessages—to indicate "what is being done by talk" (Tannen 1985:315), and how a psychotic patient coherently signals and assesses the different frames of talk that occur in the interview.

Description of the Data

The data analyzed consist of a 20-minute psychiatric interview. The patient, a lower-middle-class Brazilian woman living in Rio de Janeiro, had been taken to a mental hospital in a psychotic crisis. This interview took place two days after her admittance and before she was medicated. At that time, she was diagnosed as being in an acute manic crisis.[1]

The patient, whom I will call Dona Jurema, is 61 years old and divorced. At the time of this interview, the persons who were closest to her were her sister (Idete), her son (Francisco), and her granddaughter (Mariene). All names have been changed to preserve the patient's confidentiality.

The doctor, whom I will call Doctor Edna, is a 25-year-old woman, in her first-year internship in the psychiatric institute. Dona Jurema had been assigned to her as a patient.

In the interview, Dona Jurema displays unexpected verbal and nonverbal behavior. Consequently, coherence breaks down at a number of levels of talk. It breaks down within the exchange system: the patient does not follow the turn-taking rules: that is, she does not alternate Speaker/Hearer roles. It breaks down within the action structure: the patient does not provide the expected sequencing of actions that characterize doctor/patient interviews. And it breaks down with respect to propositional content: the patient fails to refer to what the doctor is talking about. In addition, as the interview progresses, the patient brings in several imaginary addressees who are not legitimated or ratified by the doctor. Thus, between the doctor and the patient there is only a small degree, if any, of a jointly accomplished interaction.

However, although coherence breaks down on these structural levels, the patient's discourse can be seen as serving different frames, which indicate several consistent texts, each presenting a coherence of its own. I will demonstrate that the patient's discourse obeys linguistic and social constraints that underlie the contexts she creates.

The Analysis: Introduction

When one listens to Dona Jurema's talk, one hears different speakers addressing distinct listeners—who are not in fact present. Dona Jurema takes on different roles, shifting from speaking as the patient addressing the doctor to speaking as a child addressing her mother. This is a common behavior in psychosis (Cameron 1944, Sullivan 1944, Kasanin 1944). As a child too, she talks to other family members: her sister, Idete, and her grandmother, Lena. Furthermore, she role shifts with these characters and speaks as her sister, Idete; her grandmother, Lena; and her own mother addressing the child Jurema.

The transformations that take place in this interview follow the patterns described by Goffman (1974:45) for reframings, where a systematic transformation is involved, and cues are available for establishing when the transformation is to begin. As the analysis will indicate, Dona Jurema's use of different "bits" or "chunks" of language is interrelated with the various roles assumed by the patient for herself or for her audience. These chunks of language together with other linguistic features evidence the discourse frame and the interaction that takes place.

I will argue that there are two major frames at play in the patient's discourse: the interview frame, which, although it is foregrounded for the doctor, operates in the background for the patient (only on very few occasions does Dona Jurema bring forth her role as a patient), and the frame of the psychotic crisis, which operates in the foreground for Dona Jurema. In both major frames shifts in the structure of participation occur: in the interview situation, the speaker and listener alternate turns; in the psychotic situation, the speaker (Dona Jurema) projects an addressee (the mother and other family members) and the doctor stands as an unratified participant (Goffman 1967), held at bay by the patient as someone who is not requested to participate in the occasion.

The following analysis will describe how Dona Jurema can be coherent within a frame and how frames and schemas interact in this interview. I have used a parallel column format for transcribing the data. This format captures more adequately the type of interaction that takes place here, where there is no expectation of sequential information. In the parallel column format, whenever participants overlap, their utterances occupy the same horizontal line(s) and a // (double slash) indicates the place the overlap starts. Nonverbal and paralinguistic information is indicated through the use of brackets. Most excerpts will be presented only in English. The translation portrays, as closely as possible, the sense of the talk that is taking place at that moment. I have added the Portuguese text only in those cases where a reference to the original discourse is important. The Portuguese text is available in Ribeiro (1988).

Information about nonverbal communication will be included in the transcript whenever it is relevant to the analysis. In the interview, the chairs have been arranged so that the participants can sit diagonally to each other. Dona Jurema sits on an armchair, to the right of the doctor. There is close proximity between both participants. The doctor holds a microphone pointed toward the patient. In the playback session, Doctor Edna said that Dona Jurema's unpredictable gestures and movements made it hard to attach a microphone to her gown.

The Frame of the Psychiatric Interview: *"Dona Jurema, let's talk for a little while"*

In the institutional context, the doctor is the one who frames the event as a psychiatric interview. In this frame, she attends to three types of activities: First, she requests factual information from the patient and evaluates Dona Jurema's responses to her official topic agenda. Second, Doctor Edna is concerned with the patient's physical needs. She asks her: "Do you want to walk a little?"; "Can you get up by yourself?"; "Are you tired?" Most of the time, however, Doctor Edna's questions reveal a concern for the management of the interview. Throughout the interview she requests and directs the patient to talk: "Let's talk a little bit"; "We'll keep talking for a little while"; "Answer something for me." She requests information on the patient's inability to communicate: "You can't talk to me?"; "What are you saying?" "What is 'toto'?" She monitors the communicative channel: "Can't you hear me?"

The doctor's repetitive requests for Dona Jurema to talk to her constitute an insistent invitation for the patient to "engage in a state of talk" and "reciprocal ratification" (Goffman 1967). Dona Jurema sometimes engages in talk. When she does, she alternates between participating as a patient, and thereby answering the doctor, or responding as a child addressing a mother.

When the patient does not engage in talk, Doctor Edna keeps summoning her to the frame of the interview. She uses the address form *Dona Jurema* to call the patient repeatedly, as in the following:

(1)　　　　　　　　　　　　　　　　　　Patient:
　　　　　　　　　　　　　　　　　　　[chanting and baby talk]
　　　　　　　　　　　　　　　　　　　I'm gonna tell,
Doctor:　//DONA JURE:MA!　　　//　this was,
　　　　　　　　　　　　　　　　　　　this was,
　　　　　　　　　　　　　　　　　　　this was,
　　　　　　　　　　　　　　　　　　　my secret,
　　　　　　　　　　　　　　　　　　　this was, ..
　　　　　　　　　　　　　　　　　　　this was,
　　　　　　　　　　　　　　　　　　　and this was,=
Doctor:　=Dona Jurema!=
　　　　　　　　　　　　　　　　　　　=my secret. ..
　　　　　　[acc]
　　　　DONA JUREMA!　　　　　　[singing]
　　　　　　　　　　　　　　　　　　　my little husband,

Here, we see Doctor Edna trying unsuccessfully to interrupt the patient's stream of talk. She emphatically summons Dona Jurema to the interview. Dona Jurema, however, is engaged in a speech play activity of her own. She chants and sings and does not provide any answer.

There are, however, a few moments during this interview that Dona Jurema, as a patient and interviewee, does engage in a state of talk. The excerpts that I will discuss in this section represent some of these instances when the patient briefly engages in the frame of the interview.[2]

Reframings from the Psychotic Crisis into the Interview Frame

We saw that in the institutional frame Doctor Edna keeps inviting the patient to talk. She repeats the request "Let's talk for a little while," which is often transformed into a directive "We'll keep talking for a little while." Dona Jurema responds to this request with a series of indirect negative answers. Although indirect, these answers do show her attention to the interview. Her refusal to cooperate can be captured in three different forms: (1) she turns to the doctor and expresses a complaint; (2) she shifts to nonverbal communication; and (3) she requests permission to leave and thereby close the interview. In the following discussion I will illustrate each of the three situations.

The Patient Expresses a Complaint

In the first situation, Dona Jurema shifts out of the psychotic frame into the interview frame to tell Doctor Edna that she cannot talk and to complain about the doctor's initial request to "talk for a little while."

The following example is a closing to a segment that takes place at the opening of the interview. Previous to this segment the doctor had issued an invitation: "Dona Jurema, let's talk for a while." This request opens the interview. As a response, Dona Jurema chants and sings. She holds the floor, while the doctor tries without success to take a turn. Dona Jurema ends this segment by raising her pitch increasingly while raising both hands toward the doctor. Then, she makes a supplicating gesture toward the doctor:

(2)   Patient:

                                               [whining and singing]
                              1.   [Hail:, Hail:, Hail Ma:ry,
                              2.   [Hail:, Hail:, Hail Ma:ry,

                                               [raises both hands together, raises head, raises her eyes]

                                               [whimpering]
                                               [acc]
               →   3.   what more do you want,
                                               [looks at the doctor]
                              4.   umh::? ....
                                               [freezes position:
               →   right hand shaking and pointing]

Doctor:

               [half smiling]
               [dec]
        5.   Dona Jure::ma!

                                       Patient:

                                               [whimpering]
                              6.   umh:?
               →   7.   you know that I can't::.
                                               (1.3)

                                               [freezes position: right hand shaking and pointing]

Prior to this segment, Dona Jurema has been singing and chanting (addressing her mother and referring to a secret, to her husband, and to the Virgin Mary). There has been no eye contact with the doctor. Toward the end of the hymn to the Virgin Mary (lines 1–2), Dona Jurema turns to the left, toward the doctor, and raises both hands and arms in a very slow gesture. As she raises her head, she looks up at the doctor. This is the very first time in the interview that Dona Jurema actually turns to the doctor and makes eye contact. It is also the first time that she actually talks (instead of chanting or singing). As she speaks (lines 3–4 and 6–7), she gives a negative response ("What more do you want?") to the doctor's initial request, the underlying meaning being "I have already said everything there is to know" and "You should know better than to ask me questions." She looks at the doctor and says, pleadingly, "You know that I can't::." At this moment she has shifted to the interview context, and she relinquishes the floor to the doctor.

The following is another example of the same pattern described in example (2). Again, Dona Jurema turns to the doctor and addresses her; by doing that, she relinquishes the floor to the doctor.

This segment takes place after a long stretch of talk, in which the patient addresses her sister, chants a tune about a secret, and plays with the doctor's feet as she refers to her granddaughter, Mariene. Again she sings another religious hymn (substituting her granddaughter for the Virgin Mary). At the end, she raises her head and looks up at the doctor and asks another question.

(3)   Patient:

                                        [hymn]
                                   1.   Malie:::ne:::,
                                   2.   Sa:::cred Lie:ne,
                                   3.   to me she is:::is:,
                                   4.   sanctifi::ed:,

                                        [gets halfway up in the
                                        chair, sits at the edge of the
                                        armchair, looks down, and
                                        holds posture]

                                        [whimpering, baby talk]
                        →   5.   ⌈aren't you going to=
                                   6.   =ask me questions now?=

                                        [raises her head; holds her
                                        body halfway up, hands
                                        pressing on the chair; looks
                                        at doctor]

Doctor:
   7.   =I'm going to ask, Dona Jure:ma.
                                        Patient:
                                        [sighing]
                        →   8.   what are you going to ask?
                                        [holds her body half way
                                        up]

Doctor:
        [acc]
   9.   WHERE DO YOU LIVE? ...

Again, as in example (2), Dona Jurema closes an entire stretch of talk by "touching base" with the doctor—that is, she makes eye contact and asks the doctor a question (lines 5–6). The question accomplishes two related moves: she introduces a complaint about the doctor's not managing the process of communication and she challenges the doctor to take action. She also relinquishes the floor to the doctor. Doctor Edna addresses the patient's request by stating that she will take some action (in line 7). In her next turn, Dona Jurema challenges the doctor again and requests information about what will be asked. Doctor Edna's response (line 9) is a question on the topic "place of residence," which is part of her topic agenda. She resumes, therefore, the interviewer's role which the patient had challenged.

These two segments (examples 2 and 3) illustrate how Dona Jurema may shift out of the frame of the psychotic crisis and into the frame of the interview. In both segments, the patient establishes eye contact with the doctor and shifts from singing to speaking. As she speaks, she makes a request that has the force of a complaint. She also relinquishes the floor to the doctor. Once the shift takes place, the doctor regains control over the turn system and the action structure: she takes the floor and makes the next move as she requests referential information on a given topic.

The Patient Shifts to Nonverbal Communication

The second type of response that the patient provides to the doctor's requests is a change in the communicative channel: to address the doctor's question, Dona Jurema switches to nonverbal behavior. The following segment illustrates this situation. First the patient engages in nonsensical talk. However, at the end of this segment, she communicates nonverbally her inability to engage in talk.

The following example follows an excerpt previously discussed (example 2). After the patient has stated that she is unable to talk, Doctor Edna takes a turn and asks whether the patient cannot talk to her:

(4)
Doctor:
  1.   =you can't talk to me?

                                              Patient:
                                              2.   totototototototo:.
                                                   [moves hand back to arm-
                                                   chair; looks beyond the
                                                   doctor]

                                                   ['hhh]

                                              3.   [the tototó:::!
                                                   [gesture with right hand
                                                   pointing straight ahead]

Doctor:
  4.   what's totó?

Patient:
5.   the totó totó::!
     [series of pointing gestures] $\Big\}$

Doctor:
6.   what's totó?

Patient:
7.   that totó:::.
     (1.5)
     [pointing gestures]

Doctor:
8.   what is it you're saying?

Patient:

     [acc]
9.   totodododododododododo
10. /dododododododdodo/ ...

→   [gesture with hands indicat- $\Big\}$
         ing "who knows?"; looks
         down]

Doctor:
11. you don't know, do you.

In line (1) the doctor requests the patient to confirm that she cannot talk. As a response, Dona Jurema engages in nonsensical language (line 2). She creates a form "tototó" to which she refers repeatedly (in lines 3, 5, and 7) until it becomes gibberish (lines 9–10). And when it becomes unintelligible, she gestures to the doctor, using a conventional gesture to indicate "who knows", i.e., "who knows what I'm saying" (lines 9–10). Doctor Edna picks up on this cue and responds to the patient's gesture by stating verbally what the patient has expressed nonverbally (line 11—"you don't know, do you").

The above example, like the others we have seen, portrays a situation where Dona Jurema indicates that she does not want to engage in a state of talk with the doctor. She addresses the doctor's initial question "You can't talk to me?" by engaging in nonsensical communication, thereby metacommunicating "No, I cannot (or will not) talk to you" (in line 2). The segment that follows serves to illustrate her response: she cannot talk (or will not talk) because she is talking gibberish. And she shifts to a nonverbal channel to indicate that she is aware of the fact that she is talking gibberish.

The Patient Closes the Interview

The third and last type of response represents the patient's last move in the interview: she requests permission to leave and thereby closes the interview.

(5)
Patient: can I stand upupupupupupupupup?
Doctor: yes, you can.

            can you get up by ⌈yourself?

This interview ends with Dona Jurema's requesting permission to stand up. She has been signaling from the beginning of the interview that she wanted to get up and leave: she has been swinging herself back and forth in her chair, getting up halfway and sitting on the arm of the chair; she has been asking to leave by using the word *azular* (a colloquial term for "leave," translated as "split"). In other words, she says, "it's time to leave," as in the following:

(6)
Patient: it's that time.
Doctor: it's that time for what?
Patient: it's time to go.

This last request completes a coherent set of responses through which Dona Jurema signals that she does not want to engage in talk. She first addresses the doctor, conveying a complaint (examples 2 and 3); then, she engages in nonverbal communication (example 4); and, finally she asks to leave (examples 5 and 6). All of the above constitute Dona Jurema's answer to the doctor's request for interaction within the psychiatric interview frame.

Place, Time, and Persona Cues

During this interview, Dona Jurema introduces certain cues that indicate she has the appropriate contextual *place, time,* and *persona* references of the institutional frame. I will now comment on each of these cues.

Regarding *place,* at the very opening of the interview Dona Jurema makes a reference to her "ward":

(7)
            when I get, to my ward,

Halfway through the interview, Dona Jurema says emphatically that she is "here, at the hospital." The excerpt below illustrates this segment.

(8)

[Prior to the segment below, she held the floor for a long stretch of talk, where she said that she had to get going, that she was very tired, that one could not make any noise "here."]

Doctor:
  1. ⌈HERE where, Dona Jurema?
                              Patient:
                                [baby talk]
                            2. here, here, here.=

                                [bends over, looks down,
                                speaks into the microphone

Doctor:
3.   =where are you?

Patient:
       [baby talk]
4.   here!

Doctor:
5.   mmm?

Patient:
       [baby talk]
6.   here!

Doctor:
7.   what place is this "here="
8.   =you're at now?

Patient:
9.   I am in a hospital.=

Doctor:
10. =//which hospital?

10. //I thought I'd be going=
     =to another hospital,

11. mmm.

12. and I ended up in a very=
13. =beautiful hospital. ...

While she provides the adequate referential information (being at the hospital), Dona Jurema does not give the specific information the doctor requests when she asks "which hospital?" Instead Dona Jurema introduces an evaluative remark, "I ended up in a very beautiful hospital."

However, at the closing of the interview, she mentions "the hospital" and more specifically "Pinel Hospital," the hospital she was taken to:

(9)
       that's why Chico, <last night-> ...
       came over to the house. .. to ta::ke me, ...
       to bring:: me, ... to the hos:pital. ....
       to the Pinel Hospital.

The above examples (7, 8, and 9) are place cues that the patient provides, indicating that she knows where she is (the ward, the hospital, and Pinel Hospital).

There is also a *time* cue. The only time reference that Dona Jurema makes occurs at the closing of the interview. She mentions that her son Chico had come to fetch her the night before to take her to the hospital (example 9). This interview takes place two days after she had been admitted to the hospital; hence, Dona Jurema has some time reference, but she misses a day.

Finally, Dona Jurema also has a perception about her own disability, a reference that she introduces halfway through the interview. Prior to the segment below, the doctor had been asking questions in an attempt to establish some common referential ground with the patient. She asks Dona Jurema about what she had seen on her way from her ward to the office, to be interviewed (in this segment I include the Portuguese text and I will refer to it in the discussion):

(10)

Doctor:	Patient:

1. // ⌈A SENHORA VIU=   // viu como-.
2. =ALGUM BICHINHO=
3. LA FORA,
4. // QUANDO PASSOU=   //viu como a senhora acertou?
5. =POR AQUI?

6. Dona Jure:ma?=

                                                [singing]
                                        7. =eu vi uma formigui:nha.
8. formiguinha?

                                                [singing]
                                        9. eu vi uma formigui:nha.
10. e o outro bicho,
11. que a senhora=   [baby talk]
12. //=mostrou la fora?=   //   =o outooutooutoouto⎫
                                        biso?=   ⎭
13. =qual foi?=
                                        14. =é gente grande.
                                        15. a gente nao pode fala=
                                        16. =de gente gran::de.=
17. =mmm.
                                        18. só pode falá de gente=
                                        19. =peque:na.
        →   20. e eu como sou anãozinho-

:::

Doctor:	Patient:

1. // ⌈DID YOU SEE=   // see how-.
2. =SOME LITTLE ⎫
    ANIMAL=   ⎭
3. OUT THERE,
4. // WHEN YOU CAME=   //see how you got it right?
5. =ON YOUR WAY ⎫
    HERE?   ⎭

6. Dona Jure:ma?=

[singing]
7. =I saw a little ant:!

8. a little <u>ant</u>?

[singing]
9. I saw a little ant:!

10. what about the other=
11. =animal you showed=
12. //=me outside?=

//   [baby talk]   ⎫
     =the otherotherother ⎬
     <u>animal</u>?=   ⎭

13. =which was it?=

14. =it's a [grown-up].
15. we cannot talk about=
16. =<u>grown:-ups</u>.=

17. =mmm.

18. we can only talk about=
19. =li:ttle people.
→   20. and me, since I am a little=
         =midget-

When the doctor asks about "the other animal" (lines 10–11), she is trying to see whether Dona Jurema has some recollection of having walked through the hospital patio and pointed at some chickens and ducks that were there.[3] In her answer, however, Dona Jurema refers to the people (*gente grande,* which means "grown-up"—literally, "big people") that she saw, and she adds that one cannot talk about "big people"; one can only talk about "little people," *gente pequena.* Then (in line 20) she states that she is a midget, that is, not a full-fledged adult. When she calls herself a midget, Dona Jurema uses the diminutive form *anãozinho,* which can be interpreted as a "little midget" or a "nice-cute little midget," since the suffix *-inho* can indicate an affective dimension.

Here, the asymmetry is exaggerated. We have the social asymmetry of the medical encounter, where Doctor Edna—the gatekeeper—interviews and evaluates the patient Dona Jurema, as in any medical encounter. Then, in an exaggerated dimension, we have Dona Jurema assuming the stance of "little midget" talking to a "grown-up."

Thus in the frame of the psychiatric interview, Dona Jurema presents herself as neither a full-fledged adult nor a child, but rather something in between the two. On one hand, she has grown beyond childhood; on the other hand, she does not feel like an adult who has gained the grown-up *gente grande* identity. What Dona Jurema signals here is the perception she has of her own mental disability.

In this section I have argued that both the doctor and the patient talk within the frame of the psychiatric interview. Doctor Edna attempts to interact with the patient, summoning her repeatedly to the frame of the interview, while Dona Jurema attends to very few of these requests. There

are instances, however, when Dona Jurema shifts from the frame of the
psychotic crisis into the frame of the interview. When she does this, she
relinquishes the floor to the doctor and asks for the doctor's help. Her
requests have the force of a complaint or a challenge to the doctor's authority. She also provides references for where she is, when she arrived at the
hospital, and who she is now. In the interview frame, Doctor Edna asks the
patient to talk. The answer from Dona Jurema to the doctor is "I've shown
you everything" and "you know I cannot talk."

I will now discuss the reframings that take place in the context of the
psychotic crisis.

The Frame of the Psychotic Crisis: "Mother, you know everything."

Within the interview frame is embedded the frame of the psychotic crisis.
These two frames can be represented as shown in Figure 3.1. The predominant characteristic of the psychotic frame is that the patient speaks as if she
were a child addressing her mother. At times she addresses the doctor as if
the doctor were her mother. At other times she addresses her absent mother
treating the doctor as a third party. This frame is a psychotic fabrication
(Goffman 1974:115)—a transformation of ordinary behavior, in which
Dona Jurema treats the doctor literally (not metaphorically) as her mother.
Hence to the patient there is a transformation from "the doctor who is like
my mother" (a metaphor and, in psychoanalytic terms, a transference) to
"the doctor who *is* my mother." Goffman states that "one of the upsetting
things 'psychotics' do is to treat literally what ordinarily is treated as metaphor, or at least to seem to do so" (1974:115).

Dona Jurema addresses the listener (the doctor in the mother's role) or

Figure 3.1.

the addressee (Dona Jurema's absent mother) as *a senhora* (formal "you" in Brazilian Portuguese), using a child's variants *a senhola* and *a sinola*. She also uses the address form *mãe* "mother," with emphatic stress on the last syllable mãe:, transcribed as "ma:ma::," a form used by young children when soliciting attention from the mother. The following excerpt takes place at the opening of the interview and illustrates two different frames of talk (I have included the Portuguese text to illustrate the use of forms I have just described):

(11)

Patient:

[whining]
1. mãe:!=

Doctor:
2. =Dona Jurema!

Patient:
3. mãe:! ..
4. /que é, filhinha?/

Doctor:
5. Dona Jurema,
6. vamo conversá um pouquinho. ..

Patient:

[staccato and baby talk]
7. que-qua-senhola-qué-sabê,

Doctor:
8. //viu?
          // madame-minha-mãe,
9. a-senhola-não-soube-=
10. =já-de-tudo?

/mmm/
11. ela já não mostrou=
12. =(tudo)-

: :

Patient:

[whining]
1. ma:ma::!=

Doctor:
2. =Dona Jurema!

Patient:
[whining]
3. ma:ma::! ..
4. /what, my child?/

Doctor:
5. Dona Jurema,
6. let's talk for a little while. ..

Doctor:	Patient:
	[staccato and baby talk]
	7. what-is-it-you-wish-to-know,
8. O.K.?	// madam-my-mother,
	9. Don't you already know=
	10. =everything?
/mmm/	11. hasn't she shown you=
	12. =(everything?)

At the opening of the interview two frames conflict. While Doctor Edna summons the patient to the interview, Dona Jurema creates another context of talk where, as a child, she calls her mother twice (lines 1 and 3—"ma:ma::"), and also provides the child with the mother's answer (line 4—"what, my child"). In lines 5–6 the doctor asks the patient to participate in a conversation. In Dona Jurema's next turn (lines 7–12), she addresses the doctor's request as if it had been her mother's request: "what is it you wish to know, madam my mother." She thus shifts from her own created context of talk to engage in talk with the doctor/mother.

The schema of a very powerful mother underlies the psychotic frame. Dona Jurema addresses her mother as *madame minha mãe* "madam my mother"—the one who knows everything (lines 8–10—"don't you already know everything?"). The Portuguese address form "madam" is used in asymmetrical relationships. The predominant action in the child's discourse vis-à-vis her mother is establishing and marking deference. As example (11) illustrates, this interview opens with the child's addressing her mother and asking "what do you want to know, madam my mother?" and "don't you already know everything?" The core statement "mother knows" is repeated throughout the interview, and it is often transformed:

> my mother knows
> you (the mother/the doctor) know
> grandmother Lena knows
> my son knows
> my sister knows
> only God knows

or expanded:

> mother is the one who knows
> she is the one who knows
> he is the one who knows
> you know very well
> you know better than I
> you know better than anyone

In some moments of the interview, it is part of a speech play presented as a chant reminiscent of a nursery rhyme:

(12)
>   you know that you knew. ....
>   all all that I wanted. ....
>   you are the one who knows. ....
>   it's the mother,
>   it's the mother
>   it's the mother,
>   it's the mother,
>   it's the mother,
>   it's the mother
>   it's the mother,
>   it's the mother,
>   huh:::::::!
>   ⌊it's the mother of her::: son!/

Knowledge and power come together, when Dona Jurema says:

>   you know better than I
>   you know better than anyone

This ascribed position contrasts with the child's lack of knowledge, as she states several times:

>   I don't know anything, anything, anything.
>   I didn't know.

or as she represents herself:

(13)
>   then it's with you. ...
>   then it's been since that time, ma:ma::? ...
>   then only now that I know, ma:ma::. ....
>   I was a little silly girl,
>   I didn't know anything. ..
>   I knew only how to suck my thumb.
>   (6.1)
>   [lifts right hand and puts thumb in the mouth,
>   closes eyes, turns to the doctor, opens eyes,
>   takes thumb out of the mouth.]

Within this frame of talk, the mother holds the position of authority which is expressed through Dona Jurema's repetitive statement "the mother is the one who knows" or addressed to the doctor/mother: "you are the one who knows."

Thus the schema of an asymmetrical mother/daughter relationship dictates certain constraints in the child's role while addressing her mother. This schema is signaled through the types of moves the child performs, through speech play activities that she introduces, and through her use of child language. I will now illustrate each of these cues.

Types of Moves Performed

As a child, Dona Jurema marks deference when she addresses her mother. This is what we saw in example (11), where Dona Jurema uses the address form "madam my mother," and in example (12), where she stresses that the mother is the one who knows everything. Through deference she establishes an asymmetrical relationship. In addition, Dona Jurema keeps trying to appease the authority figure of the mother, as in the following excerpt:

[Prior to this segment, Dona Jurema had been complaining about the heavy rain and then she says:]

(14)

Patient:
1. eu tou com medo da chuva. ..
   [bends more forward]
2. bem que Francisco falou,
   [moves slightly backward]
3. mãe:. ...
4. tá certo, mãe? ... ['hhh]
   [looking down]
5. tá tudo bonzinho? ...
6. tá tudo certinho? ..
   [baby talk]
7. ela assim que ele quelia?
   (1.2)
   [looks up to the right and
   tightens lips]   }

:::

Patient:
1. I'm afraid of the rain. ..
   [bends more forward]
2. Francisco has warned us,
   [moves slightly backward]
3. mama::. ...
4. right, mama? ... ['hhh]
   [looking down]
5. is everything fine? ...
6. is everything all right? ..
   [baby talk]
7. is this really how he wanted things?
   (1.2)
   [looks up to the right and
   tightens lips]

As a child, Dona Jurema introduces a series of questions through which she requests the mother's approval (lines 4–6). She repeats (with variation) three times the same request, making use of the Portuguese morpheme *-inho* for signaling affection:

> tá certo, mãe? ...
> ⟶ tá tudo bonzinho? ...
> ⟶ tá tudo certinho? ..
>
> right, mama? ...
> is everything fine? ..
> is everything all right? ...

This type of request places the mother as evaluator and judge: the mother is the one who knows. As a consequence, she is also the one who distinguishes right from wrong, and who determines when things go right or not.

In other instances, as she addresses her mother, Dona Jurema keeps trying to get her mother's attention. Here the marker *viu* "see" is used repeatedly to stress the child's effort in calling the mother's attention to some point she wants to make. The following examples (15), (16), and (17) illustrate three instances of this type of occurrence:

(15)

> Patient:
> [baby talk]
> ela tão sim:pes, viu!
> viu mãe:!

: :

> Patient:
> [baby talk]
> it was so sim:ple, see!
> see ma:ma::!

(16)

> Patient:
> a senhora-
> dodododododododdod-
> a senhora- viu,
> viu-viu-viu, viu-viu.
> [whining]
> tá vendo, mãe:.   (3.1)

: :

> Patient:
> you-
> dodododododododdod-

                                              you- see,
                                              see-see-see, see-see.
                                              [whining]
                                              y'see, ma:ma::. (3.1)
(17)

                                       Patient:
                                       viu. ...
                                       viu tanta curiosidade a-toa,
                                       tá vendo, mãe. ...
                                       viu mãe. ...
                                            [puts slippers on,
                                             takes slippers off]
                                       porque que não podia,⎫
                                       mãe?   ⎭

::

                                       see. ...
                                       see so much idle curiosity,
                                       y'see, mama. ...
                                       see mama. ...
                                            [puts slippers on,
                                             takes slippers off]
                                       why couldn't one, mama?

In the segments above, Dona Jurema calls upon her mother and points
emphatically (with the marker *viu*) to certain events, whose referents are
never clearly indicated. As a small child, Dona Jurema does not introduce
topics, or provide the antecedent(s) for her reference. Instead, she uses
pronominal forms or impersonal verbs.

    The above discussion focused on the types of moves Dona Jurema
introduces in the frame of the psychotic crisis, and how these contributions
establish an asymmetrical mother/daughter relationship. Next I will discuss
how speech play can be another cue within this frame of talk.

Speech Play Activities

In this interview, many instances of speech play recall the rhythm of children's lore and jingles. Often it is a way for the patient to refer indirectly to
topics that represent difficult matters for her. Kirshenblatt-Gimblett
(1976:73) notes that both Bernstein (1960) and Wolfenstein (1954) observe that the "'ready-made' character of the rhymes, jokes, taunts, or insults
makes the utterances impersonal and therefore helps to insulate or protect
the child from full responsibility for what he says." Thus, it is not surprising
that the patient makes use of jingles, chanting and rhymes when she refers to
or addresses her mother. We have already seen how Dona Jurema marks

deference. In the following example, she uses speech play to defy her mother indirectly, as she refers to a "secret":

(18)

	Patient:
	[singing and baby talk]
	eu vou contá,
Doctor: //DONA JURE:MA!	// ela esse,
	ela esse,
	ela esse,
	o meu segedo,
	ela esse, ..
	ela esse,
	e ela esse,=
Doctor: =Dona Jurema!=	
	=o meu segedo. ..

::

	Patient:
	[singing and baby talk]
	I'm gonna tell,
Doctor: //DONA JURE:MA!	// this was,
	this was,
	this was,
	my secret,
	this was, ..
	this was,
	and this was=
Doctor: =Dona Jurema!=	
	=my secret. ..

Here Dona Jurema ignores the doctor's (or mother's) summonses. She goes on with her own activity. In this frame of talk, Dona Jurema plays with the theme of secrecy. She chants about having said something:

(19)

eu já disse!
eu já disse!
eu já disse!

I've already said it!
I've already said it!
I've already said it!
said it, said it, said it!

She also challenges her addressee by saying that she will not provide the information, which will be kept secret:

(20)

        num vou contá!
        num vou contá!
        num vou contá!
        num vou contá!

        I'll never tell!
        I'll never tell!
        I'll never tell!
        I'll never tell!

Thus Dona Jurema, when addressing her mother, intersperses her talk with chanting and singing in a childish register. The setting is the family, and within this setting the child may play rhythmic and rhyming games "independent of any external needs" and present a series of activities that may be subject "to starting and stopping, to redoing, to discontinuation . . . and to mixing with sequences from other routines" (Goffman 1974:42).

The Use of Child Language

A third way to express the asymmetrical relationship between mother and child is through child language. In this interview, Dona Jurema introduces certain phonetic variants that are typical of young children. Of all of them, the most common is the substitution of the alveolar lateral [1] for the alveolar flap [r] as in the third person singular of the imperfect of *ser* "be" (*era/ela*); the formal "you" (*senhora/senhola*); and the form "because" (*por isso/pol isso*) that has been transcribed at times as *polisso*. The velar fricative [x] (in Rio) or the alveolar trill [r] (in São Paulo) changes to [1], in words such as *Terra/Tela* (Earth); *morrê/molê* "die." Another common consonant change is fronting: the alveolar fricative [š] is replaced by the dental fricative [s] in words like *chegá/segá* "arrive," *chove/sove* "rain"; the velar stop [k] is sometimes replaced by the alveolar stop [t] in words such as *casa/tasa* "house," *aqui/ati* "here." All of these variants, as well as others, occur asystematically throughout this interview. They constitute another cue to indicate Dona Jurema's stance as a child.

I have described here the frame of the psychotic crisis. Here the patient creates two figures: a child and a mother. Within this frame, the child's statements or requests frequently end with the address form *mãe* "mother," which has a whining and demanding tone (transcribed as mãe: "ma:ma::"). Besides the address term (*mãe*), the patient also uses the marker *viu* "see" to get the mother's attention. Within this frame, Dona Jurema, the child, marks deference vis-à-vis her mother; she seeks approval from her mother; and she teasingly defies her mother's authority.

Throughout this interview, the patient most often speaks as if she were talking to her mother, treating the doctor as if she were the mother. In the next sections, however, we will see that at times the patient also speaks as a child addressing her grandmother or her sister. In addition, she also shifts roles with these figures, becoming the mother or grandmother addressing the child Jurema.

The Emergence of Consistent Texts in the Psychotic Fabrication

In the frame of the psychotic crisis, Dona Jurema shifts roles and establishes new contexts of communication. The different characters that Dona Jurema introduces in her discourse perform different actions and accomplish different things. Here major reframings, where the patient takes on a different role, take place; that is, she presents herself as a different figure. However, it is important to bear in mind that by changing an alignment, Dona Jurema is not "so much terminating the prior alignment as holding it in abeyance with the understanding that it will almost immediately be reengaged" (Goffman 1981:155).

Thus, in the psychotic frame, the alignment between the child and the mother may be temporarily suspended and then suddenly reenacted. Furthermore, within the frame of the psychotic fabrication, there are various frame shifts. In the following analysis, I will map these reframings, which Table 3.1 illustrates:

Table 3.1

Speaker		Addressee
	↗	mother
child	→	grandma Lena
	↘	sister (Idete)
mother	→	child
grandma Lena	→	grandchild Jurema
sister	→	doctor

The Mother to the Child: "Ask to be excused, my child"

Embedded within the mother/child frame, Dona Jurema shifts roles with her own mother. This context of talk represents the mother's response to the child's anxious requests, as in the following example:

[Prior to this segment, the patient has been interacting with the doctor in an exchange of challenges concerning her name. She then pauses, catches her breath, and accelerates her pace as she calls upon her mother.]

(21)

Patient:
1. =no, only if you have, (1.3)
2. do you have?

[acc]
3. / ⌈oh, ma:ma::!/
        [bends over to get
        the slipper]

Doctor:
4. have what?

Patient:
    [acc]
5. ma:ma::! ...

Doctor:
6. mmm?

    [acc]
7. ma:ma::! ma:ma::! ...
8. she says she has, ma:ma:: ...
9. she says we can leave,ma:ma::
    ...
    [picks slipper up, pushes
    it away to the right,
    moves torso and right leg
    to the right]
→   10. then ask to be excused,
    11. my child. ..

         [looks at slipper;
         puts slipper on]
    12. it's like this that we ask.
         ..
         [bending down and
         forward, bending to
         the right, slippers on]
    13. so much curiosity, ['hhh] ..
    14. they wanted to have,
    15. didn't they child, ['hhh] ...
         [acc]
    16. to: know about you,
    17. right child,
    18. just because- ['hhh]
    19. they saw you barefooted
         out=
    20. =of doors),
    21. right child, ['hhh]
    22. they thought that you had-

Doctor:
23. Dona Jure:ma!

Patient:
24. popopodedededdddd
25. shsssssssssssssssssssssss

[raises head, looks up,
raises left hand, brings
right finger to mouth to
indicate silence, looks
beyond the doctor, points
and nods, looks straight
ahead, wide open eyes]

Doctor:
26. what's happening over there?

Patient:
27. shssssssssssssssssssssssss
['hhh] shsssssssssssss
['hhh] shsssssssssssss

[points and nods, turns
sideways to the right,
moves left arm to the
right, bends down, looks
down to the right]

The segment above has two parts. In the first part (lines 3–9), Dona Jurema addresses her mother. In line (3) she signals this frame (prefaced by the marker "oh"), as she anxiously summons her mother. She calls for her mother three times in lines (5) and (7). In lines (8–9), in a statement addressed to her mother, she makes a reference to the doctor as a bystander (Goffman 1981). Here Dona Jurema addresses her mother and reports about the doctor's "having" something (line 8) and about the doctor's allowing them (mother and child) to leave (line 9). Dona Jurema introduces two schemas here: She acknowledges the presence of the doctor and signals that she is aware of Doctor Edna's role (that is, as interviewer, the doctor must give permission for her, the patient, to leave). Second, she indicates that two people (a mother and a child) make up her identity, as she states that "we can leave." Her nonverbal behavior matches her utterances: while she is saying all this, she is also trying to figure out how to put her slippers on, so as to be able to get up and leave. Then, following line (9)—"she says we can leave, ma:ma::"—she pauses and shifts role, from the child to the mother.

In the second part, lines (10–22), Dona Jurema speaks as the mother addressing the child Jurema. She uses the address form "my child" to refer to Dona Jurema. Here, the mother introduces a schema for "taking leave," giving directives on how one should perform when one takes leave (lines 10–12: "then ask to be excused, my child", "it's like this that we ask"). She is in fact instructing the child in a schema for social behavior. Then, in lines (13–22), she makes a series of evaluative remarks on people's reactions to the fact that the child is barefooted. She shows sympathy for the child, as she complains about people's disproportionate reaction ("so much curiosity") to such a small event ("just because they saw you barefooted"). This schema about improper social behavior (going barefooted) which attracts people's attention (curiosity) may be an indirect reference to Dona Jurema's improper behavior when undergoing a psychotic crisis. And here we see the mother taking a sympathetic stance toward the child Jurema.

Thus, within the "mother/child" frame I have just described, Dona Jurema introduces two schemas for social conduct. There is a "mother as an instructor schema" by means of which the mother teaches the child how to behave in public and how to ask properly to be excused. Here she uses only directives to address the child. There is also a "sympathetic mother schema" that complains about people's social reactions to the child's improper behavior. This frame ends with Dona Jurema's shifting to nonverbal behavior, pointing and nodding as she signals a time to be silent.

The Child and Grandma Lena: "Can I speak, Grandma?"

> child: "Can I speak, Grandma?"
> grandma: "Give in, Jurema, give in.
>   This is for your own good, my child."

Dona Jurema, the child, also addresses her grandmother Lena. She is aware that Grandma Lena is dead, as the following segment indicates.

[This talk takes place toward the end of the interview. Dona Jurema has been engaged in gibberish talk; then, breathing hard, she turns to the doctor and says:]

(22)

Doctor:		Patient:	
1.	//(what have I)		//it may be at that time-
			[looking down]
2.	mmm:		
		3.	Grandma Lena is the one=
		4.	=who must know,
		5.	I'm gonna ask Grandma Lena,
		6.	O.K.?=
7.	=who is Grandma Lena?		
		8.	my grandma who is up in=
		9.	=heaven.
10.	mmm.		
		11.	can I speak, Grandma Lena?
			....

The above segment introduces the frame of talk in which the child Jurema speaks to her grandmother. Here, Dona Jurema gives her audience both time and place coordinates. First, she refers to a past time ("at that time") that contrasts with "this" "present" time. Second, in lines (8–9) she says that her grandmother is in heaven. Although she is aware (on one level) that her grandmother is dead, she decides to talk to her anyway. Grandma Lena is the one who should know something (lines 3–4). Hence, Dona Jurema decides to ask her a question and requests permission from her audience (lines 5–6). In line (11), she addresses Grandma Lena and requests permission to talk.[4]

After a pause, Dona Jurema shifts roles, as she becomes the grandmother addressing young Jurema:

(23)

Patient:
1. gi:ve in. ..
2. then give in. ...
3. give in, Jurema give in,
4. give in,
5. give in,
6. give in,
7. give in,
8. give in for your own good.
9. for your own good.
10. the youg lady is also=
11. =telling you, ..
12. it's for your own good, ..
13. then listen,
14. listen,
15. listen,
16. listen,
17. listen,
18. listen,
19. listen,
20. listen,
21. <u>listen.</u>

Doctor:
22. //Dona Jurema?

Patient:
    //so I listen.=
[turns head and torso
slightly to the left]

23. =<u>look</u>, ...
24. get up and walk=
25. //a <u>little bit.</u>

    // (it was because of this.)
[turns head and torso to the left]

Here the patient uses "Jurema" as the address form, evidence that she is speaking not as Jurema but as someone else. Grandma Lena gives directives to young Jurema. She tells her to "give in" for "her own good." She repeats this formula nine times, with small variations, thereby stressing her request to Jurema. She also refers to "the young lady" as a bystander and reports on what the doctor has said ("the young lady is also telling you that it's for your own good"). In paraphrasing the doctor, Grandma Lena endorses the doctor's position. She signals that she sides with the doctor. Then, Grandma Lena tells Jurema to "listen." At the end of this segment, there is another shift, prefaced by the marker "so" and a change in persona. Dona Jurema—as the patient/child—concludes by accepting her grandmother's advice, as she says, "so I listen."

The second segment of talk within this frame takes place further on, after an exchange where Dona Jurema indicates restlessness and anxiety. She has been referring to her son, and she has mentioned that he did not want to call the police (a reference to her crisis and to the family's response). Dona Jurema then addresses Grandma Lena:

(24)

Doctor:	Patient:
	[breathing hard]
	1. oh!!! [hhh]
	2. oh how ⌊exhausting,
	3. Grandma Lena! ...
4. you're <u>tired</u>,	
5. /Dona Jurema?/	
	6. oh, Grandma Lena!
	7. oh, Grandma Lena,
	8. here on Earth only if=
	9. =one does—
	[looks down, leans
	forward, moves legs]
	[acc]
	10. you wanted to know?
	11. I I don't know anything..
	12. y'see, Grandma Lena?

In this segment, Dona Jurema introduces a series of strong complaints. She uses the marker "oh" to express her anxiety and tiredness. She continuously uses this marker (in lines 1–2 and 6–7), followed by the address form "Grandma Lena." In line (8) she refers to the Earth indicating that she is aware that Lena is in another place (not "here on Earth"). In lines (10–11) she repeats a formula that she also uses with her mother, which reveals the child's deference toward a more powerful figure. Again she presents herself as a child who knows nothing (line 11) and reenacts the schema discussed previously in the asymmetrical mother/daughter relationship.

The third instance of this frame takes place further on, at the end of the interview. Here, Dona Jurema closes the interview by acknowledging Grandma Lena and stating that she will ask to be excused only by her.

(25)

[nonverbal behavior
from Dona Jurema]

Patient:

1. I'm leaving 'cause it's=
2. =already very late. ...

[looks up and addresses
the camera]

['hhh]

3. "excuse me". ..
4. only by Grandma Lena will I=
5. =ask to be excused. ...

[looks down, moves
right hand down]

['hhh]

6. "excuse me,
7. Grandma Lena, excuse me" ...

[moves backward
bends down]

8. that's it. y'see. this is it.

[keeps looking down, moves backward, as if putting on her slippers]

Dona Jurema singles out Grandma Lena as the one she addresses at the end of the interview (lines 4–5), the only one that she takes leave of (lines 6–7). Grandma Lena is also the one to whom Jurema complains (as indicated in example 23). And finally, she is the one who gives directives to Jurema, which Jurema accepts (as example 22 illustrates). Within this frame of talk, the patient never challenges her addressee. Rather, in Dona Jurema's schema for grandmothers, they are to be "listened to" and, therefore, in her own words, Jurema "listens" (example 22).

The Child to her Sister Idete: "Didn't I tell you, Deta?"

As a child, Jurema also addresses her sister Idete. In the interview, there are four short segments within this context of talk, of which I will describe two. The first one consists of only two utterances, where Dona Jurema seems to be proving a point as she addresses her sister:

(26)

1. oh, ohohohohohohohoh.
    [acc]
2. slowly,
3. slowly,
4. slowly,
5. 'cause it was, waswaswa-
→ 6. didn't I say so, Deta.
→ 7. didn't I say Deta=
8. =that it had- ['hhh]
9. popopopopopopopopopopopo=

Prior to this segment, Dona Jurema has been referring to her mother. Then, in line (1) as she bends over and looks down, she plays with her slippers and utters a continuous expressive remark. In lines (2–4) she seems to be monitoring her gestures as she tries to put on her slippers. Then, in lines (6–7) she addresses her sister twice. She then interrupts herself (line 8) and engages in nonsensical talk (line 9).

At another time, after having talked to Grandma Lena, Dona Jurema addresses her sister again.

(27)

> that's it, sis. ...
> little sis. ...

She uses two affective terms to refer to Idete, "sis" and "little sis." And then she reports on what she used to call her sister (example 28). This report has no specific addressee. It could be addressed to her Grandma Lena (the last addressee), to the doctor, or to the mother, who is Dona Jurema's most salient addressee.

(28)

Patient:

[smiles, raises head		
and torso; smiles,	1.	I only know it was like this,
bends forward and	2.	I only know I used to call=
speaks to the microphone;	3.	=Idetinha as Detinha, ..
looks down, raises	4.	then later I started to call
head slowly, moves	5.	=her sis:. ..
torso backward]	6.	she was plea:::sed,
	7.	plea:::sed,
	8.	but then:::,
	9.	she is ve:::ry,
	10.	she is ve:::ry,

Dona Jurema introduces factual information about what she used to call her sister and the types of responses she would get from her. Idete is the patient's caretaker and her closest relative. Here Dona Jurema signals that she wants to leave the information "on record." Her nonverbal behavior indicates that she is aware of presenting a report statement which will be recorded. In line (8) she introduces contrastive information prefaced by the marker "but" about Idete (now referred to by the pronoun "she"). She makes an evaluative remark which she leaves incomplete (in lines 9–10).

When Dona Jurema "talks to" her sister Idete, affection is expressed by the various address forms. In the beginning of the interview, for example, there is a frame break (from the child/mother context of talk to the sister/sister context of talk), when the patient looks to the far left corner, as if someone were there, and cries out loud, "Dete! Deti::nha!" Throughout the interview, within this frame of talk, Dona Jurema addresses her sister by the short form *Dete* or *Deta;* by the expressive diminutive *Idetinha* or *Detinha;*

and by the forms *mana* "sis" and *maninha* "little sis(ter)," which indicate her status as a sibling.

The Sister Idete and the Doctor: "Thank God! It's all over!"

Of all the family members evoked in Jurema's talk, there is only one figure who interacts with the doctor. It is the sister Idete. As Dona Jurema's caretaker, she is the only person who has maintained constant contact with the doctor. There are various statements from Idete to the doctor on the patient's hospital records.

In the first part of the interview there is a reframing where Dona Jurema shifts and assumes Idete's role. She addresses the doctor, states that Dona Jurema has been a bit sick but is now recovered, and closes by praising the doctor.

[Prior to this segment, Dona Jurema had been signaling "to be quiet" as she "shsssssssssss" and points forward.]

(29)
Doctor:
1.   Dona Jure:ma

Patient:
2.   popopodedededddddd
3.   shhhhhhhhhhhhhhhhh

[raises head, looks up, raises left hand, brings right finger to her mouth to indicate silence, looks beyond the doctor, points and nods, looks straight ahead, wide open eyes]

Doctor:
4.   what's happening over there?

Patient:
5.   ['hhh]
     shhhhhhhhhhhhhhhhhhhhh
6.   ['hhh]
     shhhhhhhhhhhhhhhhhhhhh
7.   ['hhh]
     shhhhhhhhhhhhhhhhhhhhh

[points and nods, turns sideways to the right, moves left arm to the right, bends down, looks down to the right]

Doctor:
8.Dona JuRE:MA!

Patient:
[dec]
→   9. |Thank God! ....

                                          [interrupts movement, raises
                                          head, looks up, turns to
                                          doctor and smiles]

Doctor:
10.   Thank God for <u>what?</u>

                                          Patient:
                                          11.   =it's all over. ....
                                          [holds the position
                                          and smiles]

Doctor:
12.   <u>what is over?</u>

                                          Patient:
                                          [dec]
→   13.   ⌐Jurema is a little dizzy,
      14.   y'know.
                                          [turns torso and head
                                          to face doctor, moves
                                          left hand down, and
                                          grabs armchair]

15.   mmm.

                                          ['hhh]
→   16.   could you give my little=
      17.   =sister a glass of water,
      18.   she didn't even know that=
      19.   =this would happen to her. ..
→   20.   you are very polite. ..

In the first part of this segment, Dona Jurema signals the doctor to be quiet
and points to the right corner of the room. Then, she turns to the right and
leans on the armchair, away from the doctor. She also looks down. This
movement takes place between lines (3) and (7). Then, in a different move,
she raises her head, turns to the left and looks at the doctor. As she shifts
movements, she also changes her role and in a higher pitch and slower pace
she speaks as Idete, her sister. She expresses relief and gives "thanks to God"
(in line 9). Doctor Edna then requests information about what is taking
place or has taken place. In line (11), Dona Jurema, speaking as her sister
Idete, smiles to the doctor as she states that "it's all over." Doctor Edna again
asks for information about what is over (line 12). In her next turn, the
patient refers to herself in the third person and provides information on
Dona Jurema's general well-being. She states that Jurema is a bit dizzy (lines
13–14). Then, she requests a glass of water for her sister Jurema. In lines
(18–19), she informs the doctor that Dona Jurema did not really know that
"this" was going to happen. "This" seems to refer to Dona Jurema's psychotic crisis. She concludes by praising the doctor (line 20).

     When the patient as Idete addresses the doctor, she accomplishes a set
of sequential moves: she expresses relief because Jurema now feels better;

she explains to the doctor what has happened; she requests an action of the doctor; she apologizes for what happened and provides an explanation; and she concludes by praising the doctor. All of the above moves integrate Dona Jurema's schema regarding her sister's behavior with Doctor Edna or doctors in general. In the terms of Tannen and Wallat (this volume), "knowledge schema" refers to "participants' expectations about people, objects, events and settings in the world" (p. 60). It seems that, in Dona Jurema's prior experiences with her own crisis, she recalls her sister's performing a series of sequential moves like the ones described above.

Conclusion

The notion of frame (Bateson 1972, Goffman 1974, Tannen 1985, 1986) provides a natural criterion for establishing "chunks" of coherent discourse in a thought-disordered speaker. Thus, in the interview discussed above, when the patient is undergoing a severe psychotic crisis, her contributions, for the most part, do not make sense. She rarely addresses the doctor's questions, she shifts idiosyncratically from one topic to another, and she engages in activities which are noninteractional (like singing and chanting). However, the discourse analyst can isolate several contexts of communication which make sense by themselves.

In this chapter, I have shown that if one looks at the different frames of talk that Dona Jurema continuously creates, several consistent texts emerge, each presenting a coherence of its own. In these different performances, two things seem to occur. First, Dona Jurema changes her role by shifting from being the patient to being a child; as a child she addresses her mother, her grandmother, her sister Idete. Second, she also shifts so as to speak as her own mother, or her own grandmother, or her own sister. Each one of these reframings contains different types of contribution from the patient.

I argued that there are two major frames at play: the frame of the psychiatric interview and the frame of the psychotic crisis. The latter is subsumed under the first. Goffman (1974) says that the "rim" of the frame defines the activities regarding its status in the real world. And the "core" of the frame defines what the dramatic "transformed" activity is. It seems that in the "psychotic fabrications" (Goffman 1974), the "core" of the frame is further removed from the "rim" of the frame.

In the frame of the psychiatric interview, Dona Jurema's responses often convey complaints about her well-being or about the doctor's unreasonable demands (bringing her to an interview); she also introduces requests that challenge the doctor's authority as the gatekeeper and interviewer.

In the frame of the psychotic crisis, Dona Jurema makes use of family figures (the mother, the grandmother, the sister) to create different contexts of talk. In each of these, she coherently performs a series of moves that reveal the frame of talk she has created.

Within each frame of talk, Dona Jurema also reveals schemas that are associated with certain referents. As a patient, Dona Jurema states that one cannot make any noise at the hospital and one must, therefore, go elsewhere to be noisy. To her mother, the child Jurema marks deference. When Dona Jurema speaks as the mother, she is the mother as instructor and also the sympathetic mother who sides with her child Jurema. Speaking as her sister Idete, she also performs appropriately according to a schema: she thanks God because Jurema feels better; she explains to the doctor what has happened; she requests a glass of water for Jurema; and she apologizes and praises the doctor.

Dona Jurema as child addresses her mother and her grandmother in different ways. Grandma Lena is the one singled out by the child when leaving. When asked by the doctor who Grandma Lena is, Dona Jurema answers that she is her grandmother, who is in heaven. To Grandma Lena, Jurema may report opinions or complain. But she very seldom marks deference to her. When addressing her mother, on the other hand, she repeatedly marks deference as she reasserts the knowledge the mother has. Within this frame of talk, she uses the address form *mãe:* "ma:ma::," demanding the mother's attention. The discourse markers *viu* "see", *ta vendo* "y'see," also contribute to stress the child's effort in getting the mother's attention.

What emerges is that Dona Jurema uses language to mirror the different social functions that each participant has in her discourse. On this level of analysis, she never "misfires" (Austin 1962), a rather unexpected accomplishment for a "thought-disordered patient."

Appendix: Transcription Conventions *

..	noticeable pause or break in rhythm, less than 0.5 second
...	half second pause, as measured by stopwatch
....	one second pause
(1.5)	numbers within brackets represent pauses in talk over one second, measured with a stopwatch
.	sentence-final falling intonation
?	sentence-final rising intonation
,	phrase-final intonation (indicating more talk to come)
•	high pitch on word
⌐	pitch shift on phrase, upward, continuing until punctuation (several marks indicate progressively higher pitch)
'	low pitch on word
∟	pitch shift on phrase, lowered, continuing until punctuation (several marks indicate progressively lower pitch)
-	glottal stop or abrupt cutting off of sound
:	lengthened sound (extra colons indicate greater lengthening)

*Most of these conventions are based on Tannen (1984).

	primary stress
underline	emphatic stress
CAPS	very emphatic stress, loudness or shouting
/words/	spoken softly
//words//	spoken very softly
( )	transcription impossible
(words)	uncertain transcription
((words))	differences in the English version
<words>	spoken with articulatory problems (slightly slurred speech)
=	two utterances linked by = indicate no break in flow of talk (latching); = also links different parts of a single speaker's talk that has been carried over to another line of transcript
[	overlapping speech: two people talking at the same time
[hhh]	audible aspirations
['hhh]	audible inhalations
[talk]	various characterizations of the talk (like singing, chanting) or tempo (like staccato) are indicated one line above the segment of talk, in square brackets
[acc]	spoken quickly (appears over the line)
[dec]	spoken slowly (appears over the line)
[whining]	high pitch (half-crying)
[creaky voice]	low pitch (half-crying)
[nonverbal]	description of nonverbal behavior (changes in posture and orientation) is indicated one line below the segment of talk in square brackets
→	at the left of line highlights point of analysis

Notes

1. This interview was videotaped as part of a training program developed by the Institute of Psychiatry of the School of Medicine at the Federal University of Rio de Janeiro, Brazil. The hospital provided me with the patient's clinical records, her medical history, and letters from her sister Idete to Doctor Edna. There were uncertainties related to the patient's diagnosis. Although she was initially diagnosed as presenting a manic-depressive psychosis, her doctor pointed also to another possibility: an organic-transitory psychotic episode. The doctor's initial description stated that the patient presented "no cooperation during the clinical examination, a decrease of attention span, hypotenacity, hypovigilance, unstable affect, indifference to the environment, childish behavior, pressure of speech, excessive talkativeness, and perseveration." She added that the patient was in a state of "delirium" throughout the interview.

2. In the playback session that I conducted with the doctor, she stated that

Dona Jurema was aware of the interview situation and that at several points the patient engaged in a conversation with her. She said that "the patient knew I was there, she knew that it was an interview, she expected me to say that it (the interview) was over, and to take her back to her ward."

3. There are some chickens, ducks, and other birds on the hospital grounds that have been there for many years. The presence of chickens is actually a topic for jokes among psychiatric students. After all, Rio de Janeiro is a developed and sophisticated urban center, and the Psychiatric Institute is considered the major state mental institution and one of the most important in the country. Hence, one does not "expect" to see chickens or ducks there.

4. The patient's medical records indicate that during a crisis Dona Jurema would address living as well as dead relatives. One should bear in mind that, in the Brazilian culture, there are religious rituals where people engage in "speaking to the dead" as well as "listening to the dead." Those rituals (called *umbanda* and *quimbanda*) are of African origin and are practiced on a regular basis among Brazilians, with no class or ethnic distinctions. Dona Jurema's medical records indicate that, at an earlier time in her life, she had been "introduced" to the rituals of *umbanda* by a previous boyfriend. Hence, for Dona Jurema, communicating with a dead relative is part of a "prior text" (Becker 1979). This can also be viewed as another schema (Tannen & Wallat this volume) that she has in this frame.

References

Austin, J. L. 1962. How to do things with words. New York & Oxford: Oxford University Press.

Becker, A. L. 1983. Beyond translation: Aesthetics and language description. Contemporary perceptions of language: Interdisciplinary dimensions (GURT 1982). Ed. by Heidi Byrnes, 124–138. Washington, DC: Georgetown University Press.

Becker, A. L. 1982. On Emerson on language. Analyzing discourse: Text and talk, (GURT 1981), Ed. by Deborah Tannen. Washington, DC: Georgetown University Press.

Bernstein, Basil. 1960. Review of The lore and language of school children by Iona and Peter Opie. British Journal of Sociology 11:178–181.

Goffman, Erving. 1974. Frame analysis. New York: Harper and Row.

Goffman, Erving. 1976. Interactional ritual. New York: Anchor Books.

Goffman, Erving. 1981. Footing. Forms of talk, 124–159. Philadelphia: University of Pennsylvania Press.

Halliday, M.A.K. and Ruqaiya Hassan. 1976. Cohesion in English. London: Longman.

Kirshenblatt-Gimblett, Barbara. 1976. Speech play. Philadelphia: University of Pennsylvania Press.

Labov, William. 1972. The transformation of experience in narrative syntax. Language in the inner city, 354–396. Philadelphia: University of Pennsylvania Press.

Labov, William and David Fanshel. 1977. Therapeutic discourse. New York: Academic Press.

Ribeiro, Branca T. 1988. Coherence in psychotic discourse: Frame and topic. Ph. D. Dissertation, Georgetown University, Washington: D.C.

Ribeiro, Branca T. 1993. Coherence in psychotic discourse. New York & Oxford: Oxford University Press.

Rochester, Sherry R., and J. R. Martin. 1979. Crazy talk. New York: Plenum Press.

Schiffrin, Deborah. 1985. Conversational coherence: The role of "well". Language 61:640–67.

Schiffrin, Deborah. 1987. Discourse markers. Cambridge: Cambridge University Press.

Tannen, Deborah. 1984. Conversational style: Analyzing talk among friends. Norwood, NJ: Ablex.

Tannen, Deborah. 1985. Frames and schemas in the discourse analysis of interaction. Quaderni di Semantica 6:313–21.

Tannen, Deborah. 1986. That's not what I meant! New York: William Morrow.

Wolfenstein, Martha. 1954. Children's humor: A psychological analysis. Glencoe, IL: Free Press.

4

Participation Frameworks in Sportscasting Play: Imaginary and Literal Footings

SUSAN M. HOYLE

Georgetown University

Introduction

Play and games provide a good locus for the study of framing, the way in which interactants jointly construct and signal their definition of a situation. All messages are framed by implicit metamessages indicating the way in which the content is to be taken, as Bateson (1972), Goffman (1961, 1974, 1981a), Tannen (1985), and Tannen & Wallat (this volume) have shown; conversationalists thus indicate their understanding of what "speech activity," in Gumperz's (1982) terms, is in progress. Framing is essential to any speech activity—and to any interaction—but it is particularly prominent during play, because play is a "nonliteral orientation" (Garvey 1977:8) toward objects, activities, or other people. Play is above all "an activity that cannot be successfully initiated or maintained if the actors do not communicate, mark, or frame their actions as play" (Schwartzman 1978:3).

In this chapter I discuss the way in which three 8- and 9-year-old boys construct a speech activity: talking like sportscasters while playing a competitive game. They continuously reframe the ongoing play as they take on

This chapter is a greatly revised and expanded version of part of my 1988 Georgetown University dissertation, "Boys' sportscasting talk: A study of children's use." I am grateful to Deborah Schiffrin for her unfailing support while I was writing the dissertation (and afterward), to Deborah Tannen and Peter Lowenberg for helpful comments and stimulating discussion about it, and to Deborah Tannen for encouraging me to write this chapter and for helpful editorial suggestions on it.

different identities, which they do largely by manipulating "footing," the term introduced by Goffman (1981a) to refer to the way in which framing is accomplished in verbal interaction. Footing is "the alignment we take up to ourselves and the others present as expressed in the way we manage the production or reception of an utterance. A change in our footing is another way of talking about a change in our frame for events" (Goffman 1981a:128). Footings and footing shifts are constituted and evidenced in large part through changes in the "participation framework" of talk, that is, the relations among speakers, hearers, and utterances.

Goffman suggests, further, that most often interactants do not simply *change* footing but rather *embed* one footing within another. Such embedding of interaction arrangements, or "lamination" of experience, permeates talk, and "each increase or decrease in layering—each movement closer to or further from the 'literal'—carries with it a change in footing" (Goffman 1981a:154). In short, Goffman concludes, "within one alignment, another can be fully enclosed. In truth, in talk it seems routine that, while firmly standing on two feet, we jump up and down on another" (1981a:155).

Here I investigate children's exploitation of the possibilities for laminating experience through the creation and embedding of participation frameworks during play. Johnstone (1987) suggests that the ability to manipulate footings effectively may be a rather late attainment (at least for some individuals). In a study of verb tense alternation in narratives about confrontations with authorities, she finds that many adult storytellers use tense switching as a resource for managing footing, encoding changes in alignment both on the level of a current storytelling interaction and on the level of a story about a previous interaction. She presents an example of a 14-year-old boy, however, who does *not* encode in his story his footing relative to an authority figure, and she suggests that his inability to manipulate footings effectively marks his narrative as immature. My data, on the other hand, show 8- and 9-year-olds to be adept at managing footing and framing shifts in their play. I suggest, then, that when children's talk and play are investigated on their own terms, rather than as compared to specific adult performances, children are seen to be skillful language users.

Description of the Data

The children whose play and tape-recorded talk provide the data for this chapter are 8- and 9-year-old boys, my own son and his friends; white, middle-class American children. In the examples, my son is always one of the participants, along with one of two other boys. The sportscasting talk that I discuss here was recorded under two different conditions. The first set of episodes arose naturally out of the boys' play. As two boys (my son and a visitor to our house) were playing a competitive game—usually indoor basketball, a computer game, or Ping-Pong—one of them would start announcing what was going on, giving a play-by-play report, as professional sportscasters on radio and television do. For example, while playing basketball (in the basement, with scaled-down equipment) a boy might start a sportscasting episode by announcing *he shoots* or *he puts another one up and it's good*—that is, reporting (in the third person) what he himself or his playmate had just done. Then—sometimes immediately, sometimes after a minute or so—the other boy would join in, and together they would continue to announce the action for anywhere from six to twenty-two minutes. When this first set of recordings, which I call the "spontaneous episodes," were made, over a period of about fifteen months, the boys were not aware that I was interested specifically in their sportscasting, and in fact I myself had not decided to focus on it.

The second set of recordings was made after I had finished collecting the spontaneous data. For these sessions, the "elicited episodes," I explicitly asked the boys to do sportscasting as they played a game and as I recorded them. The elicited episodes considered here range in length from twenty-five to forty-five minutes. My discussion is based on a total of two hours and twenty minutes of spontaneous sportscasting and two and a half hours of elicited sportscasting.

Both sets of sportscasting episodes—the spontaneous and the elicited versions—are characterized by their display of more than one distinct participation framework. The outermost frame in each case can be identified as that of the literal situation: "play" in the spontaneous version and "fulfilling a request" in the elicited version. Within the outer frame, in both cases, is embedded the frame of "sportscasting," the activity in which a sportscaster reports to an audience the actions taken by players. Of course, this situation is imaginary: the audience does not in fact exist, and the sportscasters and players are in fact the same people.

Finally, embedded within the participation framework of the sportscast, in both the spontaneous and the elicited episodes, is another participation framework, but it is not the same one in both cases. In their spontaneous sportscasting, the boys shift between speaking as sportscaster, in which capacity they report the events of the game, and speaking as themselves, in which capacity they seek to resolve procedural difficulties and keep the game going. The most deeply embedded participation framework, that is, is a literal one. In their elicited sportscasting, on the other hand, they never speak as themselves. Instead, when they shift away from announcing the action, it is in order to act out "interviews with a player," with one boy taking the part of "interviewer" and the other taking the part of "interviewee." Here, then, they are embedding one nonliteral participation framework within another.

Although the superordinate frame of each episode is that of the literal situation, it is the midlevel frame, that of the sportscast, that most distinctly characterizes both the spontaneous and the elicited versions. Sportscasting episodes are units around which the boys organize their talk. In the spontaneous episodes, the boys return again and again to announcing the action after they have dealt with interruptions, and in the elicited episodes, they return to their announcing after they stage each "interview."

Spontaneous Sportscasting

I will first discuss the spontaneous sportscasting episodes and will then talk about the differences between these and the elicited episodes. The two sets of episodes, however, have much in common, as in both cases the boys are imitating professional sportscasters. Sportscasting, as Levinson (1979:368) mentions, is an "activity type" in which there are "rather special relations between what is said and what is done." The sportscaster's task is to describe for an audience the action of a game as it unfolds, giving a play-by-play account, with the report of each action as simultaneous as possible with the action itself, or at least immediately afterward. Goffman (1981b) classifies simultaneous announcing, or "action override," as one sort of "fresh talk" (i.e., unscripted talk) engaged in by radio and television announcers: announcers (of a sporting event, an inauguration, or whatever), though they are free to choose their own words, are closely constrained as to content, since they are obligated to report those events that "participants and those familiar with the reported world would see as 'what is going on'" (1981b:233). Like the reporting of adult announcers, then, the boys' sportscasting talk is "activity-tied" (Ervin-Tripp 1977:165): it is structured largely by what is going on, at any moment, in the game.

Examples (1) and (2) illustrate the boys' spontaneous sportscasting. Note that sportscasting as the boys perform it is not dialogic, but is instead a joint monologue. The boys share the speaking role of sportscaster, but as sportscasters, they do not speak to each other. That is, they do not (for the most part) recreate the situation usually found in television broadcasts of sports events, where there are two announcers—one giving the play-by-play description of the game while the other gives the "color commentary"— who address their remarks not only to the audience but also to each other. Instead, the boys jointly produce the sportscaster's talk, alternating turns at speaking, addressing an imaginary remote audience. In (1) Josh Hoyle and Ben Green are playing Ping-Pong but pretending to play tennis:

(1)

a	Josh:	So eleven eight, Hoyle's lead.
b		Hoyle serves it!
c		Ben Green cannot get it ... over the net
d		and it's twelve eight Hoyle's lead now.
e	Ben:	Hoyle takes the lead by four.
f	Josh:	[fast] Green serving.
g		[fast] Hoyle returns it.
h		THEY'RE HITTING IT BACK AND FORTH!
i	Ben:	Ach-boo:m!
j	Josh:	And Ben Green hits it over the table!
k		And it i:s thirteen eight.
l		Hoyle's lead.

In (2) Josh and Matt are playing a computer basketball game in which each controls one of the figures on the screen, who are named after famous professional basketball players; Josh is "Doctor J" and Matt is "Larry Bird."

(2)

a   Josh: Thirty-seven t' thirty-three here at
             Whatchamacallit[1] Stadiu:m.
b   LARRY BIRD FOR A THREE POINTER.
c   HE MISSES.
d   Bu::t .... and .... Doctor J gets it.
e   Matt: But Larry Bird is in: very good position.
f   Josh: BUT DOCTOR J COMES I:N,
g   HE SHOOTS AND HE SCO::RES.
h   THIRTY-NINE T' THIRTY-THREE HERE AT
             WHATCHAMACALLIT STADIU::M.
i   [4.0]
j   LARRY BIRD FOR THREE POINTS.
k   Misses BU::T ....
l   HE JUMPS AND GETS THE REBOUND BACK ON
             THE FLOOR.
m   And he sco:res.
n   Matt: [nasal] Instant replay.=
o   Josh: =[nasal] And it's an instant replay here
             ⌈ at Whatchamacallit ⌈ Stadium.
p   Matt: ⌊ For you   ⌊ for you people(h) at
             home.

As they announce what is going on, the boys create and display their interpretation of the role of the sportscaster in three ways: by using the sportscasting register, by using expressive intonation, and by taking on a distinctive footing. Each of these elements contributes to the framing of the activity; it is by using them in combination that the boys construct the speech activity of sportscasting. As I have discussed elsewhere (Hoyle 1988, 1989, 1991), the boys have a good deal of productive competence in the register of sportscasting, which Ferguson (1983) has identified as a specialized register of English and which he and others (Crystal & Davy 1969, Green 1982, Leech 1971, Weber 1982) have described as characterized by forms and constructions that are either unusual or ungrammatical in other situations in Standard English. Examples (1) and (2) display the boys' use of several of the forms that are typical of the register. Like professional sports announcers, the boys use a very high percentage of action verbs in the simple present (e.g., *Hoyle serves it, Ben Green hits it over the table, Doctor J comes in, he shoots and he scores*). They produce a number of utterances lacking subjects (e.g., *misses*), utterances lacking auxiliaries (e.g., *Green serving*), and utterances lacking lexical verbs (e.g., *Larry Bird for three points*). All these forms and constructions are conventional means of expression in the register.

The second aspect of the boys' performance is their use of expressive prosody, another salient feature of the speech of professional sportscasters (Crystal & Davy 1969). Much of the boys' announcing exhibits increased volume, fast tempo, elongation of syllables, and wide pitch swings, features that indicate excitement and involvement. In (1) and (2) many utterances are spoken very loudly (indicated in transcription by capital letters), often with elongated vowels (indicated by colons), for example: *THEY'RE HIT-TING IT BACK AND FORTH!; BUT DOCTOR J COMES I:N, HE SHOOTS AND HE SCO::RES, THIRTY-NINE T' THIRTY-THREE HERE AT WHATCHAMACALLIT STADIU::M.* Despite the pervasive-ness of such expressive prosodic features in the boys' sportscasting, however, these features do not expressly distinguish sportscasting from other talk that goes on while the boys are playing. Competitive games by their nature engender excitement, and throughout their play the boys display signs of exuberance and involvement, whether or not they are acting as sportscast-ers. Finally, from time to time while they are sportscasting, the boys utter lines that are marked by a distinctive voice quality, as in example (2) where Matt and Josh announce an "instant replay"[2] using a markedly nasal tone. However, utterances with a distinctive voice quality are in fact the exception throughout the boys' sportscasting talk.

The third component of the boys' performances as sportscaster, and the one on which I focus here, is their adoption of a particular footing. That is, they create a participation framework in which the speaker is the sportscast-er, and the addressee is a radio or television audience. Speaking jointly as sportscaster, then, the boys report their own actions as if they were the actions of third parties, and they address their remarks to an (imaginary) audience.

The Participation Framework of the Sportscast

The first aspect of the footing that the boys take during their sportscasting is the way in which they use names and pronouns to refer to themselves and each other. When speaking as sportscaster, a boy does not call himself *I* and his playmate *you,* but instead reports both his own and the other's actions using third person grammatical forms.

For their identities as official players, the boys may either use their own names or take on temporary names. The possibilities may be seen as repre-senting various "laminations" in that they are options that are closer to or further from the literal situation. In the most literal footing, the boys use their own real names. In (1), above, Josh and Ben, jointly speaking as sportscaster, refer to each other by their real names, *Hoyle* and *Green* (or *Ben Green*). Interestingly, it is only when they are sportscasting that the boys refer to themselves and each other by last name, never at other times; this is another way in which they mimic the speech of professional announcers, who often refer to players by last name alone or by a combination of first and

last names. (The boys do not always use last names when they are sportscasting, however; sometimes they use first names, e.g., *Matt misses*. I will continue to refer to them by first name.)

A further step away from the literal is to use occasion-specific names. In
(3) Ben and Josh call themselves "Big Fry" and "Small Fry":

```
(3)                    (playing basketball)
                       (Ben is "Big Fry"; Josh is "Small Fry")
a  →  Josh:   AND BIG FRY CALLS TIME IN.
b  →  Ben:    That's ... two time outs for Big Fry.
c  →  Josh:   Aaaah! Small Fry misses.
d  →  Ben:    [fast] Big Fry coulda just went up there
                       and dunked it.
e                      [10.7]
f     Josh:   Forty-six forty-two here folks!
g     Ben:    [fast] HE BRINGS IT WITHIN FOU:R.
h                      [7.1]
i  →         ⎡ Small Fry
j     Josh:  ⎣ No:::!
k  →  Ben:    Off the- Big Fry gets the rebou::nd.
l     Josh:   HE'S COMIN' DOW::N,
m                      HE SHOOTS,
n                      AND IT'S GOO:::D!
o     Ben:    WITHIN TWO:.
p  →         [fast] Small Fry's getting nervous.
```

These names endure only for the duration of the play session from which
this example is excerpted. Although they are not the boys' real names or
nicknames that persist over time, they have a grounding in the literal situation, for they refer to the boys' relative sizes.

Even further removed from the literal situation is the adoption of the
names of real athletes. In (2), above, the players' names, as announced by the
sportscaster, are the names of professional basketball players, "Larry Bird"
and "Doctor J." Since (2) is an excerpt from a session in which two boys are
announcing a game of computer basketball, and the title of the game itself
identifies the contestants as "Larry Bird" and "Doctor J," the boys are
almost compelled to use those particular names (and not, say, the names of
other professional basketball players). However, when the boys are playing
this same game but *not* acting as sportscasters, they quite often refer to the
figures on the monitor as *you* and *I* rather than *he*. In addition, the boys often
take the names of "Larry Bird" and "Doctor J" when they are playing
regular basketball; the names are not reserved for the computer version of
the game. Example (4) is similar to (2), except that here Matt and Josh are
playing Ping-Pong and have taken the names of famous tennis players:

```
(4)                    (playing Ping-Pong)
                       (Matt is "Lendl"; Josh is "Connors")
```

a	→ Matt:	POINT, LENDL.
b		[6.0]
c	Josh:	Now he makes a stinky shot so it's ten t' ten.
d		[5.4]
e		No spectators here.
f		There used t' be two, but they left.
g	Matt:	hhh Prob'ly went to get .. a hotdog or something.
h	Josh:	Eleven t' ten. Yeah.
i	→	It's eleven t' ten Lendl here.
j		In this basement.
k	→ Matt:	Lendl ... Connors=
l	Josh:	=Eleven to eleven.
m	→ Matt:	Connors just served an ace,
n	Josh:	Eleven to eleven here,
o	→	Connors serves an ace.
p		Twelve to eleven.
q		And it is a great match.
r		[4.1]
s		IT IS TWELVE TO ELEVEN FOLKS!

Taking the names of tennis players makes sense when announcing a game of Ping-Pong (table tennis), since the boys are not familiar with any famous Ping-Pong players, and tennis matches (unlike Ping-Pong contests) are shown on television.

A final possibility, the most distant from the literal situation, is to take the name of a famous person who is not an athlete—as, in one episode, Ben gives himself the name "Leonardo da Vinci."

(5)   (playing basketball)
             (Josh is "Larry Bird",
             Ben has been "Doctor J")

     Ben: The Doctor. Has ... has ...
a little headache.
It bothers him.
[4.2]
But somebody else comes in for Doctor.

     Josh: hhh Oh man.

→ Ben: It's Leonardo da Vinci!

     Josh: hhh Who?

→ Ben: Leonar⌈do da Vinci.
     Josh: ⌊hhhhhhhhhhhhhh

→ Ben: Leonardo da Vinci⌈against Larry Bird.
Tapatapatapa::   ⌊
     Josh: ⌊hhhhhhhhhhh

Twenty-one seventeen.

That this name borders on the ridiculous is confirmed by Josh's laughter. Nevertheless, Ben continues to announce the doings of "Leonardo" without "flooding out" (Goffman 1961) himself.

Thus the first aspect of the footing that the boys adopt when taking the part of the sportscaster is to treat themselves as third parties, using third person grammatical forms, whether the names by which they identify themselves are their own or not. The second aspect of this footing is that the addressee is the (pretend) television or radio audience. This audience is addressed by the boy who is speaking as sportscaster as *folks* or sometimes simply as *you*. This is seen in examples (2) and (3) (lines repeated here), and in (6) and (7):

(2)
o   Josh: [nasal] And it's an instant replay here
                    ⌈ at Whatchamacallit ⌈ Stadium.
p   → Matt: ⌊ For you   ⌊ for you people(h) at
                    home.

(3)
f   Josh: Forty-six forty-two here folks!

(6)
        Josh: And Larry Bir:::d
        Matt: He gets a two: pointer.
        Josh: Fifteen t' thirteen Doctor J is leading:::.
   →   Matt: Instant replay folks.
   →   For you all on the TV set.

(7)
        Ben: And the ... Bird makes it twenty-eight all.
   →   Folks this is amazing.
                  If he makes one basket,
                  he'll take the lead by one.

As Goffman (1981a:138) points out, an audience differs from a fellow conversationalist in that an audience does not get the floor; and a radio or television audience is different still, since it *cannot* get the floor because it consists not of coparticipants in a face-to-face gathering but of "imagined recipients." Thus, the boys' situation is different only in degree not in kind from that of real sportscasters: the boys' audience is imaginary, whereas the audience of real announcers is imagined.

Besides explicitly addressing their remarks to an audience, the boys, like real sportscasters, from time to time identify their (supposed) location for the benefit of this audience (who, whether imaginary or just imagined, is in any case not present). The location named may be obviously not a real name, as in (2) where Josh identifies his location as *here at Whatchamacallit Stadium;* or it may be a real place as in (4) (lines repeated here), and (8)–(10):

(4)
i   Josh: It's eleven t' ten Lendl here.
j   →   In this basement.

(8)   (playing Ping-Pong)
       Josh: Three one Hoyle
                      Serving like John McEnroe.
       Ben: Oo:!=
       Josh: =But he can't get it t' slam on the table.
                      And it's three two.
                      [3.4]
                      ⌈ And it's three three.
       Ben: ⌊ My point.
       →   Three all here in Josh's basement.
       Josh: hhh

(9)   (playing basketball)
   → Ben: And it is eight t' two ... here,
                      Doctor J ... beating ... Larry Bird
       →   at Madison Square Garden.
                      This is amazing folks.
                      Bird ... used t' be good.

(10)   (playing basketball)
       Josh: It's one oh six to one oh six.
                      [6.8]
                      They play two games a day
       →   here at Boston Garden,
                      for a seven game series.
       →   The next two games will be at Los Angeles.
                      And it's one oh eight t' one hundred-
                      t' one oh six Celtics lead,
                      But Byron Scott has the ball.
                      Scott. Shoots. Scott! Makes it!

Like the choice of personal names, the identification of a stadium may be closer to or further from the literal situation. *Madison Square Garden* and *Boston Garden* are of course real places where sports events do take place, and so are appropriate locations to be named, but they are the most literally untrue. The term *Whatchamacallit Stadium* in example (2), since it refers to no real place, has no literal content; it is something of a placeholder that fulfills the wish to identify a stadium while not naming a real one. *Here in this basement* and *Here in Josh's basement,* in (4) and (8), identify the speaker's literal location, but are the most inappropriate expressions for a sportscaster to use, as Josh acknowledges in (8) by his laughter following Ben's announcement *three all here in Josh's basement.*

Speaking as sportscaster, then, involves referring to the players in the third person in order to report their actions to an audience that is not in the speaker's immediate presence.

Embedded Participation Framework: The Literal Situation

As we have seen, when they are acting as sportscasters the boys do not address each other, but instead they jointly address an audience and report the actions of the players (that is, of themselves as players). Within the participation framework of the sportscast, however, is embedded another participation framework, in which the boys speak to each other as their actual selves. That is, during the course of a sportscasting episode, the boys shift in and out of the role of sportscaster, and they signal their shifts by the ways in which they use names and pronouns to refer to themselves and to each other.

The boys commonly interrupt their sportscasting talk to conduct four sorts of exchanges: to ask questions or make comments about the score or the mechanics of the game, to argue, to mark an unexpected occurrence, and to deal with a situation that interferes with the game. All of these situations involve procedural matters whose resolution will help to keep the playing going smoothly.

Questions and Comments

Example (11) illustrates the use of unmarked personal reference to ask and answer questions about the score or the procedures of the game.

(11)   (playing Ping-Pong)
    Josh: GREEN SERVES AND IT DOESN'T GET OVER
             THE NET!
             Ten eight Hoyle's lead.
             Green serves it.
             Hoyle returns it,
             Green returns that and Hoyle,
             Green,
             Hoyle,
    Ben: Oh!
    Josh: And it's-
→   Did it bounce on your side?
    Ben: Yeah.
    Josh: So eleven eight, Hoyle's lead.
             Hoyle serves it!

Here Josh is announcing until he has a question about what has happened with the ball, which affects the score; he asks Ben, using the second person pronoun, *Did it bounce on your side?* After Ben answers, Josh resumes his announcing, once again referring to both himself and his opponent in the third person, using their last names (*Hoyle* and *Green*).

In (12) the participants speak as actual players to make explicit the status of the game:

(12)		(playing Ping-Pong)
		(Josh is "Connors"; Matt is "Lendl")
a	Josh:	Lendl makes a pitiful shot.
b		Connors makes a good serve,
c		Lendl makes a pitiful shot.
d		Thirteen eleven.
e		[6.3]
f	→	Fourteen eleven. Your=
g	→ Matt:	=My ⌈ serve.
h	→ Josh:	⌊ Your serve.

Here, as the serve changes hands, the boys use unmarked personal reference to comment on this procedure (to remind each other that it is time for the change). Josh has been referring to himself as *Connors* and to Matt as *Lendl*. But he switches to a second person pronoun to address Matt as he points out that it is now Matt's serve (lines f, h), and Matt, who realizes as well that it is time to switch serves, uses the corresponding first person pronoun (line g). Example (8) contains a similar comment:

(8)		
→	Ben:	My point.
		Three all here in Josh's basement.

Here Ben makes a claim for his point using the first person but then returns to sportscasting by referring to Josh in the third person.

Usually, then, when the boys find it necessary to discuss the mechanics of the game they do so by shifting out of the sportscaster's footing, thus breaking frame. During such discussions, the boys speak as themselves, not as the sportscaster, since the task of the sportscaster is only to report what is going on, not to regulate or decide such matters as whose turn it is or whether a ball bounced on a certain player's side. But when the question is resolved, or the comment finished, the boys return to sportscasting. Thus the footing of the literal situation is embedded within the footing of the sportscast.

Disputes

The boys also step out of the sportscasting frame to conduct disputes. A dispute may be only a brief objection or may consist of a longer exchange. Examples (13) and (14) show brief objections by one player:

(13)		(playing basketball)
	Josh:	AND HERE'S BIRD.
		BIRD MISSES!
→	Matt:	I didn't shoot.

> Josh: BIRD PASSES TO PARRISH.
> Bird- Parrish gives it to Johnson,
> BACK TO PARRISH!

(14)   (playing basketball)
>   Ben: Bird. Almost gets sent out of the game.
> → Josh: No, I haven't been sent out of the game.
>   Ben: Two shots. For Doctor.
>   Doctor misses the first one off the ceiling.

In (13), while Josh is speaking as sportscaster, Matt objects to the factual content of Josh's announcement that *Bird misses*. He protests that he ("Bird") did not miss because he did not shoot, and in his objection he uses the unmarked first person pronoun: *I didn't shoot*. In (14) Josh disputes Ben's announcement on the basis that "Bird" (i.e., Josh) is not in fact being *sent out of the game*.

Example (15) shows a more extended argument:

(15)   (playing basketball)
>   (Ben is "Doctor J")
>   Ben: The Doctor .... sets up another one.
> → Josh: Ben you can't slam it off the wall.
> → Ben: I wasn't trying to,
> →   I was trying t' make it go up.
> → Josh: Yeah I know but you still
>   ⌈ can't
>   Ben: ⌊ And the Doctor .... has not taken his shot.

Here Ben is announcing his own actions (*The Doctor sets up another one*), when Josh objects to the literal content of his behavior (Ben is bouncing the ball heavily against the wall). In his objection Josh calls Ben by name and addresses him as *you*. Ben defends himself, using *I,* claiming that his objectionable behavior was unintentional. Josh reiterates his protest, using *you*. At this point Ben ends the argument by not continuing to defend his action and by returning instead to sportscasting talk: *And the Doctor has not taken his shot*.

Example (16) is an even longer argument, consisting of several exchanges:

(16)   (playing Ping-Pong)
a   Josh: Seven t' seven!
b   Ben: <u>Eight</u> seven. =
c   Josh: =Green returns-
d   Seven seven.
e   Green returns t' oo::h!
f   Ben: Eight seven.
g   Eight <u>eight</u>.
h   Josh: Eight seven <u>now</u>!

i	Ben:	Eight eight.
j	→ Josh:	When did <u>you</u> get a point.
k	Ben:	From when it hit the net.
l	→ Josh:	NO THAT'S NOT A <u>POINT</u> FOR YOU!
m	→ Ben:	WHEN YOU <u>SERVED</u> IT JOSH.
n	→ Josh:	THAT'S NOT A <u>POINT</u> FOR YOU.
o	Ben:	Yeah it is.
p	Josh:	No it's not.
q	→ Ben:	Fine (your point).
r	Josh:	Eight seven.
s		[2.3]
t	Ben:	YEAH!
u	Josh:	Eight eight.
v		Hoyle serves it,
w		Green returns Hoyle hits it again 'n ...
x		Green hits the net first,
y		And it's nine eight!
z		Hoyle's lead.

In this excerpt Ben and Josh are arguing about the score, a disagreement that arises because Ben thinks that a let serve—a serve during which the ball touches the net—counts as a point for the receiver, while Josh maintains that it does not. At line (a) Josh announces the score as *seven t' seven*. Ben disputes that announcement (b), claiming that the score is *eight seven* (in his favor). Josh then interrupts his sportscasting talk (*Green returns-*) in order to correct Ben by repeating *seven seven*. The argument about the score continues for several exchanges (f–q). During the argument, the boys speak as themselves: they call each other *you*, and Ben uses his opponent's name as an address term (*When you served it Josh*). In the end Josh wins the argument when Ben gives in (q). The boys then resume play and Ben scores a point. Josh announces the new score as *eight eight* and resumes his sportscasting talk (v–z), in which he no longer addresses Ben either by name or as *you*, but instead refers to both himself and Ben in the third person.

Unexpected Occurrences

The third sort of occasion for which the boys often interrupt their sportscasting is an unexpected or surprising occurrence. It is, of course, impossible to identify precisely what players did or did not expect while they were playing a game, but some utterances rather clearly reflect surprise, such as those that begin with *oh!* or that are marked by laughter. In (17) Josh interrupts Ben's sportscasting talk with an aside marked by *oh* in which he refers to himself as *I* rather than *he:*

(17)		(playing basketball)
	Ben:	The Bird gets Doctor J's rebound.
		The Bird goes up.

Shoo ⌈ ts.
→ Josh: ⌊ Oh! I thought I had that.
Ben: Misses. The Doctor. Gets it!

In (18) Josh marks an unexpected event with laughter and a comment:

(18)   (playing computer basketball)
                 (Matt is "Larry Bird"; Josh is "Doctor J")
a   Matt: And that's the end of this quarter.
b   Josh: And Larry Bir:::d
c   Matt: He gets a two: ⌈ pointer.
d   Josh: ⌊ Fifteen t' thirteen
                 Doctor J is leading:::.
e   Matt: Instant replay folks.
f   For you all on the TV ⌈ set.
g → Josh: ⌊ hhh I-
h   when it was an instant replay
i →   I pushed this orange button and he jumped.
j   Matt: And Larry Bird's comin' back a little bit.
k   And Doctor J to the side.

Here the boys are jointly announcing when the computer shows an "instant replay" of "Larry Bird's" basket (apparently a particularly impressive one). Matt reports the replay, continuing to speak as announcer and addressing the audience as *folks* and *you all on the TV set* (e–f). But Josh's attention is drawn to something unexpected that happens during the instant replay: by manipulating the joystick (the hand-held lever that a player uses to control the figures on the computer monitor), he has caused an extra bit of movement on the screen (*I pushed this orange button and he jumped*). (Normally in this game, when the computer is showing an instant replay, the players cannot cause any movement until the replay is over.) Josh marks his surprise by shifting into the first person at lines (g) and (i).

Thus the boys mark an occurrence as unexpected by uttering a "response cry" (Goffman 1981c) or laughing, making some reference to the surprising occurrence and speaking of themselves in the first person. The shift to first person breaks the frame of the sportscast and interjects, fleetingly, the frame of the literal situation.

Interference

A fourth kind of occurrence that causes the boys to step out of the sportscaster role is interference with the game. In (19) Josh and Matt have been announcing their Ping-Pong game when Josh's dog gets in the way; Matt interrupts the announcing to try to get the dog out of the way, calling him by name:

(19)   (playing Ping-Pong)
      Josh: Seventeen to eleven.
→ Matt: Come on Dusty don't interfere.

Josh: Eighteen to eleven.
          It's eighteen to eleven.

Another sort of occasion that can interfere with a game is injury to a player. The usual way that the boys deal with injuries is to take "time out" from both playing and sportscasting until the injured party can continue playing, and to resume sportscasting only after the injury has been handled. In (20) Josh is hurt:

(20)   (playing basketball)
                (Josh is "Small Fry"; Ben is "Big Fry")
     Josh: AND IT'S FORTY-EIGHT FORTY-SIX
                SMALL FRY'S LEAD
                AND BIG FRY HAS THE BALL.
                AND BIG FRY ... doesn't make it
                BUT HE GETS HIS REBOUND,
                HE DOESN'T MAKE IT,
                BUT HE GETS ANOTHER REBOUND.
                AND BIG FRY COMES IN,
                And he misses again!
  →   Ow! Time time time.
                [4.4]
  →   Time in.
     Ben: Big Fry.
                He misses a little (   ).
                Rebound.
     Josh: And it's forty- ⎡ eight
     Ben: ⎣ Forty-eight forty-eight.
                Five minutes t' win this game folks.

Here Josh and Ben are playing basketball; Josh is announcing until he gets hurt. He exclaims *ow!* and calls for a "time out" (*time time time*). After a few seconds he recovers and calls *time in*. Only then does the sportscasting resume, as Ben takes a turn at announcing (*Big Fry. He misses ...*).

On occasions that concern practical game-related matters, then, a boy generally sets aside the footing that identifies him as sportscaster. On these occasions a different participation framework, in which the boys acknowledge their literal situation, is embedded within that of the sportscast. When the practical problem is resolved, the sportscasting footing is resumed.

Mixing Frames in Spontaneous Sportscasting

On some occasions, in contrast to the patterns seen so far, the boys, when faced with a dispute or a distraction, do not interrupt their sportscasting and acknowledge each other's literal selves. Instead, speaking as sportscaster, a boy reports the disruptive incident as one that his (supposed) audience would want to be informed of. An ordinarily out-of-frame segment, that is, is treated as belonging within the frame of the sportscast. Thus, by not embedding the participation framework of the literal situation in places where it would be expected or usual, the boys accomplish the mixing of frames.

Usually, for example, as we have seen, the boys handle disputes by breaking out of the sportscasting frame temporarily, to speak in their own voices and address each other. But in (21) Ben uses Josh's protest as something he can report as sportscaster:

(21)   (playing basketball)
               (Ben is "Doctor J")
      Ben: The Doctor.
      Josh: Ben what are ⌈ you doing.
      Ben: ⌊ GOES UP.
      Josh: It doesn't—
               you hafta shoot from the free throw line,
               okay?
  →   Ben: And the Doctor has t' shoot from the free
               throw line.
  →   [fast] Excuse me but the ref made a mistake.

Here Ben is announcing (*The Doctor. Goes up*) when Josh objects to the way he is acting (*Ben what are you doing*) and tells him what the rules require (*you hafta shoot from the free throw line*). Ben, however, does not respond directly to Josh's objection; nor does he tacitly accept the criticism by changing his actions without saying anything. Instead, he reports, as sportscaster, the substance of Josh's objection, repeating Josh's words but changing a second person pronoun to a third person—*the Doctor has t' shoot from the free throw line*—and blaming the incident on *the ref*. (In addition to simply incorporating an out-of-frame comment into his sportscasting line, Ben may well be saving face by shifting responsibility to the imaginary referee.)

We have also seen that, like disputes, situations that interfere with the game, such as injury to a player, commonly provoke the boys to step out of the sportscasting footing and speak to each other as their actual selves. Sometimes, however, they do not switch footing when faced with such a disruption. Instead, speaking as announcer, a boy continues to address the "audience" and reports the interference, treating it as an official part of the game. In (22) Matt hurts his hand, but instead of calling time out to recover, he treats the injury as part of the official game:

(22)   (playing Ping-Pong)
               (Matt is "Lendl"; Josh is "Connors")
      Matt: Oh: beautiful return
               and it's point Connors.=
      Josh: =And it's seventeen t' fourteen ... Connors.
      Matt: Oh: ⌈ : off the ...   ⌉ fingers.
      Josh: ⌊ Eighteen t' fourteen. ⌋

→ Matt: That's gotta hurt.
→   We'll get a closeup of Lendl after the ...
          game,
→   and see: if if that finger's bothering him.

Here Matt incorporates an injury to himself into his announcing. He hurts his hand by hitting the ball with his fingers instead of with the Ping-Pong paddle and complains about it (*Oh:: off the ... fingers*). But he continues to speak in the role of sportscaster, distancing himself from his injury. As sportscaster, he comments on what the official player "Lendl" must be feeling (*That's gotta hurt*), and informs the audience of his plans to follow up on the situation (*We'll get a closeup of Lendl after the game and see if that finger's bothering him*).

In (23) and (24) Ben and Matt both incorporate into their sportscasting talk an injury to the other player:

(23)   (playing basketball)
             (Ben is "Doctor J"; Josh is "Larry Bird")
    Ben: It's the ⎡ Bird.
    Josh: ⎣ Ow::
→   Ben: The Bird hits his head.
             Doctor! ⎡ steals the ball.
    Josh: ⎣ Ow.
             THAT DIDN'T <u>COUNT</u>.
    Ben: But-
→   BUT BIRD HAS A HEADACHE. And-
             BUT IT DOESN'T COUNT.
             BIRD GOES UP WITH A LAYUP AND IT COUNTS!
             IT IS HERE ... FOURTEEN ... TO EIGHT.
             AND BIRD SHOOTS!

(24)   (playing Ping-Pong)
             (Josh is "Connors")
    Josh: Ow.
→   Matt: And ... <u>CONNORS</u> is hurt.
    Josh: <u>Ow</u>. <u>OW</u>.
    Susan: Wha'd you do.
    Josh: Hit my hand.
→   Matt: HE HITS HIS HAND!

In (23) Josh hurts himself and says *ow* twice. Josh, we may assume, is speaking not as "Bird" but as himself when he utters this cry of pain. But Ben, speaking as sportscaster, treats the cry as if it were produced by "Bird": he reports *the Bird hits his head* and *Bird has a headache*. In (24) I am passing through the room as Josh hurts himself (hitting his hand on the edge of the Ping-Pong table). Even as I attempt to intervene, though, Matt continues announcing, incorporating Josh's injury and cry of pain into his sportscasting line, reporting *Connors is hurt* and *he hits his hand*.

Example (5), repeated here, is another instance in which a boy's disability is treated as a reportable occurrence. Ben, who has been acting under the name "Doctor J," reports that "Doctor J" has a headache and will be replaced by "Leonardo da Vinci":

(5)

Ben:	The Doctor. Has ... has ... a little headache. It bothers him. [4.2] But somebody else comes in for Doctor.
Josh:	hhh Oh man.
→ Ben:	It's Leonardo da Vinci!
Josh:	hhh Who?
→ Ben:	Leonar ⌈ do da Vinci.
Josh:	⌊ hhhhhhhhhhhhh
→ Ben:	Leonardo da Vinci ⌈ against Larry Bird. Tapatapatapa::
Josh:	⌊ hhhhhhhhhhhh
	Twenty-one seventeen.

It is not as clear in this example as it is in (22)–(24) that the boy in question is in fact hurt, since here there is no groaning or cry of *ow*. But, assuming that Ben does in fact have a headache (or even that he is just tired), this example is similar to the others in that a disability that is actually suffered by a boy is attributed to the official player.

In addition to injuries, other sorts of distractions may be treated as official, reportable occurrences. In (25) (which is part of example (4)), Matt and Josh incorporate into their sportscasting the presence and subsequent departure of outsiders—the dog and me. Prior to this excerpt we have been in the room where the boys are playing Ping-Pong, and we have just left:

(25)

		(playing basketball) (Matt is "Lendl")
a	Matt:	POINT, LENDL.
b		[6.0]
c	Josh:	Now he makes a stinky shot so it's ten t' ten.
d		[5.4]
e →		No spectators here.
f →		There used t' be two, but they left.
g →	Matt:	hhh Prob'ly went t' get ... a hotdog or something.
h	Josh:	Eleven t' ten. Yeah.
i		It's eleven t' ten Lendl here.
j		In this basement.

Unlike example (19), where the dog is treated as a nuisance and is directly addressed in an effort to get him out of the way, here the dog and I are treated as official, reportable entities within the sportscasting frame. As "spectators," we are not addressed, but are spoken about for the benefit of the supposed audience.

Any sort of occurrence can be incorporated into sportscasting. In (26) Matt announces several things that are not part of the game:

(26)   (playing Ping-Pong)
                (Matt is "Lendl"; Josh is "Connors")
   Matt: WE HAVE A SPECTATOR, LOOKS LIKE SHE'S IN
                JAIL.
                ANOTHER SPECTATOR!
   Josh: hhhhh
   Matt: All the um ⌈ ...ALL THIS RACKET MAKES ⌈ LENDL
   Josh: ⌊ hhh   ⌊ Seven
                t'seven.
   Matt: All this racket makes Lendl ... lose some
                points.
   Josh: Whoa! Eight t' seven.
                And here comes ... ⌈ and here comes
   Matt: ⌊ NOW THE FURRY ONE'S
                RUNNING AROUND THE SPECTATOR.
   Josh: Okay eight t' seven.
                I won the last match Mom.
   Susan: Good.
   Josh: Eight t' eight.
   Matt: HEY! NOW HE'S EATING ... LENDL'S BATTING
                GLOVE.

Here Matt keeps up the sportscasting line in the face of a variety of distractions: I have come into the room and Josh addresses me (*I won the last match Mom*), the dog (*the furry one*) is disrupting the game, and Matt himself is wearing a batting glove (which is inappropriate for playing either Ping-Pong or tennis and which may well be impeding his game). But Matt uses all these potentially disruptive things as material that he can report on as sportscaster. He says of the talking and noise that *all this racket makes Lendl lose some points*. He refers to me as *the spectator*. He reports the dog's actions as part of the larger situation surrounding the game itself: the dog is *running around the spectator* and *eating Lendl's batting glove*—mentioning the glove only incidentally, as if it were a normal accessory of "Lendl's."

Distractions that are treated as reportable need not be external to the game as in (26). The threat of disruption can arise from the fact that one person is not cooperating with the other's attempts to maintain the sportscasting activity. Example (27), from a game of basketball, shows one boy maintaining the role of the sportscaster as the other begins doing something different. Matt and Josh have each been taking the parts of several different professional basketball players (representing different teams); one of Matt's names is "McHale." Before this excerpt begins, they have been jointly acting as sportscaster for some time. In this segment, though, Matt drops out of the role of sportscaster, as he starts dancing and singing.

```
(27)              (playing basketball)
a     Josh:       McHale with the ball.
b                 McHale trying to be Michael Jackson. ⌈ hhhh
c     Matt:                                            ⌊ hhhh
d     Josh:       McHale, drops the ball.
e                 But(hh), McHale is doing a moon walk on the
                  basketball court.
f                 Now he is break dancing. ⌈ hhh
g     Matt:                                ⌊ hhh
h     Josh:       McHale. Shoots!
i                 NO WONDER HE MISSED, HE CAN'T PLAY
                  BASKETBALL,
j                 he should be a break dancer. h ⌈ hhhhh
k     Matt:                                      ⌊ hhhhh
l     Josh:       Byron Scott has the ball.
m                 And McHale is (    ) hhh
n     Matt:       [singing] Da da, dadadada,
o                 Da, ⌈ da dadadada, da da dadadadada
p     Josh:           ⌊ Now McHale is dancing (right in front
                  of the basket).
q     Matt:       ⌈ Da da da da da
r     Josh:       ⌊ Worthy!
s                 Worthy misses!
t                 It's ninety-two- It's ninety-four t'
                  ninety-two.
u                 Kareem, sets it out to Johnson!
v                 JOHNSON SHOOTS! and it's a tied ball game
w                 ninety-four all.
```

Josh, as sportscaster, starts by referring to Matt as the official player *McHale*. Matt, however, is starting to fool around, dancing and singing (*trying to be Michael Jackson, doing a moon walk,* and *break dancing*).[3] Josh incorporates this out-of-frame activity of Matt's into his own sportscasting talk. Rather than issuing a protest to Matt, Josh continues to refer to Matt in the third person as *McHale* or *he,* and he reports Matt's actions as if they were an official part of the game. From line (s) Josh then reports his own actions (under the various names of "Worthy," "Kareem," and "Johnson"). He thus maintains the sportscasting line despite a potential interruption.

Finally, a conflict can arise between a boy's attempt to continue speaking as sportscaster in order to incorporate outside events, and the tendency to speak as himself when dealing with procedural matters. Example (28) illustrates:

```
(28)              (playing basketball)
a  → Matt:    AND THE FURRY ONE GETS IN HIS ⌈WAY.
b      Josh:                                   ⌊hhh
c                Ele(hh)ven t' ni(h)ne.
d      Matt:    No that doesn't count.
e      Josh:    Okay.
f  → Matt:    The furry thing was in my way.
```

Here Matt begins by incorporating an outside distraction—the dog—into his announcing (line a). But when Josh reports the score as *eleven t' nine,* thus penalizing Matt for missing the point, Matt objects with *no that doesn't count* because *the furry thing was in my way.* That is, he repeats at line (f) his utterance from (a), but he changes the pronoun from third person to first person as he switches from the footing of the sportscaster to the footing of his literal self, the self who is concerned with defending his score and not being penalized by the interference, and who is ready to argue for his position.

The players, then, can incorporate outside events into the sportscasting activity, mixing frames by maintaining the footing of the sportscaster in the face of occurrences that might be expected to (and do ordinarily) trigger a footing shift. They continue to address the "audience" and report a potentially disruptive event as an official part of the sportscast. An injury can be treated as an injury to an official player and thus a reportable occurrence, an interference can be commented on by the sportscaster, and nonparticipants who happen to be present can be made into characters in the sportscasting activity. Even when one boy stops participating in the sportscasting activity, the other can keep it going by reporting the out-of-frame actions as if they belonged to the game. By announcing what is going on even when it is not a part of the game itself, the boys are abiding by Goffman's (1981b) observation that announcers continue to report to their audiences what is going on even when the officially scheduled activity is interrupted or breaks down. As sportscasters, the boys can expand the role in order to incorporate various aspects of the entire spectacle into the announcing.

Mixing frames is not just an exercise, though: the boys are clearly using this capacity in order to be funny. In (27) both Josh and Matt laugh as Josh keeps up his reporting of Matt's ("McHale's") antics, which are hardly actions expected of a basketball player. In (25) Matt laughs in response to Josh's report of "spectators," as he joins in speculating about what happened to them:

```
(25)
e      Josh:    No spectators here.
f                There used t' be two, but they left.
g  → Matt:    hhh Prob'ly went to get ... a hotdog or something.
```

And in (28) Josh laughs as Matt reports the dog's interference:

(28)
a   Matt: AND THE FURRY ONE GETS IN HIS ⌈ WAY.
b   →   Josh: ⌊ hhh
c   →   Ele(hh)ven t' ni(h)ne.

Exploiting their ability to frame ongoing experience as one sort of activity
(sportscasting) or another sort (taking care of procedural matters) is, then, a
resource for humor.

   A further dimension to the boys' exploitation of the sportscaster's footing for humor is their use of it for teasing. A boy teases his playmate by
retaining the stance of the sportscaster but including in his announcing a
derogatory appraisal of the other's performance, perhaps while praising his
own performance. Examples (4) and (12), for instance, include elements of
teasing; the relevant lines are repeated here, along with a similar example in
(29):

(4)   (Matt is "Lendl"; Josh is "Connors")
a   Matt: POINT, LENDL.
b   [6.0]
c   →   Josh: Now he makes a stinky shot so it's ten t'
                    ten.
d   [5.4]
e   No spectators here.

(12)   (Matt is "Lendl"; Josh is "Connors")
a   →   Josh: Lendl makes a pitiful shot.
b   →   Connors makes a good serve,
c   →   Lendl makes a pitiful shot.
d   Thirteen eleven.
e   [6.3]

(29)   (playing Ping-Pong)
         Ben: Seven five, lead by Hoyle.
                    Lead's by two!
         Josh: And it's eight five!
         Ben: Lead's by three.
                          [3.4]
     →   STUPID SERVE BY HOYLE!
         Josh: He cannot seem t' ... slam.
                    Eight six.

In each instance inappropriate lexical items are chosen to characterize a
performance: *stinky, pitiful, stupid*. While such terms are, perhaps, referen-
tially apt, they are incongruous in the context of sportscasting, where the
boys for the most part are using forms that are more technical and certainly
less derogatory. The boy who is teased, in each case, does not seem to take
the teasing utterance as a serious criticism, for he does not object to the

characterization. In (4) and (12) the boy who teases continues to speak, either before (12) or after (4) a silence, without any comment from the other. In (29) Josh not only does not object to Ben's assessment that he has made a *stupid serve* but continues with a similar—although less insulting— criticism of himself (*he cannot seem t' slam*).

In their spontaneous sportscasting, then, the boys use the capacity to switch footings in order to embed one within another, while keeping the first on hold; and in addition, they exploit their knowledge of when such embedding is usual in order to break the pattern for humorous effect. That these children do this is perhaps not startling, for Goffman characterizes everyday talk as composed of just this sort of activity, but their performance illuminates the competence that adults are often surprised to find in younger speakers.

Elicited Sportscasting

I turn now to the elicited sportscasting episodes. For these sessions, I explicitly asked the boys, two at a time, to "do sportscasting" while I recorded it. They agreed but attached some conditions to their performance. They insisted that the only sort of game they could announce would be a computer game, since a computer game can be set up so that one person plays against the computer, leaving the other, who is not playing, free to act as sportscaster. They claimed that it is impossible to play a game and act as sportscaster at the same time. They had, of course, done so on many occasions, spontaneously. The explanation for their reluctance to try it deliberately is twofold. First, it seems that they have a tacit understanding of the complexity involved in managing multiple tasks and the related footings, although they could not explain (when I asked them) exactly what the difficulties would be. Second, as I will describe, their elicited sportscasting turned out to be a more elaborate performance than the spontaneous version, and they may have been quite right that they could not stage it and compete against each other at the same time. So, in the elicited episodes, unlike in the spontaneous ones, the talk of the sportscaster is always the production of one boy rather than a joint production, although both boys do play a speaking role in each elicited episode.

The frame of the sportscast in the elicited episodes is created through the use of the same devices as in the spontaneous ones: register-marking grammatical features, expressive prosody, and creation of a participation framework in which the speaker is the sportscaster and the addressee is the (imaginary) audience. The register is even more strongly marked by means of formal features than is the case in the spontaneous version, for several register-marking forms appear more often in the elicited version: sentences with no subject (e.g., *gets the rebound*), with no auxiliary (e.g., *Doctor J working for a good shot*), or with no lexical verb (e.g., *Doctor J with the rebound*). In addition, during elicited sportscasting, the boys use a large number of passives, a construction which is typical of adult sportscasting

(Weber 1982) but which these children use very rarely in spontaneous sportscasting. For example, (30) is a short excerpt from Matt's announcing of a game that Josh is playing against the computer; Josh is manipulating the figure "Larry Bird," while the computer controls that of "Doctor J":

(30)

	Matt:	Nice steal inside by Larry Bird!
		He takes it back.
		In the corner,
		he gets around him,
		but he loses his positioning.
		That's a twenty-four second violation,
		Doctor J's ball once again,
→		blocked by Larry Bird,
		inside,
→		blocked again,
		rebou:nd!
		Larry Bird.
		[fast] He gets it inside
→		but the ball's stolen.

The boys' heavy use of passives in the elicited episodes to report what happens to the ball shows that they know that this construction is appropriate to sportscasting. They probably do not use it during their spontaneous sportscasting because it fulfills no practical function for them. For professional sportscasters, using the passive allows mention of an agent (a player) to be delayed until the sportscaster can ascertain the player's identity (Green 1982). For the boys, though, figuring out players' identities is not a problem. However, they can and do use the passive frequently—as Matt does in (30)—when they are consciously trying to sound like sportscasters. As Ferguson (1983) notes, even syntactic constructions that may serve some practical purpose become, in addition, conventionalized register markers. Thus the boys, like professional announcers, recognize that passives—like other sportscasting forms—are appropriate and conventional, and use them for this reason and not always because their use serves an immediate practical function.

The most striking difference between the spontaneous episodes and the elicited ones, however, and the difference that influences the footings that are taken, is that in the elicited version there is less need for verbal management of the game. Whereas in their spontaneous sportscasting both boys have to pay attention to both announcing and playing, in the elicited episodes the roles of sportscaster and player are kept completely separate. The boy who is playing does not have to worry about announcing, and the announcer does not have to worry about playing. In the elicited sportscasting, every utterance is part of the sportscasting performance; there is not any frame shifting of the same sort that occurs in the spontaneous episodes. Since the boys are not competing against each other, there is no rivalry about the score, and there are hardly any disputes or questions. In addition, the boys do not tease each other or make jokes by mixing frames. Their literal situation, that is, is not brought into their sportscasting.

However, the boys do create another frame shift in their elicited sportscasting, one that reveals a knowledge of the various characters and participation frameworks involved in the genre of the sportscast. Specifically, they know that sportscasts on television and radio include not only the play-by-play announcing but also, prominently, interviews with players. Within their elicited sportscasts, then, the boys stage "interviews." Thus the participation framework that they embed is one in which the participants are not the boys' real selves but are instead dramatized characters.

Embedded Participation Framework: Interviews

During an "interview with the player," the boy who has been acting as sportscaster takes on the part of interviewer, and the boy who has been playing speaks as the interviewee. Unlike the play-by-play announcing, which is basically monologic, the interviews are dialogic: the participants address each other. An interview consists of a series of questions (by the interviewer) and answers (by the interviewee, the player). Whereas during the play-by-play announcing it is the audience who is addressed as *you,* during an interview the interviewer and interviewee address each other as *you* and by name.

The boys know that during real sports events that are broadcast on television, interviews with the players are not generally conducted by the sportscaster himself (the announcer who is giving the play-by-play account of the game). Instead, the camera shifts to another person who does the interviewing, and after the interview is concluded, the camera goes back to the sportscaster, who resumes his announcing. A typical interview sequence, then, involves three participants: the sportscaster, the interviewer, and the player (the interviewee).

Since there are only two boys, they must create these three participants with only two people. In order to create enough participants for an interview sequence, the boy who is acting as sportscaster takes on the part of an interviewer, as seen clearly in (31):

(31)

a	Josh:	Or will Larry Bird WIN [fast] LARRY BIRD WINS!
b		THIRTY-SIX THIRTY-THREE,
c		WHAT A SHOT BY LARRY BIRD!
d →		Now let's go down t' Irv Cross for an interview.
e →		Well Larry what d' you think about that.
f	Matt:	Well I had planned t' do that,
g		because today I've been shooting pretty good three pointers.

h		So I decided I'd call time,
i		be nice and fresh,
j		right off the bench,
k		and try t' get the lead in the last second.
l	Josh:	Well you certainly did that, Larry Bird.
m	Matt:	Well I'm ... <u>still</u> mad about a couple of those calls.
n		I wouldn't've had t' even even <u>think</u> about that- trying something like that,
o		if any of those calls were not called.
p	Josh:	Okay and there's another game going on right now.

Here Josh, as sportscaster, reports excitedly that Larry Bird has won the game (a–c). He then calls on "Irv Cross" (the name of a real sports broadcaster) to conduct an interview with "Larry Bird" (d), indicating, through the term *go down,* that this interviewer is (supposedly) in a different location from the sportscaster (*down* on the court). Speaking as "Irv," then, he poses a question, *Well Larry what d' you think about that.* Notice that Josh's role switch, from speaking as the sportscaster to speaking as the interviewer, is indicated only through the form and sequencing of his utterances; that is, he does not adopt a different voice quality in order to speak as "Irv." The interview proceeds as Matt, the player, speaks as "Larry," describing his strategy in the just-finished game.

Not every interview introduces the interviewer as a separate character as explicitly as (31) does, although the shift in participation framework is always evident. In (32), for instance, Ben announces just that an interview is about to take place, but he does not summon an interviewer:

(32)

a		Ben:	It's stolen by Bird,
b			Bird misses,
c			Bir:d rebound,
d			shoots it up it's goo::d!
e	→		We're gonna have a ref's time out here.
f	→		And we just called Larry Bird over
g			to talk to us.
h	→		Now Larry, you have a one hundred and
i			[3.5]
j			you have <u>over</u> a one hundred point lead.
k			How do you feel about that.
l		Josh:	Well y'know Vince, I-
m			I just feel great about that,
n			and I like the way I'm playin' ball,
o			and I think I- I'm gonna score
p			over three hundred points today.

q	Ben:	Three hundred!
r		You have ... all you need is sixty-four points.
s		Do you think you'll get 'em this quarter?
t	Josh:	U:m y'know- maybe not this quarter but close to it.
u		I'll score in the early fourth quarter.
v	Ben:	Okay.
w		And now back t' the game.
x		Doctor J for two,
y		It's no good.

At lines (e–f) Ben indicates that an interview is forthcoming, and at (h) he shifts his footing, from addressing the audience to addressing "Larry." Throughout the interview, then, until lines (v–w), Ben continues to speak as interviewer rather than as announcer, addressing Josh as "Larry," and Josh responds to Ben's questions, addressing him by the name of "Vince" (1). Thus the shift in participation framework, although not explicitly introduced, is clearly marked.

The interviews, then, are set apart from the play-by-play announcing through a shift in participation framework which involves two closely related elements: a change in the characters who speak and are spoken to, and a change from monologue to dialogue. The boy who has been speaking as the announcer begins to speak as the interviewer, turning from play-by-play reporting to asking questions, and the boy who has been performing the nonspeaking role of the player takes on a new role as a conversationalist, speaking as an interviewee who answers questions. The boys thus embed one imaginary participation framework within another.

Conclusion

The boys' sportscasting, in both the spontaneous and the elicited versions, shows their playing with the possibilities for framing that are opened up by the activity, specifically by manipulating participation frameworks. Their performances illustrate two related ideas: first, that analytical attention to framing leads to a greater appreciation of children's discourse abilities, and, second, that attention to children's framing of their play illuminates the human framing capacity in general.

The discourse of school-age children in nonacademic settings has been a relatively neglected area, and their capacities sometimes tend to be underestimated. With some notable exceptions (e.g., M. H. Goodwin 1990, M. H. Goodwin & C. Goodwin 1987, Shuman 1986), most studies of older children are conducted in controlled situations, such as the classroom or the experimental laboratory, with a focus on their acquisition of referential and literacy skills. However, as Evans (1985:130) notes, concentrating on the classroom discourse and the experimenter-directed talk of school-age children, while overlooking the language of their spontaneous interaction, creates "an incongruous characterization of preschool-aged children as competent communicators with a reasonably sophisticated understanding of discourse rules and conversational strategies, but slightly older beginning school-aged children as communicatively inept, hindered by limited processing skills."

The framing capacities of school-age children are one way in which their discourse abilities are clearly anything but limited. By juggling and embedding footings, the boys discussed in this chapter turn a basically nonverbal, physical activity (playing games) into a speech activity (sportscasting). They use their implicit knowledge of how framing works, in the spontaneous version of sportscasting, to compete and cooperate at the same time, and they exploit their appreciation of framing for humorous effect. In the elicited version, they eliminate the element of competition. But even though they are freed of the need to embed the participation framework of the literal situation within the imaginary one, they continue to create layers of footings, embedding one imaginary participation framework within another. Their doing this indicates, I suggest, that they recognize, tacitly, that all discourse is layered. So even when frame shifting may not be absolutely required by a discourse task (in this case, my request to "do sportscasting"), it *is* necessary in order to create a vivid episode.

Children's exercise of their framing capabilities during play exposes several aspects of the way that framing can work in general. The framing capacity is always available for creating discourses that are prosaic or inventive, serious or humorous, with practical objectives or just for fun. It is not only during play that framing is vital to the organization of talk, but the creative ability that is manifested during play sets in relief the capacities that all communicators use in constructing their discourse. It is during play that we routinely see the most elaborate interweaving of literal, possible, and fanciful participation frameworks.

For participants in interaction, framing is a resource for gracefully managing divergent tasks. These might be tasks that are normally thought of as conflicting (such as simultaneously competing and cooperating), or they might be tasks that simply require different displays of attention to interlocutors and to ideas (such as producing a monologue in a specialized register and engaging in conversation). For the analyst, identifying the ways in which interactants manipulate frames helps to explain how discourse is at once anchored in literal experience yet not restricted by it. Identifying the outer frame of an activity, the points at which it is most firmly linked to the literal world, is only a starting point in exploring what is going on. More revealing of the nature of an activity, often, is the way in which participation frameworks, assembled out of such ordinary discourse elements as address terms and reference forms, are layered and mixed.

Appendix

Transcription conventions, based on Tannen (1984), are as follows:

.	sentence-final falling intonation
?	sentence-final rising intonation
,	continuing intonation
!	sentence-final falling intonation, with animated voice quality
..	noticeable pause, less than .5 second
...	half second pause; each extra dot represents additional half second pause
[3.5]	numbers in brackets represent pauses, in seconds
<u>underline</u>	emphatic stress
CAPITALS	extra emphatic stress
h, (h)	laughter
( )	empty parentheses indicate transcription impossible
(words)	filled parentheses indicate uncertain transcription
⌈	Brackets between lines indicate overlapping speech
⌊	Two people talking at the same time
=	second speaker's talk is latched onto first speaker's without a noticeable pause
:	lengthened sound (extra colons represent extra lengthening)
-	glottal stop: abrupt cutting off of breath
→	highlights point of analysis
[fast]	information in brackets applies to the talk that follows; continues until punctuation

Notes

1. *Whatchamacallit* represents the way *what you may call it* (i.e., "whatever the name is") is pronounced in rapid casual American English.

2. An *instant replay* is a videotape of an especially impressive or unusual action (e.g., a basket shot from a long distance) which is shown on television sportscasts immediately after the original occurrence, for the benefit of viewers who may have missed it or who may like to see it again. In the computer basketball game that the boys play, "instant replays" are shown from time to time on the monitor, triggered by the distance from which a figure has successfully shot a basket.

3. Michael Jackson, a black rock singer and dancer popular in the 1980s, when these data were recorded, is noted for his performance of the *moon walk,* a type of *break dancing,* which are skilled dance routines typically associated with urban teenagers of that time.

References

Bateson, Gregory. 1972. Steps to an ecology of mind. New York: Ballantine.

Crystal, David, and Derek Davy. 1969. Investigating English style. Bloomington: Indiana University Press.

Ervin-Tripp, Susan. 1977. Wait for me, roller skate! Child discourse, ed. by Susan Ervin-Tripp & Claudia Mitchell-Kernan, 165–88. New York: Academic Press.

Evans, Mary Ann. 1985. Play beyond play: Its role in formal informative speech. Play, language, and stories: The development of children's literate behavior, ed. by Lee Galda and Anthony D. Pellegrini, 129–145. Norwood, NJ: Ablex.

Ferguson, Charles. 1983. Sports announcer talk: Syntactic aspects of register variation. Language in Society 12:153–72.

Garvey, Catherine. 1977. Children's play. Cambridge, MA: Harvard University Press.

Goffman, Erving. 1961. Encounters: Two studies in the sociology of interaction. Indianapolis: Bobbs-Merrill.

Goffman, Erving. 1974. Frame analysis. New York: Harper & Row.

Goffman, Erving. 1981a. Footing. Forms of talk, 124–59. Philadelphia: University of Pennsylvania Press.

Goffman, Erving. 1981b. Radio talk. Forms of talk, 197–330. Philadelphia: University of Pennsylvania Press.

Goffman, Erving. 1981c. Response cries. Forms of talk, 78–123. Philadelphia: University of Pennsylvania Press.

Goodwin, Marjorie Harness. 1990. He-said-she-said: Talk as social organization among black children. Bloomington and Indianapolis: Indiana University Press.

Goodwin, Marjorie Harness, and Charles Goodwin. 1987. Children's arguing. Language, gender and sex in comparative perspective, ed. by Susan U. Philips, Susan Steele, and Christine Tanz, 200–248. Cambridge: Cambridge University Press.

Green, Georgia. 1982. Colloquial and literary uses of inversions. Spoken and written language: Exploring orality and literacy, ed. by Deborah Tannen, 119–153. Norwood, NJ: Ablex.

Gumperz, John J. 1982. Discourse strategies. Cambridge: Cambridge University Press.

Hoyle, Susan M. 1988. Boys' sportscasting talk: A study of children's language use. Unpublished doctoral dissertation, Georgetown University.

Hoyle, Susan M. 1989. Forms and footings in boys' sportscasting. Text 9:153–173.

Hoyle, Susan M. 1991. Children's competence in the specialized register of sportscasting. Journal of Child Language. 18:435–450.

Johnstone, Barbara. 1987. 'He says . . . so I said': Verb tense alternation and narrative depictions of authority in American English. Linguistics 25:33–52.

Leech, Geoffrey. 1971. Meaning and the English verb. London: Longman.

Levinson, Stephen C. 1979. Activity types and language. Linguistics 17:365–399.

Schiffrin, Deborah. 1987. Discourse markers. Cambridge: Cambridge University Press.

Schwartzman, Helen. 1978. Transformations: The anthropology of children's play. New York: Plenum Press.

Shuman, Amy. 1986. Storytelling rights: The uses of oral and written texts by urban adolescents. Cambridge: Cambridge University Press.

Tannen, Deborah. 1984. Conversational style: Analyzing talk among friends. Norwood, NJ: Ablex.

Tannen, Deborah. 1985. Frames and schemas in interaction. Quaderni di Semantica 6:326–35.

Weber, Elizabeth G. 1982. Going, going, gone: Verb forms in baseball sportscasting. Unpublished M.A. thesis, University of California, Los Angeles.

5

The Pulpit and Woman's Place: Gender and the Framing of the 'Exegetical Self' in Sermon Performances

FRANCES LEE SMITH

Grand Canyon University

> *But the minister who is forceful uses language which rings with reality. He is never vague, ethereal, or effeminate. . . . He has the power to stab awake the conscience of men. He speaks like a man!*
>
> *Steps to the Sermon* (H. C. Brown, Jr., et al. 1963:158)

This excerpt from a textbook written at a large Baptist seminary in Texas expresses a traditional belief that persuasive, truthful speech equals direct,

This article is based on my dissertation, "Gender and the Framing of Exegetical Authority in Sermon Performances," completed at Georgetown University in May 1990. I would like to thank my mentor, Deborah Tannen, for her encouragement, patience, and perceptive comments. I am also grateful to my readers, Ralph Fasold and Deborah Schiffrin, for their suggestions and support.

The professors, instructors, and students at the seminary where I conducted this study also unselfishly offered their cooperation.

The phrase "The Pulpit and Woman's Place" is derived from the title of Robin Lakoff's provocative treatise on gender and language, *Language and Woman's Place* (1975).

forceful speech equals masculine speech. The authors of these statements were verbalizing a widely held value judgment about the ways men and women use linguistic resources to construct credibility. From a sociolinguistic perspective, credibility is closely associated with what Erving Goffman calls the "textual self." In "The Lecture" (1981:160–195), Goffman identifies the textual self of a speaker as "the sense of the person that seems to stand behind the textual statements made *and which incidentally gives these statements authority* [emphasis mine]" (173).

This projection of self can also be defined in relation to footing. "Footing" is Goffman's term for the alignment between a speaker and the other participants that is constantly being changed through various "projections of self" signaled by pitch, volume, rhythm, stress, and other paralinguistic, lexical, and syntactic cues (1981:128). In the case of a performance such as a lecture or a sermon, the "textual self" footing is the central or core alignment between the speaker and audience.

During the summer of 1986, I sat in on three preaching classes at the seminary where the cited textbook was written. I found a group of young adults who shared a common religious and educational background—a heritage whose ideology has nonetheless traditionally discriminated between women and men regarding who is eligible and/or qualified to preach. I decided to explore how these men and women framed their presentations of the "textual self" in their sermon performances.

The sermon is a complex, highly ritualized discourse genre made up of the specialized performance tasks of exegeting a fixed sacred text, illustrating it with narratives or poems, and exhorting the audience to change their behavior on the basis of its message. Thus, in a typical sermon performance, the preacher displays a textual self as exegeter, illustrator, and exhorter, according to the task in which s/he is currently engaged. I limited my examination to the preacher's presentation of self as exegeter.

A frame-analytic study of the relationship between gender and language in the context of preaching extends our knowledge of both gender and framing. First, it shows that the display of gender is integral to the structure of a sermon performance, just as other research has shown for conversations. Second, it delineates how this display is accomplished through the linguistic strategies the speaker uses for framing the performance. I now discuss the relationships between my study and other research on these issues.

Background: Studies on Gender and Framing

In *Gender Advertisements* (1979:8), Goffman suggests that there is no such thing as "gender identity," only a "schedule for the portrayal of gender." To participants in social situations, however, the portrayal of gender is synonymous with gender identity. Goffman's use of the term "gender display" in this article is based on an ethological approach to male/female distinctions in the ritualized behavior of animal communication, which is a fundamental feature of the natural order. Thus, for Goffman, gender display belongs to the realm of ritual and performance.

Goffman further claims that social relationships are built on the principle of "portraiture." That is, human beings are constantly constructing "artful poses" of themselves and "glimpsed views" of other people for the benefit of their audience. Goffman showed how this portraiture or framing is accomplished through posed pictures constructed by advertisers. However, speakers are engaged in the same process as they verbally portray themselves and other females and males as figures in their discourse.

Recent research supports the argument that gender differences in language are cross-cultural differences which are best explained as differences in the way women and men frame the forms of talk which shape their lives. The "cross-cultural" view, which has roots in the work of Gumperz (1978, 1979, 1982) on interethnic communication, has been advocated by Maltz and Borker (1982) and Tannen (1986, 1989a, 1990a,b) and validated with studies by Tannen (1990a,b), M. H. Goodwin (1980a,b, 1982), C. Goodwin (1986), and Goodwin and Goodwin (1987), among others. I discuss here only the findings to which my study is most directly related.

Tannen (1990b) uses the cross-cultural differences paradigm to explain the differences in the way males and females construct topical cohesion and physical alignment in conversations. This study is based on twenty-minute videotapes of eight pairs of friends, one female and one male pair of second graders, sixth graders, tenth graders, and twenty-five-year olds, respectively. Tannen found that "in both the alignment of posture and gaze and the development of topics, the girls and women focused more tightly and more directly on each other than did the boys and men" (1990b:202). However, she argues that this is not an indication that the females were more "engaged" than the males were. Rather, she maintains that these data support the argument that males and females have different ways of expressing engagement and conversational involvement. Similarly, I have found that men and women have different ways of constructing ritual engagement and involvement between themselves and an audience in their performances of exegetical arguments.

The joint and separate studies of Marjorie Harness Goodwin and Charles Goodwin show that human beings frame forms of talk such as everyday arguments and narratives according to interpersonal goals. That is, people acquire and use certain discourse strategies in order to shape the social organization of the activities in which they participate. The findings of these two researchers fall under two major categories. First, they show that the embedding of alignments is central to the construction of narratives and arguments. Second, they demonstrate how the cultural ideology about the social identity of the performer shapes the form of a discourse performance.

In their study of children's arguing, Goodwin and Goodwin (1987) observe that the girls embedded other forms of speech (requests, explanations, excuses, stories, etc.) within the "opposition moves" that constituted the overall structure of their arguments. Goodwin and Goodwin conclude that because of the ability of argument structure to incorporate not only various types of speech activities but also paralinguistic features capable of distinguishing various "'voices', displays of affect, and thus dramatic personae, arguments become vehicles for dynamic social drama" (238–239).

I suggest that sermons, as specialized forms of argument, provide a discourse arena for similar dramatic display. I have demonstrated that the "textual self" footing (i.e., alignment) is a useful construct for analyzing sermon arguments because it reveals how the framing strategies that preachers employ to create ritual alignments among themselves, the audience, and a fixed written text affect the structure of their arguments.

Second, the work of both H. Goodwin and C.Goodwin deals with the relationship between the form of a discourse performance and the cultural ideology about the social identity of the performer. In her study of the "instigating" stories of black adolescent girls in Philadelphia, M. H. Goodwin (1990) shows how the larger cultural framework affects the structuring of narratives. The girls used indirect forms and carefully chose the characters and actions in their narratives in order to provoke their listener into a future confrontation that would reorganize the social identities of the group in a way that was satisfactory to the narrator. That is, the participants relied on their background knowledge (i.e., their knowledge of the relevant cultural ideology) in using the performance of a narrative to transform old alignments into future realignments, and this affected its structure significantly.

C. Goodwin's analysis (1986:283–316) of a story told by a man to male and female friends at a backyard picnic also shows that there is a relationship between the discourse form of narrative and an implicit, presupposed ideology about the nature of men and women that is shared by a speaker and his or her audience. He found that certain "properties" of the narrative "—such as the characters in it, the activities in which they are engaged, the themes that motivate its drama, and the words selected to tell it—show that some of those present (specifically, the men) are a more appropriate audience of what it has to offer than others" (295).

In this chapter, I show that the same kind of relationship exists between the discourse form of a sermon and the implicit, presupposed ideology about the nature of men and women that is shared by a preacher and his or her audience. I also demonstrate how the larger cultural framework of shared background knowledge shapes and is shaped by the framing strategies preachers use to embed certain types of alignments in their sermon performances.

Models of Framing and Involvement Strategies

My theoretical perspective on the textual self is based primarily on the discourse model proposed by Goffman in "The Lecture," although it is also indebted to the one advanced by Deborah Tannen in *Talking Voices* (1989b). Therefore, before discussing my study in more detail, I briefly summarize the relevant insights from these paradigms.

Goffman: Framing, Footing, and "Fresh Talk" Strategies

For Goffman, the study of "framing" is the study of the organization of experience. In *Frame Analysis* (1974), he articulates the implicit conventions that distinguish one way of organizing experience (e.g. dreams, trances, games, rehearsals) from another. In *Forms of Talk* (1981), he applies his frame analytic method more specifically to the study of discourse.

The fundamental constructs of Goffman's theory are "ritualization," "participation framework," "production format," and "embedding." He describes "ritualization" as the process whereby

> the movements, looks, and vocal sounds we make as an unintended by-product of speaking and listening . . . acquire a specialized communicative role . . . looked to and provided for in connection with the displaying of our alignment to current events. (1981:2)

"Participation framework" refers to the participation statuses of speakers and hearers in relation to the production and reception of an utterance, respectively. The "production format" is made up of the self-projections of the speaker of an utterance as "principal," "animator," and "author." The "principal" is the "social actor" in the current activity, who is presenting himself or herself as "animator" (a physical body that speaks) and "author" (a mind that has chosen the sentiments and words that express them). "Embedding" refers to the way participation frameworks and production formats are manifested in the construction of utterances.

In "The Lecture," Goffman addresses "the ultimate claims that society makes upon a person who performs" (1981:192). He suggests that, in order to present oneself successfully in a performance role, the performer must create the impression that she or he has "effectively put himself at the disposal of an occasion and hence its participants, opening himself up to it and to them, counting the rest of himself as something to be subordinated for the purpose" (192).

In other words, the success of the performance lies in the performer's ability to convince the audience that they not only are experiencing the privilege of hearing a text, but also are gaining added access to the heart and mind of the author of the text, an author who is surrendering himself or herself to the current occasion for the benefit of the audience (186–195). That is, success depends on the speaker's creation of what Goffman calls the "illusion" that s/he is being responsive to the audience and the occasion (189).

Speakers create this illusion or impression by constantly "laminating" or "rekeying" the textual-self footing with other footings whose functions are to present projections of self which modify the speaker's display of textual-self authority in various ways. Goffman identifies and discusses four categories of these additional footings—"rekeyings," "text bracketings," "text parenthetical remarks," and "management of performance contingencies" (173–186).

What these four footings have in common is that in each one, the lecturer as "principal" splits his or her animator self off from the author self in order to qualify or modify either the current spoken text (as in rekeyings, text brackets, text parenthetical remarks) or the performance situation (as in management of performance contingencies) (173–186).

Besides sharing the feature of splitting animator from author and fore-grounding the animator's role, all four of these footings often appear as "fresh talk," or at least simulated fresh talk. That is, the linguistic structures through which they are manifested are designed to appear as though they have been spontaneously formulated and produced by the performer (186–191).

Responsiveness, in turn, is displayed through the following three forms of "fresh talk," or its simulation: "parenthetical embroidery" (191), "hyper-smooth delivery" (i.e., the absence of hesitations, restarts) and "high style" (i.e., word plays, metaphors, parallelisms) (189).

Goffman suggests that "high style" frames the lecturer as authoritative because it makes him or her look as though s/he has applied his or her intelligence diligently to the presentation of the text for this particular audience (189).

Similarly, "hypersmooth delivery" signals that the performer is doing more than just "aloud reading"—s/he is monitoring the formulation process of the speech in order to prevent any "hitches" that would interfere with the clarity of the message (188–189).

The use of "parenthetical embroidery," on the other hand, makes the speaker appear as though s/he is wearing his or her warranted authority "lightly," or is politely declining it in deference to the audience. In this form of "fresh talk," the speaker-as-animator speaks both for himself or herself as lecturer and on behalf of the audience, presenting all of the participants in the current performance as fellow "appreciators" of the text (191–193).

Finally, Goffman says that what underlies these three types of "fresh talk" strategies is "the style or register of spoken discourse itself" (189). He employs a written/spoken framework for his observations, stating that "what makes for 'good' writing is systematically different from what makes for 'good' speaking, and the degree to which the lecturer uses the normative spoken form marks the degree to which it will appear he has delivered himself to a speaking event" (189).

Tannen and "Involvement" Strategies

As we have seen, the central theme of Goffman's model is that, in order to present oneself successfully in a particular speaking role, the performer must create the impression of being fully engaged with both the topic and the audience. For Goffman, this is accomplished through the "localizing" or "indexicalizing" of a text through "fresh talk."

According to Tannen's model, this process would be described as creating an impression of "involvement." *Talking Voices* (Tannen 1989b) is a study of involvement and the strategies through which it is constructed in conversational discourse and across a variety of other discourse genres.

Tannen claims that "involvement" underlies all human communication. Furthermore, "understanding is facilitated, even enabled, by an emotional experience of interpersonal involvement" (34). This emotional experience is the source of communication in that it provides the impetus for the poetic function of language, the purpose of which is to fire the individual imagination by creating patterns of "sound" and "sense" (16, 34). "Involvement strategies" are patterns of sound and sense which, when shared by interlocutors, create an "aesthetic response," a concept Tannen borrows from Becker (1982), which in turn generates "connectedness," "rapport," and "coherence" (13–17).

Tannen identifies the involvement strategies that she has found in her own and others' research as follows:

> The strategies that work primarily (but not exclusively) on sound include (1) rhythm, (2) patterns based on repetition and variation of (a) phonemes, (b) morphemes, (c) words, (d) collocations of words, and (e) longer sequences of discourse, and (3) style figures of speech (many of which are also repetitive figures). The strategies that work primarily (but never exclusively) on meaning include (1) indirectness, (2) ellipsis, (3) tropes, (4) dialogue, (5) imagery and detail, and (6) narrative. (17)

Tannen demonstrates how involvement strategies "contribute to the point of the discourse, presenting the subject of discourse in a way that shapes how the hearer or reader will view it" (28–29). She states that "in the terms of Gregory Bateson's (1972) framework, they contribute to the metamessage, the level on which a speaker's relationships to the subject of talk and to the other participants in talk are negotiated" (29).

This level, which has much in common with what Goffman describes as "footing," is where Goffman's and Tannen's models interface. Both Goffman's "fresh talk" strategies (high style, hypersmooth delivery, and parenthetical embroidery) and Tannen's "involvement strategies" represent linguistic strategies through which a text is localized and particularized in and through a specific performance. That is, the presentation of self and the creation of involvement are mutually constructed through verbal and nonverbal strategies at the level of footing.

In applying both of these models to eighteen sermons preached by seminary students, I found that there were significant inter- and intragender differences in the strategies the students employed for framing their exegetical arguments. The men as a group employed certain ritualized references to self and the audience, discourse markers, question/answer sequences, intensifiers, and modals to put themselves "on record" as exegeters of the written text more often than the women did. The only woman who used these discourse strategies as frequently as the men was also the only woman who did not express uncertainty about the appropriateness of her preaching to adults. The other women rarely used them. Moreover, one woman employed an atypically formal register throughout both of her arguments; another used framing strategies common in stories told to children. In both cases, the ritual authority of the text was foregrounded and that of the performer was backgrounded. Overall, then, the men foregrounded their textual-self (i.e, exegetical) authority more than the women did.

In the remainder of the chapter, I present a summary of the study, the data, the method of analysis, the findings, and the conclusions.

The Study

The Scene

The art of preaching is taught in two courses that are required for students in the M.Div. (Master of Divinity) program at this seminary. The students must take the class on how to *write* a sermon, called "Principles of Preaching," before enrolling in the "preaching lab," where they are taught how to *deliver* a sermon. In the latter course, each student preaches a minimum of two times. The participants explicitly define these performances as being simultaneously "academic assignments" and "real sermons."

Until 1980, the seminary had different requirements for male and female students seeking the Master of Divinity degree. According to several professors in the Preaching Department, prior to 1970, "school policy" prohibited women from taking the preaching lab course. I was told that this policy was based on an "off-record" consensus of faculty members and administrators. During the seventies, the preaching lab was officially a required course for men, an elective for women. In 1980, the lab was made a required course for all students enrolled in the M.Div. program.

The seminary has an annual enrollment of about four thousand students. During the summer of 1986, the preaching labs were open only to students who were planning to graduate in August. One lab had twenty-four students, including three women; the second lab had twenty-two students, with one woman; the third had twenty-one students, with no women. Thus, the total enrollment was sixty-seven students, four of whom were women. Because of scheduling conflicts, none of the labs was taught by a professor. Instead, two Ph.D. candidates and a recent Ph.D. recipient (all men) served as the instructors.

According to a questionnaire that I gave to students toward the end of each course, the average age was between 25 and 30. All but three had been born in the United States; these three were a Korean, a Jamaican, and a Cuban.

The questionnaire was designed to provide demographic data, information about career goals, and self-reports of attitudes toward what a preacher's preaching style should be like. For example, I asked, "Are there any stereotypes about how to preach that you plan to avoid in your preaching?" In a second, expanded version of the questionnaire, I added a number of questions, two of which were about women and preaching: "Have you heard a woman minister preach?" and the two-part follow-up question, "Would you like to again? Why or why not?" Nineteen students said that they had heard a woman preach before; seventeen said they had not. One man responded ambiguously that he had heard a woman "share," possibly indicating a belief that women "share" rather than preach. One woman stated that women "teach" rather than preach. And one student, the only Mexican American in the study, returned his questionnaire to me rather angrily with only the question about age answered.

To the follow-up question "Would you like to again? Why or why not?", ten replied "yes," eight responded "no," and one said "maybe." The eight students who answered "no" were men. To the question "Why or why not?" four of the eight claimed that it contradicts Scripture; one claimed that it does not please God; one said that he didn't agree with it; one simply added an exclamation point to the word "no" that he had written; and one answered with "They sound like children. They look out of place and they seem out of character being forceful and emphatic."

The picture that develops from these answers is that only about half of the participants in two of the labs had heard a woman "preach" before (nineteen of thirty-nine), and that about half of these (eight of nineteen) offered strong opinions about not wanting to do so again.

Thus, although the sermon performance situation would appear to be the same for the female and male students when viewed etically, because of the religiocultural tradition that has supported only the men's performance of this discourse form until recently, emically the situation is different for the two groups. The men who engage in the task are following long-established community expectations; the women are going against them. Furthermore, although policies have changed at the institutional level and none of the students would challenge the new requirements openly, a large portion of the students' attitudes toward women as preachers appear to remain ambiguous or negative.[1]

Collection of the Data

I first obtained written permission from the Preaching Department to observe and tape the three preaching labs. I introduced myself to each class as a graduate student doing sociolinguistic research on communicative styles in preaching. I also added a release statement to the questionnaires that I distributed in each class which said that the student was aware the classes were being taped. Ninety-one percent of these questionnaires were returned signed by the students. None of the other 9 percent of the students explicitly opposed the procedure.

Lab sessions were held for two hours, four days a week. After one to three days of introduction (depending on the instructor), each class session consisted of a series of student performances which the lab personnel taped from a booth in the back of the room. In the prerequisite sermon writing class, all students had to write sermons based on the same Scripture text. For the two sermons which they preached in the lab, students could choose their own text. In response to my general request for volunteers, however, several students in each of the three labs (a total of thirteen) agreed to preach on the story of "The Ten Lepers" in Luke 17:11–19.

While they were taping, the audiovisual assistants in the booth simultaneously recorded a second copy of the sermons on Luke 17 for me. I sat with the students in the audience, audiotaped the classes, and took notes while the class members were occupied performing for each other and filling out evaluation forms.

After the three courses had ended, I transcribed eighteen sermons in their entirety as well as thirty-two sermon introductions. I followed the established practice of many discourse analysts by chunking the data into lines according to intonational patterns, discourse markers, and/or pauses of varying lengths. (For a list of the transcription symbols, see the Appendix.)

The Data

The data consist of the sermons preached by the women who were enrolled in the labs as well as the sermons by ten of the eleven men who volunteered to preach on "The Ten Lepers." I transcribed both of the sermons preached by each of the four women, one by each of the ten men. I decided to omit one male volunteer's sermon from my analysis because he was from Jamaica. He was also in his fifties, whereas the other volunteers ranged in age from twenty-four to thirty-three.

All ten of the men's sermons are based on the story of "The Ten Lepers." Four of the women's sermons are derived from narratives—two on "The Ten Lepers" and two about Abraham. The other four sermons by the women are based on either God's instructions to the Israelites or the apostles' instructions to the early churches. Since an exegetical argument based on a Scripture passage is incomprehensible without access to the passage itself, I provide a copy of the passage which served as the basis for most of the transcribed sermons:

Luke 17:11–19
(King James Version)

11   And it came to pass, as he went to Jerusalem, that he passed through the midst of Samaria and Galilee.
12   And as he entered into a certain village, there met him ten men that were lepers, which stood afar off:
13   And they lifted up their voices, and said, Jesus, Master, have mercy on us.

14   And when he saw them, he said unto them, Go show yourselves unto the priests. And it came to pass, that, as they went, they were cleansed.
15   And one of them, when he saw that he was healed, turned back, and with a loud voice glorified God,
16   And fell down on his face at his feet, giving him thanks: and he was a Samaritan.
17   And Jesus answering said, Were there not ten cleansed? but where are the nine?
18   There are not found that returned to give glory to God, save this stranger.
19   And he said unto him, Arise, go thy way: thy faith hath made thee whole.

Analysis

By performing both quantitative and qualitative microanalyses of each of the eighteen sermons, I found that each student had constructed his or her argument to display one of four types of "exegetical authority" footings. I have labeled each of these footings in terms of the projection of textual self which it manifests. They are (1) "the preacher as 'on-record' exegeter," (2) "the preacher as 'low-profile' exegeter," (3) "the preacher as narrator," and (4) "the preacher as 'high-style' exegeter." In the first footing, the ritual authority of the preacher is foregrounded through the speaker's use of explicit references to the participation framework (e.g., "I see," "we see," "you see"); in the second, it is downplayed through the use of fewer such references; and in the fourth, it is backgrounded through the repeated citing of the Scripture as its own authority. In the third footing, the preacher primarily retells the Scripture passage rather than explains it, thus transforming "exegetical" authority into "narrative" authority.

I first present what I identified as "text-exegeter" framing strategies and show how their distributions in this group of sermons create discourse patterns through which these four footings can be seen. Then I provide excerpts of sermons to illustrate each footing.

The "Text-Exegeter" Framing Strategies

Certain discourse strategies and linguistic devices foreground the exegetical authority of a preacher by making salient the preacher's ritual presence as leader in the exegetical task. Some do so explicitly, others implicitly. However, according to my framework, they are all optional devices, and, therefore, they all do so, in Goffman's terms, "parenthetically" (i.e., as a type of "parenthetical embroidery").

Schiffrin's (1987) study of discourse markers provides sociolinguistic insight into Goffman's parenthetical embroidery. According to Schriffrin, discourse markers "provide contextual coordinates for utterances: they index an utterance to the local contexts in which utterances are produced and in which they are to be interpreted" (326). These markers can be drawn from many linguistic categories such as particles, conjunctions, lexicalized clauses, perception verbs, time and location deictics, adverbials, quantifiers, interjections, and metatalk (327–328). Schiffrin suggests that an expression can be considered to be a marker if it is syntactically detachable from a sentence, is often used in initial position of an utterance, has a range of prosodic contours, and can operate both globally and locally and on different planes of discourse. Furthermore, its meaning may be reflexive of the language or the speaker (328). According to these guidelines, the text-exegeter strategies I found in the sermons would be considered discourse markers.

The self-references "I believe," "I think," "I see," "I find," "it appears to me," and "it's interesting to me" signal explicitly that the preacher is the author of the adjacent statement. They also present the preacher as having weighed the evidence for his or her evaluative comment. Thus, they convey that the statement is a result of a cognitive process of interpretation for which the preacher is claiming responsibility.

A preacher also displays herself or himself as spokesperson on behalf of the audience by structuring evaluative comments in the form of *that* complements embedded in "we see," "we can see" and "we find" statements. All of the verbs in these formulas have to do with examining and interpreting something; thus, in this interactional context, their use presents the speaker explicitly as an interpreter speaking on behalf of the audience as well as himself or herself.

These three "we" constructions create the impression that the same inner cognitive process of interpretation is going on simultaneously in both the preacher's and the audience's minds with the result that they have come to the same interpretation of the text. Since in reality this is very unlikely, the listeners understand "We see," "We can see," and "We find" to be ritual formulas through which the preacher is indirectly requesting that they pay attention to the preacher's interpretation and agree with it.

A preacher can also make explicit appeals for the audience's attention with the following "you" constructions: direct imperatives such as "listen," indirect imperatives like "you'll remember" and "you'll notice," and interrogatives like "do you remember?" and "did you notice?" These forms are also recognized by the participants as ritual formulas that the preacher uses to focus the audience's attention on an upcoming remark. Another "you" construction that is often used is the generalized "you" form with which the preacher is able to embed the listeners as figures in the argument itself.

Another form which functions similarly to the other "you" constructions just described is "you see" or just "see." It frames a proposition as information that the speaker is offering to a listener. This discourse marker displays the speaker as a sharer of new information and the audience as listeners who are fully capable of understanding it. Thus, although the footing it creates is asymmetrical, "you see" also creates a focus of attention on the ability of the listeners to learn rather than on the speaker's ability to inform.

These various "I," "we," and "you" constructions manifest exegetical authority explicitly. Their repeated use in an argument not only verbally defines but also explicitly foregrounds the current ritual participation framework and the preacher's position within it as leader in the exegetical task.

Other discourse and linguistic strategies mark exegetical authority implicitly. One such strategy for presenting oneself as a textual commentator is to answer one's own question in a rhetorical question/answer sequence. When a performer does this, s/he implies that s/he has the competence and the authority to provide an answer for the audience to consider.

Certain discourse markers also foreground the preacher's exegetical authority implicitly. "Now" is the most common one. According to Schiffrin (1987:245), "now" is often used to mark evaluative statements that contain views or interpretations that a speaker favors.

A response marker which also contributes to a preacher's presentation of himself or herself as a coherent and approachable text exegeter is "well," as in "*Well*, what should I say?" Schiffrin (1987:127) suggests that "'well' shows a speaker's aliveness to the need to accomplish coherence. . . ." It also conveys the speaker's responsiveness (i.e., his or her ritual presence) to the current interactional situation (128).

Intensifiers and modals are other linguistic strategies through which a speaker can be presented as a textual commentator implicitly. They share the function of displaying the speaker as a conjecturer or hypothesizer in relation to the world the statement is about. They also signal various types of commitment to one's statements.

Intensifiers such as "obviously," "of course," "actually," "basically," "simply," and "surely" convey a strong sense of certainty about what is being said. The modals "had to" and "must've" also convey the speaker's strong commitment to the hypothesis that is being presented. These intensifiers and modals convey that the statement in which they occur is endorsed by the speaker. Thus, they put the speaker on record implicitly.

In sum, all of the strategies I have described, both explicit and implicit ones, present the preacher as a figure who is commenting on his or her textual statements in such a way as to put himself or herself on record as exegeter. I claim that they form a subset of parenthetical embroidery because they all present the speaker as, in Goffman's terms, "a broker of his own statements, a mediator between text and audience" (1981:177). Both types of markers contribute to the saliency of the preacher's ritual leadership as exegeter in the performance.

Quantitative Analysis of the "Text-Exegeter" Strategies

The explicit strategies for putting oneself on record that I quantified are "I think," "I believe," "we see," "we can see," "we read," "we find," "we notice," "we look," "(you) notice," "(you) find," "(you) note," "(you) listen," "(you) remember," "(you) look," and the discourse marker "you

Table 5.1   Number of Text-Exegeter Strategies Employed by Each Student
             Arrayed According to Footing

Preacher as "On Record" Exegeter		Preacher as "Low-Profile" Exegeter		Preacher as Narrator		Preacher as "High-Style" Exegeter	
Meg1	28	Don	11	Carol2	4	Marge1	5
Tim	27	Mat	10	Len	4	Marge2	3
Rick	24	Tom	10				
Joel	22	Jim	8				
Meg2	17	Ann1	8				
Bill	15	Ann2	5				
		Todd	4				
		Carol1	4				

see/see." The implicit strategies for putting oneself on record that I quantified are rhetorical question/answer sequences; the discourse markers
"well" and "now"; the intensifiers "obviously," "obvious," "of course," "actually," "simply," "surely," and "basically"; and the modals "must
have"/"must've" and "had to."

Table 5.1 summarizes the distribution of the text-exegeter strategies.
Because I included two sermons by each woman in my data, I designate
them with "1" and "2" after the woman's name.

Table 5.1 shows that Meg was the only woman who constructed an "on
record" footing, whereas four of the men did so. And in the "low-profile"
footing, the men used the text-exegeter strategies more often than the
women did. In the four remaining sermons in the other two footings, few
text-exegeter strategies were used. Three of these four sermons were
preached by women.

Table 5.2 presents the average number of occurrences of individual text-
exegeter framing strategies per argument by footing. (For a breakdown of
the number of occurrences of individual strategies employed by each student, see chapters 3–6 of the original study.)

In Table 5.2 we see that Footing 1 contains more occurrences per
argument of each of the framing strategies, except modals, than does any of
the other footings. However, because of the very low number of strategies
employed in Footings 2, 3, and 4, I point out only major tendencies in the
patterns.

According to the table, Footing 1 had an average of at least six times
more occurrences of "I believe" and "I think" per sermon than did any of the
other footings. Thus, we may conclude that the preachers in Footing 1 made
explicit a separate participation status for themselves as leader in the exegetical task more often than the other preachers did.

The preachers who constructed Footing 1 also employed "we" and
"you" references (including "you see") about twice as often as those in
Footing 2. There were no occurrences of these markers in Footing 3, and

Table 5.2   Average Number of Occurrences of Individual Text-Exegeter Framing
Strategies per Argument by Footing

	Footing 1: Preacher as "On Record" Exegeter	Footing 2: Preacher as "Low-Profile" Exegeter	Footing 3: Preacher as Narrator	Footing 4: Preacher as "High-Style" Exegeter
"I think/believe"	3.00	.25	.50	.00
"We see/can see/read/find/ notice/look"	3.33	1.50	.00	.00
"(You) notice/find/note/ listen/remember/look"	3.00	1.13	.00	1.00
"You see/see"	1.50	.87	.00	.00
Rhetorical question/ answer sequences	1.83	.75	.50	.50
"Well"	.83	.50	.50	.00
"Now"	4.17	.63	.00	.00
Intensifiers	3.83	.63	1.50	.50
Modal intensifiers	.67	1.25	1.00	2.00
Average number per argument	22.17	7.50	4.00	4.00

only two "you" references were employed in Footing 4. From this pattern, we may conclude that the preachers in Footing 1 also foregrounded the ritual presence and participation status of the audience more often than the other preachers did. Therefore, we may say that the "on record" preachers made more explicit references to the participation framework of the performance.

As for implicit strategies, not only did the arguments in Footing 1 contain more rhetorical question/answer sequences, as shown in the tables, but not shown, ten out of eleven of them contained self-references and/or were prefaced with the response marker "well" or the speaker-focused discourse marker "now." These framing strategies were not employed by the preachers who constructed the other footings. Thus, we may say that the rhetorical question/answer sequences in Footing 1 were framed to call attention to the preacher's ritual presence, whereas those in the other footings were not.

The response marker "well" occurred most often in Footing 1, although not by as large a margin as some of the other strategies. This is because "well" was not used frequently in any of the sermons.

There was a dramatic difference in the average number of occurrences of "now" across footings, ranging from slightly over four per sermon in Footing 1 to none in Footings 3 and 4. These two markers signal implicitly the interactional presence of the preacher.

The "intensifiers" entry reflects the figures for the use of the following intensifiers: "obviously," "obvious," "of course," "actually," "simply," "surely," and "basically." Again, intensifiers were most common in Footing 1.

Finally, as I noted earlier, the modal intensifiers "must have"/"must've" and "had to" occurred more often in Footings 2, 3, and 4 than in Footing 1. I suggest that these modals are functional equivalents of "I believe" and "I think." The difference between them is that the modals serve as embedded evaluation devices through which the preacher puts himself or herself on record implicitly, whereas the self-references serve as external evaluation devices through which the preacher is put on record explicitly.

In sum, a quantitative analysis of the "text-exegeter" strategies reveals that Footing 1 is constructed with many markers of the preacher's interactional presence as exegeter in the performance situation, whereas in the other three footings these markers are employed much less frequently.

Illustration of the Footings

The Preacher as "On Record" Exegeter

Five student preachers assumed a footing that I call "the preacher as 'on record' exegeter." This footing is characterized by the frequent use of two types of framing strategies for structuring the exegetical argument. One is that the preacher not only provides definitions and paraphrases of key linguistic items from the archaic text in an expository register, but also elaborates on the text in the contemporary spoken register of the audience. With this strategy, s/he presents her- or himself as a Biblical scholar, on the one hand, and as a mediator of the text's message who is a member of the same world as the audience, on the other. Thus, the preacher is displayed as an expositor of the text who is also "responsive to the concerns of the audience" (1981:177).

In the second framing strategy for presenting oneself as an "on record" exegeter of the text, the preacher also frequently claims responsibility for the credibility of the translations, paraphrases, elaborations, interpretations, and evaluative statements that s/he makes about the written text by employing the explicit and implicit "text-exegeter" framing strategies that I described earlier. Thus, the preacher is displayed as an expositor who accepts responsibility for the statements s/he makes as spokesperson.

The sermon I selected as representative of this footing was preached by Meg, a woman in her late twenties who had grown up in New Mexico and had been a schoolteacher. Her immediate career goal was to work with college students as a campus minister. Her long-range goal was to work in Mexico as a missionary. On her written questionnaire, she responded to the question "How long have you been preaching?" with "I have only 'preached' [quotation marks are hers] in class." However, in an answer to another question, she said she believed that women can be called to preach. Thus, we may conclude that her attitude toward women as preachers was positive.

Meg preached on "The Ten Lepers" narrative. In the following excerpt, she is refocusing the audience's attention on the task of analyzing the Scripture text. She foregrounds the ritual presence of the participants in the task by referring to herself and the audience as "we" (line 80) and to the participation framework with "our passage" (line 81). (Line numbers correspond to those in the whole transcribed sermon, which is presented in Smith [1990]. Underlining highlights segments that are relevant to analysis.)

80   And then <u>we come</u> to verse fifteen,
81   perhaps the turning point of <u>our passage</u>-
82   "Now ONE of them-
83   when he saw that he had been healed,
84   turned back."
85   <u>In OTHer words,</u>
86   The OTHer nine did NOT turn back to offer and express
87   their gratitude to Jesus-

In these lines, Meg uses expository expressions like "the turning point of our passage" (line 81) and "in other words" (line 85). By framing her exegetical comments with such expressions, Meg displays herself as an informed or "expert" mediator of the meaning of the original text to the current audience.

Meg now asks the question,

88   Why didn't they?

By asking this question, she is again presenting herself as, in Goffman's terms, "a mediator of the text" who is aware of the "concerns" of the audience and is being responsive to them. Meg's question and the answer sequence which follows it in lines 89–123 display her as having anticipated the key question that the audience might have about the text. The sequence also conveys that she has tried to find answers to that question for the sake of the audience. Thus, it presents her as someone who has "given" herself to her audience.

Meg introduces her lengthy answer to her question with an explicit claim of responsibility for it.

89   I've done a lot of <u>thinking</u> about that
90   and I came up with several possible reasons.

By elaborating the prototypical form for claiming responsibility for one's interpretive statements "I think" into "I've done a lot of thinking about that and I came up with several possible reasons," Meg creates a focus of attention on her claim of responsibility for the credibility of her interpretation of the text and on herself as exegeter.

Later in the sermon, Meg inserts another revealing self-reference into her comments:

125   Do you have a history of ingratitude-
126   ˆ in YOUR life?

```
127  ^ Are you too PROUD?
128  ^ too independent-
129  ^ too busy?
130  to ^ get on your knees before God and say
131  "God- thank you,
132  I have not deserved all of the many things
133  that You have done for me-
134  in my life,"
135  I'd like to-
136  insert something here a- and just uh-
137  i- in passing,
138  make a point that I think is-
139  specifically related to us as ministers
140  in this passage.
141  You'll notice that Go(d)- that Jesus HEALED
142  all ten lepers,
143  knowing that only one was going to come back-
144  and offer gratitude.
145  In OUR line of work,
146  there's no guarantee of gratitude.
147  And God tells us to minister to people
148  whether we EVer get a pat on the back,
149  whether anyone EVer says- "Thank you."
150                              [That's right=
151                               amen amen]
```

In this text-parenthetical sequence, Meg displays a high degree of approachability. Regardless of whether the hesitations in "I'd like to- insert something here a- and just uh- i- in passing, make a point that I think is-" (lines 135–138) are intentional or not, they convey the message that her remarks are being spontaneously formulated. She also constructs the impression of spontaneity by explicitly stating what she is doing—making a point that is specific to this particular audience (lines 138–140). And she provides explicit verbal cues of spontaneity—the verb "insert" and the qualifier "in passing."

Meg maintains her leadership footing by claiming responsibility for her evaluative comments with "I think" (line 138) and by focusing her listeners' attention on her point with "you'll notice that . . . " (line 141), telling them what they are supposed to find in the text.

Meg also identifies herself with the audience as a professional colleague of theirs three times, referring to "us" as ministers twice ("specifically related to us as ministers" in line 139 and "God tells us to minister to people" in line 147) and to "our line of work" (line 145). Meg is the only one of the four women to refer to herself and the audience explicitly as members of the same profession. Carol once referred to her audience with "you as pastors," thus explicitly separating herself from her audience in terms of this professional role. Marge once referred to herself and the audience with "we as leaders in our churches"; however, "leaders" is a nonprofessional term. Beth did not make any such references. None of these three women presented herself as a clergy member in her statements.

All of these "fresh talk" devices are effective in boosting Meg's authoritative stance, as is evidenced by the feedback she gets from the audience—a "That's right" and a couple of "amens" (lines 150–151). This is because, according to Goffman's model, she has successfully employed "fresh talk" devices to convince the audience that she has given "herself" to them in this particular performance. Or, in terms of Tannen's model, she has successfully employed "involvement strategies" to achieve this interpersonal goal. This is the only place in her argument where members of the audience respond with spontaneous verbal affirmations.

In the final example, Meg again makes explicit her acceptance of responsibility for her statements as exegeter:

168   And then in verse nineteen,
169   Jesus says to the man,
170   "Rise- and GO your way.
171   Your faith has saved you."
172   This could be translated,
173   "Rise,
174   go your way- your FAITH
175   ⟩ pardon me=
176   "Rise- go your w-"
177   ˘ originally i- in my version it says
178   ˘ "Rise and go your way- your faith has made you WELL."
179   ˘ Some translators translate it-
180   "RIse- go your way- your faith- has SAVED you."
181   And I believe that's a better translation,
182   for you see there were TEN HEALINGS,
183   that day on the border between Samaria and Galilee,

Here Meg provides a translation for the key word "well" or "whole" or "saved." She comments on how it could be translated (line 172), cites an interpretation by other translators (line 179), then offers her evaluation of their translation (line 181). She claims responsibility for this evaluation explicitly by prefacing it with "I believe" (line 240). Thus, she again foregrounds the exegetical task and puts herself on record as exegeter. She also continues her pattern of using the marker "you see" to focus the audience's attention on statements that are important to her argument (line 182).

By examining the framing strategies with which Meg constructed her argument, we have seen how she presented herself as an authoritative exegeter of the text's message. She and four men constructed a "preacher as 'on record' exegeter" footing by framing their arguments to convey three distinct but overlapping metamessages: (1) "I am presenting an exegetical interpretation of the text's message," (2) "I am explicitly claiming responsibility for the interpreted message that I am presenting," and (3) "I am both explicitly and implicitly displaying a strong commitment to what I am telling you." In this way, these performers foregrounded their exegetical authority.

The Preacher as "Low-Profile" Exegeter

Five men and three women constructed a "preacher as 'low-profile' exegeter" footing. They rarely put themselves "on record" as exegeters of the text. Instead, they often created focuses of attention on the text, their interpretation of the text, and/or the audience without claiming authorship for their statements. In this way, they downplayed their exegetical authority.

The representative sermon I chose for this footing was preached by Mat, a man in his midtwenties who had grown up in a small town in East Texas, graduated from a Baptist college in that area, and currently pastored a small church there. He had been preaching full-time for two years.

Theologically, Baptists believe that there are only two requirements that a person must meet in order to pastor a church: (1) s/he must have experienced a personal "call" from God to be a pastor, and (2) a local congregation must validate that call by electing him or her to the office of pastor. However, the majority of Baptists have also traditionally believed that God calls only males to preach. There are no other requirements. Formal education, seminary training, and ordination have been encouraged for the last century or so, but, from a theological standpoint, they are not necessary. Thus, Mat was pastoring a church while attending the seminary. Like Meg, he was one of the students who volunteered to preach on "The Ten Lepers."

In the following excerpt, Mat invites the audience to participate in the exegetical task:

10 Let's consider the situation-
11 of these lepers.

By requesting the audience's participation with "let's consider . . . " Mat downplays the fact that he has already studied the text for the purpose of providing them with information to which they would not otherwise have access. Instead, he presents the audience as co-exegeters with him in the current task.

The location of this "let's" request in his argument has strategic significance. By beginning his exegesis with this request form, he defines the overall participation statuses of the participants as that of fellow interpreters of the text. However, this is the only time he uses a "let's" construction. Moreover, he does not employ "we see," "we find," or "we notice" anywhere in this sermon. In other words, he rarely refers to himself or the audience.

The following excerpt contains the only rhetorical question/answer pair in Mat's argument. Like Meg's, it is a paraphrase of the climactic question in the narrative "Why didn't- the other nine come?"

62   Why didn't- the other nine come?
63   Maybe they thought Jesus d- OWED 'em- healing,
64   because of who they WERE-
65   after all they WERE JEWS.
66   ˜ "Now that Samaritan he oughta be thankful,
67   [inhale] He didn't deserve anything." [exhale]
68   One rabbi taught that-
69   gentiles were created to fuel the flames- of hell.
70   "So he OUGHTA be thankful."

Rather than use a self-reference to mark his interpretation of the lepers' thoughts as being on record, Mat instead employs constructed dialogue to create involvement with the written text. "Constructed dialogue" is Tannen's (1989) term for what has been traditionally called "reported speech." She suggests that when speech is reported in a context other than the one in which it was supposedly uttered originally, it is transformed by the new speaker. Thus, it is a new utterance constructed by the current speaker to fit the new context.

In lines 66–70, Mat uses constructed dialogue to present the lepers' thoughts ("Now that Samaritan he oughta be thankful; he didn't deserve anything"), then echo the imaginary thoughts of the lepers ("So he OUGHTA be thankful"). With constructed dialogue, he focuses the audience's attention on the interpretation of the text, not on whether he is putting himself on record as its interpreter. Mat does not frame his "constructed dialogue" utterances anywhere in this sermon with text-parenthetical devices that make explicit his role as interpreter of the utterance he is quoting.

Mat downplayed his role as interpreter of the text's message in this sermon by constructing a low-profile ritual presence for himself in his evaluative and interpretive statements.

The Preacher as Narrator

Of the fourteen student preachers in the study, two students, a male and a female, presented themselves primarily as narrators rather than as traditional exegeters. Instead of foregrounding their expertise as exegeters through frequent claims of responsibility for their statements, they constructed a sustained focus of attention on their retelling of the Biblical narrative by unobtrusively incorporating exegetical information into its structure. However, the woman, Carol, took this framing strategy a step further by reframing the Biblical story itself. In her retelling, she prefixed the recorded Biblical narrative with nontextual events in which a main character appeared as a child.

Carol was in her early thirties. She had spent about half of her life in the state of New York and half in Texas. She and her husband planned to return after graduation to New York, where she would be teaching Bible courses in a Christian college. At the beginning of the course, Carol expressed concern both to me and to the instructor about her ability to "preach." She explained that although she had experience in and felt comfortable preaching "children's" sermons in separate worship services planned for them and teaching college-level Bible courses to adults, she was not comfortable preaching to adults because of the sacredness of the responsibility that the task entailed. For her first sermon, she had tried to memorize her written version. She began her performance of it with an apology for her nervousness, mentioning her experience in leading children's worship services; during the sermon she made several elaborated self-corrections, and at one point she appeared as though she were going to give up and sit down.

For her second sermon, which was based on the "Ten Lepers" narrative, she made several changes in strategy. She rehearsed in her own church's empty auditorium several times. And she had her husband come to the class and sit on the front row. Carol was the only married female preacher, and although spouses were allowed to sit in on these classes, only two other spouses of the sixty-seven preachers that summer did so.

Carol began her exegetical argument in the second sermon with the following words:

1   [inhale] <u>A little boy,</u>
2   <u>grew up</u> in a Samaritan village.
3   He had a happy childhood=
4   And [inhale] sometimes his parents would take him
5   to the neighboring villages
6   to market or-
7   o- m-
8   occasionally they might even go to Galilee
9   to the sea for (a) vacation.

By employing a story-opener formula as for a children's story—"A little boy grew up . . . "—Carol signals a metamessage that instead of presenting herself as an exegeter of the text, which is what the audience expects her to do, she is going to present herself as a narrator.

That is, she creates a new footing. Moreover, not only is she not presenting a traditional exegesis of the passage, but the story that she is telling is not the one recorded in the Scripture. At this point, the audience has no way of knowing whether or not the little boy in her narrative is the same character as the Samaritan leper in the written story. Nor do they know that she will present an exegesis after she has retold the story. Thus, she creates involvement by making the audience participate in the sense making of her performance.

Carol could have followed the prescribed rhetorical model and still have involved the audience with the Biblical narrative. I argue that she invents new narrative events in order to present a narrative told from a child's point of view not just in order to create a high degree of involvement, but also to create a certain kind of involvement, the kind of involvement that is created when stories about children are told. Her story-opener formula is a formula commonly used in children's stories told in Western literate societies.

Although Carol's audience is familiar with such formulas and strategies, they are not used to hearing them as part of an exegetical argument (hers was the only one in my data), especially when all of the characters in the Biblical passage are adults. Thus, Carol flouts the norm for the presentation of an exegetical argument not only by presenting herself as a narrator, but, more significantly, by presenting herself as the narrator of a story about a child.

Later in her narrative, Carol refers to the Samaritan as "our little Samaritan boy."

58   ⟨ And as <u>our little Samaritan boy</u>
59   stood there watching these people,
60   he was moved with compassion
61   ˜ And he left some food there by the side of the road.

Thus, at this point in her story, she has reframed the adult Samaritan figure of the original Biblical story not only as a child, but also as a child who is related to her and the audience.

Only at the end of her narration did Carol shift footing to display herself as an "on record" exegeter of the text. The following excerpt, in which she refers to herself for the first time, occurred toward the end of the sermon. Here again, though, she employs atypical framing strategies. Rather than use "I believe" or "I think," or even "I've done a lot of thinking and . . . ," to present a cognitive reaction to the text, Carol uses constructed dialogue and a colloquial register to display an atypically affective reaction:

152   ⟨ <u>At first the time I read this</u> I-
153   I thought "ˆ <u>Well that's strange</u>
154   ˆ <u>I kind of identify with the</u> ˆ nine,
155   They were doing what ˆ Jesus TOLD them to.
156   ⟨ They were heading off to the PRIEST.
157   <u>You know but and this guy he's a Samaritan,</u>
158   and he wouldn't be welcome at the temple <u>ANYway,</u>
159   <u>so why not?</u>=
160   <u>sure you'd go back</u> and praise the Lord,"
161   hm [she chuckles]

Carol presents herself as being emotionally involved with the text by particularizing the display of her reaction to it (lines 152–154). She does this with several framing strategies. First, she states that her reaction occurred at a particular point in time with "At first the time I read this I- I thought. . . ." Then she presents her thoughts as constructed dialogue. By expressing her reactions with "that's strange," she conveys the metamessage that her reactions are more affective than cognitive. In lines 157–160, she presents an exegetical interpretation of the text as if it were part of an informal conversational dialogue by using "you know," "well," "kind of," "but and," "this guy he's," "anyway," "so why not?," and "sure you'd. . . ." These linguistic choices are more typical of a casual conversation than they are of a scholarly argument. I suggest that this sequence in which Carol is presenting herself as exegeter of the text also simultaneously provides a source for the stereotype cited earlier that women preachers sound like children, look out of place, and seem out of character being forceful and emphatic.

This analysis has shown that Carol did not follow the norms for constructing an exegetical argument nor for displaying oneself as exegeter. She constructed her performance in such a way that, while involving the audience with her exegesis of the text, she also presented herself as a nontraditional exegeter. That is, in Goffman's terms, she "bled" her desire to be heard as a preacher of children's sermons rather than as a professional minister into her text by presenting herself as an intelligent and artful narrator but not as an "objective" exegeter.

The Preacher as "High-Style" Exegeter

The performance style of another woman was more "formal" than that of the other students. She paraphrased and elaborated on the written text not in a contemporary, typically spoken register but in a "high-style" register. 'High style' is Goffman's term for "elegance of language—turns of phrase, metaphor, parallel structures, aphoristic formulations" (1981:189). However, I use "high style" to refer to both the formal literary register of Biblical commentaries and the formal, detached essayist literacy register of dictionaries and other reference works.

The woman who constructed this type of "exegetical authority" footing in her sermons was in her midtwenties. As the daughter of a missionary doctor, Marge had grown up in Indonesia, although she had also lived in South Carolina and Louisiana. Before attending the seminary, she had been an art teacher. She was engaged to a young man who was enrolled in the same preaching lab and who was present when she preached.

On the questionnaire I discussed earlier, Marge answered the question "Have you heard a woman minister preach?" with "I have heard two kinds teach—ones out to promote self and prove a point and the one who desires to humbly serve the Scripture." Another question I asked on the questionnaire was "Is your style more (a) literate/literary or (b) conversational?" She circled (b). However, on the basis of the two sermons she preached in class, this answer was not realistic.

Marge's first sermon was based on the narrative in Genesis in which God asked Abraham to sacrifice his son Isaac. Just as Abraham raised the knife to kill his son, "the angel of the Lord" called out to him and told him to stop, because he had already shown his faithfulness. Abraham then became aware of a ram in a nearby thicket, which he offered as a burnt sacrifice instead of Isaac.

In the following excerpt, Marge presents a brief paraphrase of a Scrip-

ture verse in lines 1–3. However, instead of then reparaphrasing the paraphrase with an elaboration in a contemporary conversational register, she
constructs a lengthy elaboration in a formal, literary register in lines 4–18.

1   [inhale] Abraham in verse three ROSE
2   EARly in the MORNing-
3   and prepared to LEAVE

[Pause while she looks at her notes;
then she looks up.]
[inhale]

4   The CLARity of the directions
5   that God gave him,
6   were as a STAB-
7   in his HEART.
8   ˜ in his parental heart.
9   HE: was willing to believe imparent-
10 apparent IMpossiBIlities and OBEY-
11 rather than to DOUBT- his GOD.

[She looks down briefly again, then looks up.]

12 [smacks lips] It's easier to reach the HEIGHT
13 of oBEdience,
14 SELF-SAcrifice,
15 in some moment of e:nTHUsiasm
16 [inhale] than to keep it there
17 through the commonplace details
18 of slowly passing DAYS.

Both her actions and her linguistic choices show that Marge has carefully
worded her written comments and is trying to present them without resort-
ing to reading them. In lines 7–8, she self-corrects from "in his heart" to "in
his parental heart." She constructs a formal, literary style through her choice
of lexical items and by her repetition of the genitive phrase structure
throughout this sequence as, for example, in "the clarity of the directions,"
"the height of obedience," "some moment of enthusiasm," "the commonplace details of slowly passing days," and "a stab in his parental heart."

Marge's second sermon is as uniquely formal in its expository style as
her first one was in its literary style. She constructs her points, definitions,
and elaborations in a formal register. She does not refer explicitly to herself
or the audience as examiners of the text with "I" or "we." Moreover, she cites
Scripture verses other than the text her sermon is based on as a primary
strategy for constructing her argument. She either reads, quotes, or paraphrases other Scripture texts a total of fourteen times in this sermon, whereas the most often that any other student did so was six times.

At the beginning of the exegetical argument in her second sermon,
Marge reads her Scripture text, First Peter 5:5–7, which is a series of

exhortations to the younger men of the church to be humble and submissive to their elders and to God. She then immediately paraphrases the verses in the following way:

16   In verse FIVE-
17   Peter speaks of TWO
18   OPPOsing ATTitudes found in MAN-
19   and God's response to both of them.
20   Then in verse SIX,
21   ⁻) and seven
22   according to the provision of gra:ce
23   which God supplies-
24   he commands sharpl-
25   Peter sharply commands
26   "Humble yourselves-
27   and cast your anxieties upon Him."

Her paraphrase is formal in syntax and vocabulary (e.g., "two opposing attitudes found in man" in line 18 and "according to the provision of grace" in line 22). Throughout her sermons, Marge refers to people as "men."

Next Marge states her points:

28   God is opposed to the PROUD.
29   But TRUE grace,
30   which He supPLIES-
31   is effectual for TRUE humility.
32   The:re's where God
33   ⁻ manifests His GLOry..

Here again, she employs a formal expository register, signaled, for example, by "is opposed to," "is effectual for," and "manifests." She follows her points immediately with a restatement of the first one:

34   God opPOSes the PROUD.

This is followed with a formal definition of pride:

35   [inhale] Pride is the antithesis of huMIlity:
36   It's the ROO:T and the ESsence-
37   of SI:N
38   and it attributes to SELF
39   the HONor that is due to GOD.

Again, her expository stance toward the text is signaled by syntactic and lexical choices. She employs declarative statements and words such as "antithesis," "essence," and "attributes."

Next Marge shifts into illustrating these points and her definition of pride by citing a number of Scripture verses. Her argument becomes a recitation of verses with very little elaboration or paraphrase interspersed between them. These verses are also verses of God's judgment. They depict a God of wrath rather than a God of mercy. This is in keeping with the impression of "sternness" which this whole sermon conveys.

Thus, in both of her sermons, Marge employs a formal or "high" style through which she foregrounds the ritual presence and exegetical authority of the sacred text rather than that of herself or the audience.

Discussion

The men and women in this study differed in the way they displayed themselves as exegeters of a fixed sacred text. First, they differed in the degree to which they employed what I have identified as "text-exegeter" strategies. These are discourse markers and strategies which create, in Goffman's terms, fleeting "focuses of attention" or "glimpsed views" of the preacher as the author of adjacent evaluative utterance(s), an author who is committed to their validity. They also present the preacher as the mediator of the message of the ancient text to the current audience. Thus, they foreground the exegetical authority of a preacher by making salient his or her ritual presence as leader in the exegetical task.

My analysis has shown that whereas these strategies occurred ten or more times in seven out of the ten sermons by the men, they occurred that often in only two of the eight sermons by the women. Thus, we may conclude that, as a group, the men foregrounded their textual-self authority both by putting themselves on record as exegeters of the text and by calling attention to the current participation framework in the exegetical task more often than did the women.

Second, the women used a greater variety of framing strategies for creating the textual-self footing in their exegetical arguments than the men did. Meg, who was the only one of the four women who did not express a negative attitude toward the task of preaching to men, was also the only female to present herself as an "on record" exegeter of the text. On the other hand, two of the other women, Carol and Marge, employed strategies which none of the men used. Carol constructed an atypical kind of involvement, the kind that is created when a narrator tells a children's story. Marge distanced herself as exegeter from the audience by consistently employing a "high" exegetical style. The fourth woman, Beth, downplayed her authority as exegeter by not making explicit references to her separate participation status as exegeter. In both of her sermons, she constructed a "preacher as low-profile exegeter" footing. Thus, although their strategies differed, all of the women who were negative or uncertain about the appropriateness of females' preaching presented themselves as mediators of the text more indirectly than the men did.

In sum, this group of seminary students framed their performances to reflect the ideology of our culture that it is more appropriate for men to present themselves as powerful mediators of a fixed sacred text than it is for women.

Conclusions

Language, like other forms of behavior, is ritualistic and can be understood only when the framing strategies its users employ are understood. Interpersonal ritualization strategies such as Tannen's "involvement strategies" and Goffman's "fresh talk" strategies are ways of localizing talk within a particular performance. Our lives are made up of a continuous stream of such performances. In this study, I have shown that what is true of the framing strategies females and males use in everyday conversations is also true of those they employ in constructing their performances of more static, monologic, formally ritualized discourse forms such as sermons. We have increased our understanding of gender by observing that gender display is as integral to one's performance in the pulpit as it is to other forms of interaction. And by focusing on the linguistic strategies through which this gender display is accomplished in sermons, we have deepened our understanding of framing.

Appendix: Transcription Symbols

I have transcribed what I heard on the tapes and what was written on the questionnaires in such a way as to capture, as accurately as I could, exactly what was spoken or said. Therefore, the apparent "errors" in the transcripts are those of the students.

.	clause final falling intonation
?	clause final rising intonation
,	continuing intonation
	(If "." "?" "," symbols are doubled, the intonation contour is followed by a noticeable pause)
=	elision with word on next line, no break or pause
-	hesitation or self-interruption with glottal stop
˘	faster pace
^	raised pitch
(	louder
)	softer
:	lengthened vowel
CAPS	emphatic stress
()	uncertain transcription
[]	extralinguistic sounds, comments by transcriber; or, if on separate line within transcript, audience responses

Note

1. In August 1992, I checked with the seminary about their current enrollment and policies regarding women taking the Preaching Lab course. I found that the

total enrollment for Fall 1991, Spring 1992, and Summer 1992 for 811—532 Preaching Laboratory: The Delivery of the Sermon was 345 (325 men and 20 women). I also found that the course description in the seminary catalog is followed by this footnote: "Female students may substitute an approved course for 811—532." A second footnote specifies substitute courses that international students "for whom English is a second language or who may not be preparing for an English language ministry" may take. However, the courses women may substitute are not specified in the catalog. Instead, a woman may pick up the list and description of the courses in the Preaching Department office. The four substitute courses the women may choose from are: Voice and Speech Improvement, Training the Speaking Voice, Speech for Christian Workers, and Oral Interpretation.

References

Brown, H. C., Jr., Gordon Clinard, and Jesse J. Northcutt. 1963. Steps to the sermon: A plan for sermon preparation. Nashville, TN: Broadman Press.

Goffman, Erving. 1974. Frame analysis. New York: Harper and Row.

Goffman, Erving. 1979. Gender advertisements. New York: Harper and Row.

Goffman, Erving. 1981a. Footing. Forms of talk, 124–159. Philadelphia: University of Pennsylvania Press.

Goffman, Erving. 1981b. The lecture. Forms of talk, 160–195. Philadelphia: University of Philadelphia Press.

Goodwin, Charles. 1986. Audience diversity, participation, and interpretation. Text 6(3):283–316.

Goodwin, Marjorie Harness. 1990. He-said-she-said: Talk as social organization among black children. Bloomington: Indiana University Press.

Goodwin, Marjorie Harness, and Charles Goodwin. 1987. Children's arguing. Language, gender, and sex in comparative perspective, ed. by Susan U. Philips, Susan Steele, and Christine Tanz, 200–248. Cambridge: Cambridge University Press.

Gumperz, John. 1978a. The conversational analysis of interethnic communication. Interethnic communication, ed. by E. Lamar Ross, 13–31. Athens, GA: University of Georgia Press.

Gumperz, John. 1978b. Dialect and conversational inference in urban communication. Language in Society 7(3):393–409.

Gumperz, John. 1979. The sociolinguistic basis of speech act theory. Speech act theory ten years after, ed. by Julian Boyd and S. Ferrara. Milan: Versus.

Gumperz, John. 1982a. Discourse strategies. Cambridge: Cambridge University Press.

Gumperz, John. (ed.). 1982b. Language and social identity. Cambridge: Cambridge University Press.

Lakoff, Robin Tolmach. 1975. Language and woman's place. New York: Harper and Row.

Maltz, Daniel N., and Ruth A. Borker. 1982. A cultural approach to male-female miscommunication. Language and social identity, ed. by John J. Gumperz, 195–216. Cambridge: Cambridge University Press.

Schiffrin, Deborah. 1987. Discourse markers. Cambridge: Cambridge University Press.

Tannen, Deborah. 1986. That's not what I meant!: How conversational style makes or breaks your relations with others. New York: William Morrow.

Tannen, Deborah. 1989a. Interpreting interruption in conversation. Papers from the 25th Annual Regional Meeting of the Chicago Linguistic Society. Part Two: Parasession on Language in Context, ed. by Bradley Music, Randolph Graczyk, and Caroline Wiltshire, 266–287. Chicago: Chicago Linguistic Society.

Tannen, Deborah. 1989b. Talking voices: Repetition, dialogue, and imagery in conversational discourse. Cambridge: Cambridge University Press.

Tannen, Deborah. 1990a. You just don't understand: Women and men in conversation. New York: William Morrow.

Tannen, Deborah. 1990b. Gender differences in conversational coherence: Physical alignment and topical cohesion. Conversational organization and its development, ed. by Bruce Dorval, 167–206. Norwood, NJ: Ablex.

6

Cultural Differences in Framing: American and Japanese Group Discussions

SUWAKO WATANABE

Portland State University

Introduction

As relations between the United States and Japan become close and important, more interactions between Americans and Japanese are seen in ordinary, informal situations than in those involving government officials or business executives. In the past several years, the number of Japanese who study in the United States has increased rapidly. Some Japanese are enrolled in EFL programs, and others are in regular programs at undergraduate or graduate levels. As a matter of course, they experience cross-cultural communication, whether it is successful or unsuccessful, as everyday occurrences in their public and private lives.

Among the many speech events in which Japanese students may experience cross-cultural miscommunication, this study will examine a particular speech event in the school setting, that is, group discussion. The communication problems in this speech event occur not only because of the language

I am greatly indebted to Deborah Tannen, who offered valuable suggestions and comments in the course of writing this chapter as well as my dissertation, "Framing in American and Japanese Group Discussions," from which this chapter has been adapted. I am also grateful to Deborah Schiffrin and Miwa Nishimura for their helpful comments on the dissertation; to all the students who participated in the group discussions; and to Sarah Koch, who helped me with editing. Nevertheless, all remaining errors are my responsibility.

difference but also because Japanese students are accustomed to different framing strategies for group discussion than American students. In other words, they have a set of expectations about how to interact in a group discussion that is different from American students'. According to Japanese students studying in the United States, they tend to get lost in the middle of discussion because sometimes opinions, questions, and so forth, expressed by American students are not as relevant to the topic or what has preceded as they expect these utterances to be, and they lose track of what is going on in a discussion and/or view the group discussion as incoherent and disorganized.

This chapter attempts to shed light on a cultural aspect of framing by demonstrating differences between American and Japanese university students in their framing of the speech event, group discussion. A further aim of this chapter is to demonstrate the application of theories of frames to the study of cross-cultural communication.

I have found the following differences between Americans and Japanese in their framings in the group discussions: (1) Americans promptly began and ended group discussions while Japanese were deliberate as they talked about procedural matters before discussions and, when ending, a leader punctuated the end by checking and announcing it. (2) When the participants were asked to give reasons, Americans framed their giving of reasons as "briefing" while Japanese framed theirs as "storytelling." (3) When they discussed a controversial topic, Americans used a "single-account" argumentation strategy (one account per discussant at a time) while Japanese used a "multiple-accounts" argumentation strategy (multiple accounts per discussant at a time).

In this chapter, I first discuss relationships among theories of frames, communication process, and cross-cultural communication; second, I discuss two characteristics of Japanese communication: nonreciprocality of language use and the tendency toward nonconfrontational communication, both of which are most relevant to the findings in this study. Then I demonstrate the analyses of the beginnings and the endings of the group discussions, presentation of reasons, and argumentation strategies. After this, I suggest the sources of these differences in discourse strategies at the level of framing. Finally, I discuss some theoretical and practical implications of my findings.

Theoretical Background

The notion of frames goes back to Bateson (1972), who identified three different levels of communication: (1) the denotative level (i.e., referential level), (2) the metalinguistic level (i.e., the purpose of communication is to talk about language), and (3) the metacommunicative level (i.e., communication concerning the relationship between the speakers). On the metacommunicative level, people send, intentionally or unintentionally, a message that tells the intention of the communication. For example, when one says,

"I hate you," on the denotative level, s/he may send signals telling that the communication is intended to be "joking." The term "frame" is used to refer to messages defining intentions of communication in the sense that a picture frame delimits the picture within it and distinguishes the picture from the surrounding wall. Accordingly, Tannen (1984:23) defines "frame" as "a superordinate message about how the communication is intended." Bateson's identification of the metacommunicative level of communication enabled the study of language to break the barrier of intrasentential levels of meaning and to further investigation of context-dependent, sociocultural meanings. Gumperz (1982) and Tannen (1984, 1985) have demonstrated that interactants send messages at various levels and have shown how these messages can be analyzed.

Frames and the Communication Process

Tannen (1986) writes that, in interaction, "meaning is never totally determinate but rather is . . . a joint production" (146). This suggests that, even in a verbal exchange between two people, the interactive process consists of not only two utterances produced by the two but also the hearer/addressee's interpretation appropriate at that particular moment. Without the addressee's proper interpretation, communication may fail in the worst case. In this sense, meaning is a joint production. However, the question arises, "How do we arrive at a proper interpretation?" An example of an exchange between two secretaries given in Gumperz (1981) suggests that sharing a language is not sufficient. The following is the exchange:

A: Are you going to be here for ten minutes?
B: Go ahead and take your break.

(Gumperz 1981:326)

Gumperz (1981) points out that although A's first utterance is a yes-no question, B does not give a yes-no answer, but an imperative one. This is because B interprets A's utterance as requesting B to stay while A takes a break, and, accordingly, B suggests that A take her break. The appropriateness of B's interpretation is confirmed by A's later line: "I won't take long." What is it, then, that is shared by the two secretaries? According to Goffman (1986:10–11), people within a society share frames, defined as "principles of organization which govern events—at least social ones—and our subjective involvement in them." It is because the two secretaries shared, besides the language, principles of organization which govern the event of "taking a break" that they understood each other and made appropriate moves.

   In situations, interactants are always figuring out what it is that is going on, and on the basis of the interpretation, they act accordingly. Frames guide interactants to appropriate interpretations of what is going on in situations at each moment. Tannen (1985) and Tannen and Wallat (this volume) have incorporated the various notions of frame and redefined frame as "sets of expectations about people, objects, events, settings, and ways to interact." Tannen and Wallat demonstrate how frames function for interactants to arrive at a plausible interpretation of the situation. The situation they present as an example is a telephone conversation in which one suddenly said, "You stop that." The hearer understood this as "disciplining a dog" not "talking to her" because she "drew on her familiarity with the use of linguistic cues to signal frames . . . [b]ut she also drew on the knowledge that her friend was taking care of someone's dog" (207). A contextualization cue, which Gumperz (1982:131) defines as "any feature of linguistic form that contributes to the signalling of contextual presupposition," is another example of framing in the sense that it signals what the speaker means by what s/he says and guides the hearer to a plausible interpretation.

Gumperz (1982:132) further points out that "conversationalists have *conventional* expectations about" interaction (italic mine). To the extent that these sets of expectations about people, objects, events, settings, and ways to interact are conventional, some parts of them may vary from culture to culture. For example, Tannen (this volume) shows differences between Americans and Greeks in their expectations about events and objects. The study was based on an experiment in which subjects were to watch a film which had no sound effects and to tell a story of the film to someone. It was found that the American subjects were conscious of their roles as "subjects of an experiment" because their narratives tended to be longer and more detailed than the Greeks', and that the American narratives contained more evidence of expectations about "films as films" and the role of "film viewer" than the Greek ones. The film was the same, but interpretations of it by the American and the Greek subjects were different.

If two people from different cultures do not share the same expectations about how to interact, that is, perceive differently the unmarked or marked linguistic features that signal a superordinate definition of what is being done by the talk, it is possible that differing interpretations of the situated meaning of what is said are processed by the interactants. On the surface, it looks as if they understand each other, but it is likely that they will find later that they have misunderstood each other. For the study of cross-cultural communication, it is useful to analyze various speech events from the perspective of the theories of frames. By closely examining communication, linguistic cues signaling frames in a given culture can be identified. The frames that are found in one culture can be, then, compared with those found in another.

Characteristics of Japanese Communication

In this section, two characteristics of Japanese communication, non-reciprocality of language use and a tendency toward nonconfrontational communication, will be discussed. First, it has been repeatedly confirmed that Japanese communication is nonreciprocal. It is reflected in the vast variety of honorifics which are an essential part of the Japanese language

(Harada 1976). Benedict (1946:47) writes that in Japanese "Every time a man says to another 'Eat' or 'Sit down' he uses different words if he is addressing someone familiarly or is speaking to an inferior or to a superior." The choice of language is strictly determined by the hierarchical social structure. According to Nakane (1972:30), a social anthropologist, the Japanese social structure is based on vertical hierarchy, and a Japanese is always expected to use appropriate language according to his/her rank in relation to the addressee. Thus, information about the interactants such as age, social rank, occupation, gender, the schools they have graduated from, and the social profile of their families is drawn together to determine the relational position to others in every situation, which enables individual interactants to interpret the communicative intent of others and to make an appropriate move toward it.

The second characteristic of Japanese communication that is relevant to this study is the tendency toward nonconfrontational communication which is reflected in indirect and ambiguous communication (Tsujimura 1987, Ramsey 1985). The social motivations for nonconfrontational communication are strong emphasis on harmony within a group and sensitivity to face. An ethnographic study of interpersonal relations and behaviors of employees in a Japanese bank revealed that harmony was a high-ranking value (Rohlen 1974). Studies of management in Japanese companies (Ouchi 1972, Stewart 1985) also found that "group orientation," which puts a strong emphasis on "consensus," is the key to their success. In Japanese society, confrontation is to be avoided since it disrupts harmony within a group. Moreover, it is considered almost prohibited when it is against the superior in the social hierarchy because it causes the superior's loss of face. Hirokawa (1987:146–147), in his study of communication in Japanese business, attributes deliberate ambiguity to the Japanese "desire to avoid embarrassing both themselves and others." He continues: "The Japanese appear to be particularly sensitive to the concept of 'face' (i.e., one's dignity and self-respect) and thus make every effort to avoid or prevent the 'loss of one's face' (i.e., the loss of self-respect and dignity resulting from public humiliation and embarrassment)." Furthermore, Yamada (1992) examined business meetings participated in by Americans and Japanese and found in the Japanese interaction the tendency to avoid confrontation.

In sum, (1) nonreciprocal language use and (2) nonconfrontational communication are characteristics of Japanese communication. These two characteristics, along with the social motivations underlying them, are important to relating the communicative behaviors of the Japanese participants in the group discussions to their expectations about interactions in that speech event.

The Data and the Analytic Focuses

Seven group discussions were set up and tape-recorded.[1] Each group discussion was made up of four participants who spent approximately fifteen to twenty minutes, in a school setting, spontaneously discussing three topics without formally appointing a leader. Depending on circumstances, some of the conditions were modified. For example, if a group felt the topics were not exhausted, they could spend more than twenty minutes discussing them.

There were four American groups and three Japanese groups, labeled A-1, A-2, A-3, A-4, J-1, J-2, and J-3.[2] All the participants were students of Georgetown University, Washington, D.C. Each group consisted of two males and two females, except A-2, which consisted of one male and three females.[3] All American participants were undergraduates, ranging from freshmen to seniors, studying Japanese in the intensive courses I taught. Members of J-1 were students in the EFL program at Georgetown University. Both the J-2 and J-3 groups consisted of one undergraduate and three graduate students.[4]

The three topics that were discussed are as follows:

1. Why did you decide to learn Japanese? (for A-1, A-2, A-3) Why did you decide to study abroad? (for J-1, J-2, J-3, and A-4)[5]
2. Many people say that, for Americans, Japanese is hard to learn compared to European languages. Do you agree or disagree? Why?
3. Discuss misunderstandings that are likely to occur between Americans and Japanese because of the language and cultural differences, giving specific examples of misunderstandings.

The transcripts were analyzed in order to identify linguistic features signaling framing differences. Analysis indicated two kinds of framing. One kind is found in the beginning and ending phases of the group discussions. It is what Goffman (1986:251) calls brackets, defined as "a set of boundary markers" that mark off a social activity from other ongoing events. Bracketing is another way of framing in the sense that, just like brackets used as punctuation in writing, they frame what is between them. The beginning and ending phases, in one sense, mark off the actual discussion frame; yet, in another, they are partial elements of the speech event as a whole. The analyses of these beginning and ending phases have revealed that the Americans and the Japanese bracketed the discussion frame differently.

The other kind of framing is identified in what is termed a communicative act such as requesting or joking. The assigned topics triggered two communicative acts in all the group discussions. One is to present reasons for a certain decision made in the past, in relation to the first topic; the other is to argue, in relation to the second topic. The Americans and the Japanese framed these two communicative acts differently.

In the following three sections, I analyze the beginning and ending phases, presentation of reasons, and argumentation, in turn.

The Beginning and Ending Phases
of the Group Discussions

How They Began the Discussion

The American and Japanese participants began discussions differently. The Japanese participants took a longer time than the American participants getting into the actual discussion frame as the Japanese talked about the order of turns and/or the procedure in which they would discuss the topics while the Americans did not. In every group, after I explained the procedures and turned on the tape recorder(s), I told the participants to begin, saying something like "Go ahead" or "Please." The American participants, on one hand, directly began to discuss without talking about procedural matters. In groups A-1 and A-2, the participants acknowledged my telling them to start with "Okay," then one participant began telling his/her reason for studying Japanese. In group A-3, when I was out of the discussion room, one member said, "Okay::," signaling the discussion frame. The discussion was immediately begun by another's directly asking a topic question. In general, the American groups gave the impression that the discussions started promptly.

The following excerpt is from the A-3 group discussion, which starts from Jenny's beginning her comment about the tape recorders, which was interrupted by my telling the participants to begin. Before then, Mike, pointing to the tape recorder in front of him, said, "Tsk, tsk, tsk." He had already indicated that he did not like being tape-recorded, the experience of which reminded him of taking an oral test. Immediately after Mike's reaction to the tape recorder, Jenny began as follows:

[Excerpt 1][6]

| 1 | Jenny: | I hate- ⌐   ⌐Oops. |
| 2 | Suwako: | └ Go ahead. ┘ |

| 3 | | [pause:3.5 seconds; sounds of opening and closing a door as I left the discussion room] |

4	Beth:	Okay:: ⌐
5	Mike:	└ So, Beth, why ⌈ did you decide to learn →
6	Sean:	⌊ Why.
		Japanese.

| 7 | Beth: | Uhm... I guess I decided to learn Japanese [Beth continues.] |

During the pause (3), I was leaving the discussion room. When the door was closed and I was out, Beth said, "Okay::," (4) which signaled the discussion frame. Immediately, Mike called on Beth and asked her a question: "So,

Beth, why did you decide to learn Japanese?" (6). Beth simply took up the turn and started with a hedge: "I guess I decided to learn Japanese. . ." (7). There was no discussion about how the group would go about discussing the given topics. Instead, there was a three-and-a-half-second pause during which the participation alignment changed from that of a prediscussion frame, mostly concerning the procedural matter of the experimental group discussion involving the four participants and me, to that of a discussion frame in which the four participants engaged in discussing the given topics.

In the A-1 discussion one member, Stan, asked the group who would talk first. However, it was very brief and did not turn immediately into a discussion:

[Excerpt 2]

(1)   Suwako: Begin:: whenever you're ready::
(2)   Kris: Okay. ⌐Okay. ⌐
(3)   Joan: ⌐Who's first... I'll go.
(4)   Stan:

When Stan asked the others, "Who's first?" they remained silent for one second. Stan interpreted the silence to mean that he should talk first, so he took a turn: "I'll go," (4).

In contrast to the American groups' prompt beginning, the Japanese groups took more time getting into discussion frame as they talked about procedural matters, such as the order in which they would take turns and the order of the topics to be discussed. For example, in the J-1 discussion, after I told them to begin, one member (Satoko, female) raised the question of how they would begin each topic. After discussion, they decided that one member (Teruo, male) would read each topic to the group. In the J-2 discussion, there was negotiation in terms of who would speak first. The most extensive beginning was that of group J-3 because they talked about both the turn order and a way of conducting the discussion. Let us look at their segment which begins with a line in which I told the participants to begin on their own. (An English translation follows the Japanese.)

xcerpt 3]
:panese]

1)   Suwako: JA   ONEGAI SHIMASU.
              then ask

2)   Yasuo: EETO, YAPPARI ANO ICHIOO JUNBAN-O FUNDE
              well   as you see uhm   number-OP following

3)   Keiko: SOODESUNE, ICHIBAN, NIBAN,   SANBAN TO.
              right   number one number two number three

4)   Fumiko: H-H-H-H

5)   Yasuo: HN. HAIRI-YASUIDESU-NE.⌐
              hm   enter-easy-FP

6)   Keiko: ⌐SOODESU-NE. JAA.. MAA U-
                                      right   -FP   then uhm

ICHIBAN   UE-WA HITORI HITORI HANASU
number one top-TP one   one   talk
SHIKA NAI KASHIRA.⌐
only   NEG wonder |
(7)   Fumiko: ⌐SOO-NE.
                                       right
(8)   Yasuo: SOODESU-NE.. JUNBAN KARA. DOO-SHIMASU-KA...
                 right-FP   turn   from   how-do   -QP
(9)   Ikuo: REDII FAASUTO.
                 lady   first   ⌐
(10)   Fumiko: ⌐DOOZO.
                                       please
(11)   Yasuo: AA IIDESU-NE, SORE-WA.⌐
                 oh good-FP   that-TP |
(12)   Fumiko: | [laugh]
(13)   Keiko: ⌐[laugh]
(14)   Keiko: JA ⌐ WAKAI KATA KARA [laugh]
                 then| young person from   ⌐
(15)   Fumiko: ⌐DOOZO.   ⌐[laugh]
                     please
(16)   Fumiko: IYA IYA ONEESAMA [laugh]
                  no   no big sister
(17)   Keiko: EE::?
                  what
(18)   Ikuo: DOTCHIDEMO II-JA NAI DESU-KA.
                  either one   okay NEG   -QP
(19)   Keiko: YAPPASHI [Keiko takes turn.]
                  as you see

[English]
(1)   Suwako: Then, please.
(2)   Yasuo: Let's see, as you see, uhm, basically we'll follow
                 the number. ⌐
(3)   Keiko: ⌐[That's right. Number one, number →
(4)   Fumiko: ⌐H-h-h-h.
                 two, and number three.
(5)   Yasuo: Hm. It's easy to get in. ⌐
(6)   Keiko: ⌐That's right. Then..
                 well, the top one, each one of us has to talk in
                 turn, I wonder. ⌐
(7)   Fumiko: ⌐That is so. ⌐
(8)   Yasuo: ⌐That's right...
                 following numbers, how are we going to do...
(9)   Ikuo: Ladies first. ⌐
(10)   Fumiko: ⌐Please.

(11)   Yasuo: Oh, that sounds good. ⌐
(12)   Fumiko: | [laugh]
(13)   Keiko: ⌐ [laugh]
(14)   Keiko: Then, from ⌐ the younger one. ⌐ [laugh]
(15)   Fumiko: ⌐ Please   ⌐ [laugh]
(16)   Fumiko: No, no. Big sister. [laugh]
(17)   Keiko: What?
(18)   Ikuo: It doesn't matter, does it.
(19)   Keiko: As you see, [Keiko takes turn]

First, in line 2, Yasuo suggested a discussion method by saying that the group would discuss according to the topic number. Keiko confirmed this and elaborated it: "Like number one . . . number three," (3). Second, in line 6, Keiko suggested a way to discuss the first topic: "each one of us just has to talk in turn," as in a round-robin system instead of a free discussion. Keiko's suggestion was immediately confirmed by Fumiko (7) and Yasuo (8).

Then, third, Yasuo raised the question of turn-taking order, saying, "how are we going to do . . ." (8). Ikuo suggested that ladies should go first (9). Almost at the same time, Fumiko said, "Please," (10) indicating that she conceded the first turn to someone else. Here, both Ikuo and Fumiko are making a concession. Yasuo, then, enthusiastically agreed with Ikuo, saying, "Oh, that sounds good," (11). Fumiko and Keiko interpreted this as meaning that one of them was to talk first, and they mutually made a concession in lines 14–17. Keiko invited "the younger one," Fumiko, to go first (14), and Fumiko invited "big sister," Keiko, to go first (15 and 16). It was when Ikuo said, "It doesn't matter, does it," in line 18, that Keiko volunteered to be the first speaker and began to tell her reason (19).

The pattern of the beginnings of the Japanese group discussions suggests that they did not want to be engaged in discussion unless procedural matters were agreed upon within the group. Because of this, the Japanese groups appeared to be deliberate in beginning the discussions. The question of who speaks first seems to be very important. No one simply decided to speak first; instead, there were invitations to take the first turn, concessions to others, and suggestions of who should talk first. In the end, in all the Japanese group discussions, a female member started, followed by the other female member, then by the younger male member, and last by the oldest male member. This consistent pattern of the turn-taking order in the Japanese group discussions further suggests that in the beginning segments, the Japanese members were negotiating not only the procedural matters but also a hierarchical order within a group. The hierarchical order is an essential part of Japanese communication to the extent that language style and vocabulary are carefully chosen according to the hierarchical relationship between the speaker and the addressee. It seems very natural for a Japanese to discern rank order within a given group because it is important information which enables him/her to choose appropriate linguistic forms with which to communicate.[6]

Furthermore, the importance of hierarchy is also reflected in the sequence of turns. One result of failing to use an appropriate linguistic form is loss of face. In general, the face of a highly respectable person is to be protected at any cost. This tendency was observed in the negotiation of turn-taking order in the Japanese group discussions in the sense that the oldest male member, who is considered the most superior, was given the last turn. From the Japanese perspective, in a meeting like these group discussions, in which the contents of the discussion are spontaneous and unplanned, the first turn entails the chance of making premature, wrong, or ignorant statements, resulting in loss of face, since it is too early to know what would be an appropriate statement. Thus, turn-taking order is indirectly arranged in the way that juniors/inferiors take earlier turns perhaps because their face is considered dispensable while seniors/superiors take later turns when they can express their opinions without losing face.

In brief, the American participants began group discussions promptly without talking about procedural matters, while the Japanese participants negotiated the discussion procedures and the turn-taking order before they began the actual discussion.

How They Ended the Discussion

There was a difference between the Japanese and American participants in the ways they ended their group discussions. When the Japanese participants ended their discussions, an assumed leader led the ending by asking about the group's intention to end and/or officially announcing the end. In contrast, in the American group discussions, there were no instances in which someone, acting as a leader, asked the group of its intention to end or officially announced the end of the discussion. The American groups ended their discussions when they exhausted the third topic that was assigned to them. For example, a relatively long pause indicated when topics were exhausted as in the A-1 group discussion.

The following segment is from the A-1 group discussion, which begins with Kris's saying that she thought it was right for them to start learning the polite style of Japanese rather than the direct style, which sounds blunt and too casual to a nonintimate person, because using the former saves them from the possibility of being rude unknowingly.

[Excerpt 4]

1	Stan:	What we're doing now certainly gets
2		difficult /?/..because.. Oh-⌐
3	Kris:	└ But it's a
4		good thing ⌈ we're beginning the other →
5	Stan:	└ That's-

6	Kris:	stuff first because if you slip up,
7		⌈ you'll always remember the more polite..⟶
8	Stan:	⌊ Yeah.
9	Kris:	⌈ instead of more casual. Yeah.
10	Ken:	⌊ /? ? ? ? ? ? ? ? ? ? ?/
11 ⟶		[pause: 5 seconds]
12 ⟶	Stan:	OWARIMASHITA. [said to investigator]
		(Finished.)

When Kris finished her turn in line 9, there was a long pause (11). This pause signaled the end of the discussion. Note that previously in (5) Stan started to say something, but he did not restart it when Kris and Ken were finished. Instead, he turned his face to me and reported the end in Japanese, saying (12), "OWARIMASHITA (Finished)." Similarly, in the A-2 group discussion, a long pause occasioned the end of discussion.

The A-3 group's ending is slightly different from the other American groups' in that there was no long pause, yet neither were there indications of a leader's asking the other members of their intentions and announcing an end. In the A-3 group discussion, when episodes of misunderstanding were nearly exhausted, Sean was put on the spot because he had been relatively quiet. The segment starts with Mike's question directed to Sean.

[Excerpt 5]

1	Mike:	So, do you think of any other reason
		you decided to learn Japanese, ⌈ h-h-h.
2	Beth:	⌊ H-h-h.
3	Sean:	Well, back to that, yes. Uh.. ⌈ no.
4	Jenny:	⌊ Well,
		/we're past/ twenty minutes. ⌐
5	Beth:	⌙ Yeah.
6	Jenny:	We don't have to force the conversation.
7	Sean:	/It's/ up. ⌐
8	Mike:	⌙ Let's.. go get sensei.[7]
9	Jenny:	Okay. ⌐
10	Sean:	⌙ So who wants to go.
11	Jenny:	I'm designated to get her.
12	Mike:	Sensei getter.
		[The discussants continued to joke about the
		expression "sensei getter."]

In A-3's group discussion, the fact that Mike returned to the first topic indicates that they had exhausted the material for the third topic. When Sean responded to Mike's question in (3) ("Well, back to that, yes. Uh.. no"), Jenny mentioned the time: "Well,/we're past/twenty minutes," (4). Beth acknowledged this in (5): "Yeah." Jenny continued to say in (6) that they did not have to force the conversation. Jenny's mentioning the time, reminding them that it was unnecessary to continue, and, perhaps, Sean's utterance "/It's/up" (7) signaled that the discussion was over.

Then, Mike proceeded to initiate the next step in the procedure, that is, to call me back into the room. He said, "Let's go get *sensei* (teacher)" (8). Note that Mike neither asked the others whether they wanted to end the discussion nor officially announced the end. Jenny acknowledged Mike's request in (9) and identified herself as the designated person to get me in (11) in response to Sean's inquiry, "So, who wants to go?" (10). As Jenny was leaving the room, the others joked about the expression "*sensei* getter" and started to talk about subjects completely different from the discussion topics.

Let us turn to the endings of the Japanese group discussions. In the Japanese groups, the oldest male member was assumed to be the leader and he punctuated the end either by asking whether the other members intended to end the discussion, or by officially announcing the end, or both. In what follows, Group J-3's ending segment will be examined. As the J-3 group discussed the third topic, which was concerned with misunderstandings between Americans and Japanese, it turned into negative criticism of the Japanese education system. After Ikuo's long presentation, there were two long pauses, which indicated that the topic had been exhausted. Then Ikuo reminded the group that he had to go to a class. The segment begins with the final part of Ikuo's criticism.

[Excerpt 6]
[Japanese]

(1)	Ikuo:	DAKARA KODOMO-NO UCHI-NI
		so child -of within
		SOOYUU ARUSHU-NO-NE, KEIKEN-O
		that a kind-of-FP experience-OP
		SASERU-NO-GA II INSPIRATION-NI
		let do -SP good inspiration-P
		NARUNJA-NAI-KANA TOKA OMOIMASU-KEDOMO-NE.
		become-NEG-wonder think- -but -FP
(2)	Keiko:	N::
		hm
(3)		[pause: 7.0 seconds]
(4)	Keiko:	SOOYUU HANASHI-GA ARIMASU-NE,
		that story-SP be -FP
		KORE-TO KANKEI NAI KEDO.
		this-to relation NEG but
(5)		[pause: 3.0 seconds]
(6)	Ikuo:	SORO-SORO IKANAKEREBA, JUGYOO-GA.
		about now if not go class-SP
(7)	Yasuo:	A, SOODESU-NE.
		oh right-FP

(8)   Keiko: IMA MOO NAN-JI   DESU-KA.
                    now already what-time be-QP

(9)   Ikuo: JUU-NI-JI   MOO YON-JUP-PUN.
                    twelve-o'⌈clock already forty-minutes

(10)   Keiko: ⌊HAN?
                            half

(11)   Yasuo: ICHI-JIKAN.
                    one-hour

(12)   [pause: 2.5 seconds]

(13)   Fumiko: TOTEMO II   OHANASHI-O [laugh] KI-,
                    very   good story-OP
                    KIKASHITE ITADAITA-TO YUU
                    let hear   received-P   like
                    KANJI-DE, H-
                    seem

(14)   [pause: 2.0 seconds]

(15)   Yasuo: JA, KONO ATARI-NI SHIMASU-KA.
                    then this   point-P   make-QP

(16)   Ikuo: HAI, SOO SHIMASHOO..
                    yes so   let's make

(17)   Keiko: KORE-DE YOROSHII,   KORE-DAKE-DE→
                    this-with   okay   ⌈this-only-with

(18)   Ikuo: ⌊YONDE KIMASU
                                          call   come
                    YOROSHIINDESU-KA, KONO, YOOSURUNI,
                    okay-QP   this   namely
                    KORE /?/
                    this   ⌐

(19)   Yasuo   ⌊SAN-BAN-MO DETANJA-NAI-DESU
                            three-No.-too   expressed-NEG
                    -KA-NE.
                    -QP-FP   ⌐

(20)   Keiko: ⌊DEMASHITA-NE.
                            expressed-FP⌐

(21)   Yasuo: ⌊N.
                                          hm
                    [Pause followed for 12 seconds until I
                    returned to the room.]

[English]

(1)   Ikuo: So, letting them (Japanese) have a kind of
                    experience while they are young would be a good
                    inspiration, I guess, but, you know.

(2)   Keiko: Hm::

(3)   [pause: 7.0 seconds]

(4)	Keiko:	There is a story like that, although
(5)		it's not related to this.
		[pause: 3.0 seconds]
(6)	Ikuo:	If I don't go about now, my class will-
(7)	Yasuo:	Oh, that's right.
(8)	Keiko:	What's the time now?
(9)	Ikuo:	Twelve ⌐ already, forty minutes past.
(10)	Keiko:	└ Half past?
(11)	Yasuo:	One hour.
(12)		[pause: 2.5 seconds]
(13)	Fumiko:	It seems like I had an opportunity to
		hear very good stories, h-.
(14)		[pause: 2.0 seconds]
(15)	Yasuo:	Then, ⌈ shall we call it off around here?
(16)	Ikuo:	└ Yes, let's do so..
(17)	Keiko:	[To Yasuo] This is okay, ⌈ only this is okay?→
(18)	Ikuo:	└ I'll get her.

This, I mean, th ⌈ is /?/
(19)   Yasuo: └ I suppose we discussed number three

enough, didn't we. ⌐
(20)   Keiko: └ Discussed, right. ⌐
(21)   Yasuo: └ Hm.

[Pause followed for 12 seconds until I
returned to the room.]

This segment shows that Yasuo, the oldest male group member, assumed a leader role and played it out by confirming the other group members' intention to end the discussion. Ikuo's mentioning his having to leave in (6) and inquiring what time it was in (8–11), Fumiko's postdiscussion remark in (13), and pauses in (3, 5, 12, and 14) signaled that the discussion was over. Appropriately perceiving this, Yasuo checked on the group's intention to end the discussion by asking, "Shall we call it off around here?" (15). Note that Yasuo did not use the consultative *shimashoo,* which is equivalent to "let's." In the previous excerpt from the A-3 group discussion, Mike took the initiative in proceeding to call me back by saying, "Let's go get *sensei.*" In contrast, Yasuo's taking the initiative is expressed in a question form. This indicates that Yasuo perceived that the other members thought that the discussion should be ended at that time and he was confirming it.

Moreover, at the same time, Yasuo's position in the hierarchy within the group qualifies him to punctuate the end. Note that before Yasuo asked the group about ending the discussion, Fumiko perceived that the topics were exhausted and signaled that the discussion was over by saying, "TOTEMO II OHANASHI-O KI-, KIKASHITE ITADAITA-TO YUU KANJI-DE (It seems like I had an opportunity to hear very good stories..)" (13). She was using an expression that is typical in ending in Japanese TV talk shows. A talk show host often expresses gratitude at the end of the talk by saying something like "KYOOWA TOTEMO II OHANASHI-O KIKASETE ITADAITE, ARIGATOOGOZAIMASHITA (Today, we/I have benefitted from your wonderful stories, thank you very much)." However, Fumiko's expression in (13) did not punctuate the end of the discussion because she was not operating in the capacity of leader. When Yasuo, who was assumed to be the leader in the discussion, consulted with the group as to whether they wanted to end the discussion, Ikuo agreed with Yasuo. It was the leader's consulting with the group and the subordinates' subsequent acknowledgment that officially sealed the end of the discussion.

On the basis of the differences in their ways of ending, I suggest that the Japanese participants perceived the activity of group discussion as one that they were to carry out as a group, in which a superior leads subordinate members. From the hierarchical order within a group, role differences evolve. When the group shifts from the discussion frame to a postdiscussion frame, the leader leads the subordinate members so that every member shifts at the same time. In contrast, the American participants perceived the activity of group discussion as an activity wherein four individuals are relatively equally bound together only for the purpose of discussion, but when the purpose is fulfilled, there is no binding force.

On the whole, the Japanese discussants appear to be deliberate both in beginning and in ending the discussion frame. They negotiated the procedural matters before they actually discussed topics, and they had a leader punctuate the end of the discussion by asking the group of its intention to end and/or officially announcing the end. On the other hand, the American discussants promptly began and ended the discussion frame. They quickly adjusted their participation statuses as they were getting into and out of the discussion.

It seems that the deliberateness with which the Japanese began and ended discussion is due to their tendencies toward group orientation and social hierarchy, which are essential elements in Japanese communication. To the Japanese, these considerations are always in their minds when communicating among themselves, whatever the situation. In order to act properly, a Japanese must be deliberate, determining hierarchy within a given situation and acting as a member of a group within which hierarchical order governs its members.

Expectations about Presenting Reasons in a Group Discussion

The first topic, "Why did you decide to learn Japanese or study abroad?" directly asked the discussants to present reasons. Every group, both American and Japanese, decided that each member should take a turn as in a round-robin system. Although the turn-taking system was the same, the average time of each member's presentation in the Japanese group discussions was much longer (71.5 seconds) than that in the American group discussions (23.1 seconds). When I closely examined the transcripts, I found that the time difference is the result of differences in expectations about the presentation of reasons between the American and Japanese participants. The Japanese participants framed their reasons as "stories." They seemed to have the expectation that they should present details as fully as possible, in chronological order, which built up to the situation in which they decided to study abroad. Telling small details and presenting them in chronological order made their reasons "stories." On the other hand, the American participants framed their presentations of reasons as "briefing" or "reporting." Their reasons were short and to the point, and they tended to use flat intonation. This pattern parallels Tannen's (1980) comparison of Greek and American narratives about a film, in which she found that the Greeks framed their narratives as storytelling and the Americans framed theirs as a memory test.[8]

In the following section, I will first demonstrate the two characteristics of the Japanese members' presentation: organizing in chronological order and describing contexts in detail. Then, I will demonstrate two characteristics of the American members' presentations: keeping to the point and using flat intonation.

Japanese Presentation of Reasons

First, the Japanese participants tended to organize their reasons according to chronological order. They followed the chronological sequence of the process in which they decided to study abroad. Moreover, the most directly and immediately related reason was postponed until the end since presentation began from an original past event and built up to the point at which they made a decision. The following excerpt is Satoko's presentation, which contained a chronological sequence.

[Excerpt 7]
[Japanese]

(1) WATASHI -WA   JUUHAS-SAI   NO   TOKO-NI..
     I   -TP   18-years old   of   time-at
     ANO..   ASOBIDE..   LOS ANGELES-NO   HOO-E
     uhm   for fun   Los Angeles-of   area-to
     IKKAGETSUKAN   HOOMUSTEE   SHITA-NO-NE.
     for one month   homestay   did   -you know
(2) SOREDE   NANKA..
     and then   uhm
     IROIRO   KOTCHI-NO   REGYURAA-NO-HITO-TO
     various   this-of   regular-of-people-with
     TOMODACHI-NI   NATTE...
     friends   became
(3) DE..   NANKA   SOOYUUNO   MITETE
     and   uhm   that things   seeing
     NANKA   EIGO   HONTOONI

```
        somehow    English    seriously
        BENKYOO-SHI-TAKU    NATTE-NE
        study              -want      became-FP
(4)     ZUTTO..    KOYOO TOKA    OMOTTE
        long       come                thought
        SORE-
        and
```

[English]

(1) In my case, when I was eighteen years old,
    uhm.. I went to Los Angeles.. for fun,
    homestayed for a month, you know.

(2) And then, somehow..
    I became friends with people from the regular courses.

(3) And.. as seeing things like that,
    I became seriously wanting to study English, you know.

(4) For all those years, I was determined to come.
    And-

Satoko's most direct reason is that she wanted to study English seriously. Instead of directly stating so, she referred to a time when she went to Los Angeles. This event further unfolds in (2). She said that she became acquainted with some (Japanese) students who were studying in a regular college program. In (3), she stated that she was influenced by these students and what they were doing ("things like that") and became serious about studying English until she actually came back to the United States to study. The events in (1), (2), and (3) are chronologically sequenced.

Furthermore, the beginning of her statement of her reason was an orientation to a time in the past, in the expression "When I was eighteen years old" (1). A similar kind of orientation to a time was found in other Japanese participants' comments. Beginning with a particular point in the past is a way to set up a context for a story to unfold, and it is one way of framing a reason as a "story" in the sense that the audience is led to expect something to happen.

It also should be noted that Satoko used temporal connectives and phrases. First, in (2), she used *sorede* (and then); second, she began (3) with *de* (and). In the reasons presented by other Japanese participants, there was frequent use of temporal connectives and phrases, which indicates their tendency to follow a chronological sequence.

Second, the Japanese participants tended to describe contexts in detail, as if they were explaining each step in the process of reaching the decision. These details include background information directly or indirectly related to the point such as names of schools, the kind of company one had worked for, one's age, and psychological states, such as how one was eager to go abroad or was concerned about past circumstances.

The difference between the Japanese and American styles is illustrated

by the following two examples. I will compare Minako's discourse in J-2
with Jill's in A-2 because their reasons are similar in that both referred to
their fathers' experiences. Jill, on one hand, mentioned her father's experience in Japan briefly; Minako, on the other, extensively described her father's experience in the United States. In the following, the first excerpt is
Jill's reason, and the second is Minako's.

[Excerpt 8]

Jill: And my dad went over to Japan
        to set up exchange programs
        and he really liked it.
        So I decided to take Japanese.

[Excerpt 9]
(Japanese)

Minako: EETOO, WATASHI-WA CHIISAI-KORO-KARA
        well   I   -TP little   -when-from
        GAIKOKU-NI IKI-TAI-TTEYUU KIMOCHI-WA
        abroad   -to go -want-that   feeling-TP
        ATTAN-DESU-YO-NE.
        had   -P -FP
        DE, WATASHI-NO CHICHI-GA.. MOO NANTE YUUKA
        and I   -of father-SP   what   say
        AMERIKA-BIIKI TTEYUUKA..
        America-fan   that say
        ANO.. UCHI-NO CHICHI-JISHIN-GA KOTCHI-DE
        uhm   I   -of father   self   -SP here   -in
        BENKYOOSHI-TAKUTE ...
        study   -wanting
        DEE, U OF M, UNIVERSITY OF MISHIGAN TO
        and U of M University   of Michigan   and
        ATO UCLA TO NI ANO
        also UCLA and to uhm
        KENKYUUSHI-NI ITTARI TOKA SHITE
        research   -to go   etc.   did
        MO TONIKAKU SOTCHI-NO-HOO-NI
            anyway   that-of-direction-in
        ANO WATASHITACHI-NO-KOTO-MO
        uhm we   -of-thing-too
        IKASE-TAI   TTEYUUKA
        make go-want or
        SOOYUU-KANJI DATTA-NODE,
        so   -like   was   -so
        SOREDE JOJONI-NE
        therefore gradually-FP

KOTCHI-NO-HOO-NI IKOO-KANA
this-of-direction-in   go   -wonder
TTE KANJI-NI NATTE KITE.
that   like-P   become   came

(English)

       Well, I, since when I was little...
       had had a desire to go to a foreign country.
       And my father was..
       what should I say,
       an American fan, if I could say..
       y'know.. my father himself
       wanted to study here...
       And he went to U of M, University of Michigan
       and, also UCLA, y'know,
       to do research or did things like that.
       Anyway, in that direction, y'know,
       he wanted to make us go, or
       since it/he was like that,
       therefore, gradually, y'know,
       I had come to feel like
       "How about going this way?"

Jill's reference to her father's account is very succinct ("And my dad went over to Japan to set up exchange programs and he really liked it.."). In contrast, Minako's reason is extensive in that she explains her father's motivation for going to the United States ("my father himself wanted to study here"), mentions which U.S. universities he attended (U of M and UCLA), and tells of his hopes for his children ("he wanted to make us go").

In Jill's segment, the fact that her father influenced her was expressed only through a logical connective "so" in "he really liked it. *So* I decided to take Japanese." In contrast, Minako explicitly stated how she was influenced in "therefore, gradually, y'know, I had come to feel like 'How about going this way?'"

Furthermore, in Minako's segment, it is observed that the main point was presented toward the end. In the beginning, she explained her father's experience. Then, at the end, she stated that she had come to consider studying in the United States. From the viewpoints of the speaker who was telling what happened in the past and the other participants who expected to hear a story, it was natural that the main event was postponed until the end.

I have shown in the previous section that the reasons of the Japanese participants contained the features of (1) chronological organization and (2) detailed description of past contexts. These features suggest that the Japanese participants framed their reasons as "stories."

American Presentation of Reasons

While the reasons presented by the Japanese participants were extensive, the reasons presented by the American participants were relatively brief. The best term with which to characterize the way in which the American participants presented reasons is "briefing" or "reporting." They tended to use flat intonation and to keep their reasons short by directly making the point. The following comparison of two deliveries by the same person (Mark in the A-3 group discussion) demonstrates the way he differentiated the use of intonation according to his perception of the ongoing communicative task. The first excerpt is a segment from Mark's episodic example of a cross-cultural misunderstanding in response to the third topic ("Discuss misunderstandings that are likely to occur between a Japanese and an American because of the language and cultural differences. Give specific examples of misunderstanding."). The episode concerned his difficulty in arranging to send flowers to his mother, who was living in Japan, on Valentine's Day. In Japan, it is the custom for girls to give chocolates to boys on Valentine's Day, which is the opposite of the custom in the United States. To make the situation more complicated, Mark was in the United States when he called a flower shop which was near his parents' house in Japan.

[Excerpt 10]

(1) So I was calling up this flower shop..
     near my house[9]
(2) and I was trying to like
     all the Japanese I could /?/
     to convince this guy to send like uh..
     five thousand or eight thousand yen,
     take flowers to my mom's house on Valentine's Day.
(3) And he was like, you know, basically, he-,
     I had to go through like three people
     and eluding me all around,
(4) and they couldn't conceive the concept
     that I was sending,
     me a guy,
     sending flowers,
     why flowers,
     on Valentine's Day you send chocolate, you know,
     to a girl, you know,
(5) he was-, couldn't conceive it at all.
(6) And I tried and tried,
     finally he gave up, you know,
     and he, uhm, and uh,
     I just, I had like someone else deal with
     the whole thing.
(7) But it's, it was really hard...

When Mark was telling this episode, his intonation rose and fell frequently. For example, in (2) he used an exaggerated tone for "convince." He also emphasized "flowers," "mom's," and "Valentine's," which were key words for the point of the story. In (4), after he said, "I was sending," he put emphasis on "me" and more emphasis on "guy," by quickly raising and dropping intonation on each word, to explain that the concept of a male sender was contrary to the Japanese expectation. Furthermore, the intonation he used when saying, "Why flowers," was a skeptical one, not the one for innocently asking for a reason, because from the Japanese perspective, it was obvious that the flowers made no sense. He also emphasized contrastive key words such as "chocolate" and "girl."

The second excerpt is Mark's presentation of the reasons why he decided to learn Japanese, in which he used flat intonation.

[Excerpt 11]
(Mark)

(1) I decided .. when I was, I spent a summer over there, visiting friends.
(2) And I've never taken a language /where/ I can speak.
(3) And uhm.. people seem nice.
(4) [Beth: [laughter] People. [as if she were saying Mark's line] "I like people."]
(5) [laughter] So I.. went back to.. decided to take it.
(6) And my parents got a job there...
     which gave me more incentive...
(7) That's why.

Compared to the various uses of intonation in the previous excerpt, the intonation contour in this presentation is weak in its rise and fall. The intonation is, in a sense, flattened. For example, in the last word "friends" in (1), the intonation fell on the primary stressed syllable instead of rising.

When Mark remarked about the Japanese people, "people seem nice" (3), Beth laughed and said, "I like people," teasingly, as if she were reminded of a funny story which she and Mark shared.[10] She used dramatic intonation, putting strong emphasis on "like" and dramatically differentiating the stress level on the two syllables in "people." The intonation that Beth used was different from the one which Mark had been using. Beth's remark also prompted Mark's laughter (5), but as he immediately resumed what he had been saying, his intonation became flat again.

Second, the American participants tended to keep their reasons short by reaching the point directly. An extreme example is Linda's reason in the A-4 group discussion, when the participants were asked of their reasons for deciding to study abroad. She said:

[Excerpt 12]

To figure stuff out for going to college..
waste a year before I went to college..

The point of Linda's reason was a purpose for studying broad. She directly reached her point by starting with the infinitive "to," the function of which is to express a purpose. In contrast to the Japanese ways of telling reasons, Linda did not describe what the circumstances were, nor give specific information such as names, nor explain how she had felt about going to college before she ultimately decided not to begin college at that time.

Another way of briefly expressing one's reason is to summarize details. An example of this is found in Steve's presentation. He was the only one of the American participants who organized a reason in chronological order. In the following excerpt, Steve began by referring to an exchange program and explained the process, from applying for the scholarship to arriving in Japan.

[Excerpt 13]

    1   Well, I went on YFU also.
    2   And.. it was just the opportunity,
    3   I was interested in Japan,
    4   and the opportunity came up...
    5   So the, uh, scholarship to spend a year there,
    6   so . . I just applied for it..
→ 7   One thing led to another, and..
    8   then, I was there

In (6), Steve said that he applied for a scholarship. Then, in (7), he summarized details of many events that might have happened by using the expression "One thing led to another." Instead of describing in detail how he was selected as an exchange student before he arrived in Japan, he used a shortcut expression to bridge the gap between the point of application and the point of his arriving in Japan. This shortcut enabled him to keep to the point and make the reason clear without going into a lengthy story.

The previous two sections have shown characteristics of the ways in which the American and the Japanese participants presented reasons. The chronological organization and the elaboration with details found in the Japanese participants' reasons suggest that they framed their reasons as "stories." On the other hand, the flat intonation and briefness found in the reasons presented by the American participants indicate that they framed their presentation of reasons as "briefing" or "reporting."

Being given the same or a similar topic, the participants from the different cultures framed their task differently. The communicative task that they shared in common, in this case, may be termed as "responding to a why-question, which asked reasons why certain kinds of decisions were made in the past, within a group discussion." If this question were asked in a casual conversation, perhaps Americans would have framed reasons as "stories." However, the speech event of "group discussion in a classroom setting" seems to be a major factor in their framing reasons as "briefing" rather than "stories" because it is expected they should reach the point directly. In a situation in which two or more people get together to get a job done within a certain time limit, the American expectation is that one should "get to the point" instead of "beating around the bush." To the Japanese participants, getting to the point seemed to have little impact on their ways of presentation. From the Japanese perspective, direct point making is generally avoided, while its opposite trait, indirectness, is preferred as it is considered a convenient tool for preventing frictions or conflicts from damaging harmony within a group. The Japanese participants, thus, seemed to have used the framing of "storytelling" as in talk shows, interviews, and casual forum/roundtable-type discussions which are commonly set up by the media in order to elicit personalized stories.

Argumentation Strategies

The major communicative task which was triggered by the second topic is to make an argument. The second topic was "Many people think that, for Americans, Japanese is harder to learn than European languages. Do you agree or disagree? Why?" Naturally, the participants were to choose whether or not they agree with the proposition of the topic and to give support for their choice. Thus, the task of arguing in this study was to express one's position on whether Japanese is difficult, as proposed in the topic, and support it. Analysis showed that the American and Japanese participants argued differently. Each American participant tended to state clearly his/her position, giving one argumentative account per turn. I call their style "single-account" argument. As only a single argumentative account is presented per turn, each turn tended to be short, and more exchanges were observed. In contrast, the Japanese participants tended to give arguments in a round-robin system, with each one's giving multiple argumentative accounts per turn. I called this way of arguing "multiple-account" arguments. As each participant presented inclusive accounts, each turn tended to be extensive. Their multiple argumentative accounts included both supporting and contradicting ones.

Let us, first, look at an example of the Japanese characteristic of argument, that is, a "multiple-account" argument. The following excerpt is Kazuko's opinion, which exemplifies the tendency to review or examine many aspects of the issue at one time. In this excerpt, Kazuko discussed the difficulty of learning Japanese in regard to four aspects of language learning: basic structure, *kanji* (a set of Chinese characters), reading, and nuances. HNU is Higashi Nihon University in Japan.

[Excerpt 14]
(Japanese)

1 SOODA-NA.. YAPPARI   MUZUKASHII TO OMOU
   so   -FP   as is expected hard   QT think
   [mumbles]
2 TOKUNI NAN-TE-YUUNO-KA-NA..
   especially what-QT-say   -Q -FP

3 UCHI-NO-BAAI-WA..
  I   -of-case-TP
  A, SOKO-DE, HNU-DE, YAPPA   NIHONGO-NO KOOSU
  oh there   HNU-at   as you see Japanese-of   course
  TOKA-TTE ARUNDESU-NE, AMERIKA-NO, KOTCHI-KARA
  like -QT exist   -FP America-of   here   -from
  MUKOO-NI ITTE TOKA-NO KOOSU-TOKA-GA ATTE,
  there-to   go like-of   course-like-SP   exist
  DE KEKKOO INTENSIVE-NI YATTE..
  and quite   intensively   do
4 KIHONTEKINA STORAKUCHAA-TOKA MI-NI TSUKU-KEDO,
  basic   structure   -like body-to attach-but
5 KEKKYOKU KANJI-NO RYOO-TOKA-MO OITSUKA-NAI-SHI,
  after all   kanji-of amount-like-too   catch up-not-and
6 SOREDE IKURA SONO UE-NO-HOO-NO-KOOSU-MADE
  and   even   the   up-of-direction-of-course-till
  ITTE-MO.. TATOEBA, SHINBUN YOMU TOKO-MADE
  go-even   for example newspaper read   point-till
  IKA-NAI.
  go-not
7 DAKARA WATASHI-TACHI-DA-TTARA SONNA BAA TOKA
  so   I   -plural -are-if   that   ONO. like
  KOTCHI-NO EIJI   SHINBUN-TOKA YOME-NAI-KEDO,
  here-of   English newspaper-etc.   read-not-but
  ICHIOU BA-TTOKA MITE WAKARU-KEDO,
  tentatively ONO.-like seeing understand-but
8 KO, KOTCHI-NO-HITO-GA TATOEBA ADOBANSUDO-NO
     here   -of-people-SP for example advanced-of
  REBERU-NI IRU-HITO-GA, JA, SORE-DAKARA
  level-in   are-people-SP   then   it   -so
  JA, SHINBUN YOMERU, WATASHITE YONDE-MI-NASAI
  then newspaper can read handing   read-try-ORDER
  TTE IT-TARA TABUN YOME-NAI-TO
  QT say-if   probably read-not-that
  OMOUNDESU-YO-NE.
  think-FP-FP
9 DAKARA, SOOYUU-TOKORO MUZUKASHII-TO OMOUSHI,
  so   that   -point   difficult   -that think
10 TO ATO, NYUANSU-TOKA.. DOKO-MADE WAKATTERUNO-
   and also nuance-like   where-to   understand
   KA-NA TTE-YUU-KI-GA-SURU.
   QP-FP QT-like-feeling-SP-do

(English)
1 Let's see.. As it is expected, I think it's hard.
2 Especially, how can I say..

3 In the case of my university...
oh, there, at HNU, they have like a Japanese course,
like, Americans, they go from here to there, and they study
quite intensively..
4 Like basic structure, they can master,
5 but after all, they can't keep up with the amount of kanji,[11]
6 and no matter how far they advance, they don't reach a
certain point, say, to read a newspaper.
7 So, like ourselves, we can't read like an English
newspaper that fast, but, at least, we can understand by
roughly skimming it.
8 But, if the people here, for example, those at the
advanced level, well, if we gave them a newspaper and can
they read(?) if we told them to read it, probably they can't
read it, I think, you know.
9 That's why I think that part is hard,
10 and also, as for like nuances.. I wonder how far, deep, they
understand....

In the very beginning, Kazuko stated her position that the Japanese language is hard for Americans by saying, "As it is expected, I think it's hard" (1). This is followed by four different argumentative accounts. In (4), she stated that it was possible for Americans to master the basic structure of Japanese. In (5), she said that they could not keep up with the large number of *kanji* characters. In (6)–(8), she argued that students learning Japanese, even at an advanced level, were less likely to be able to read a Japanese newspaper with ease while Japanese who study English could at least skim an English newspaper. Finally, in (10), she expressed skepticism about Americans' ability to understand the nuances of the Japanese language. The way in which she expressed her opinion was to examine more than one aspect of language learning.

Moreover, Kazuko's argumentative accounts included both supporting and contradicting ones. Her position was, as stated in the beginning, that the Japanese language, compared to European languages, is hard for Americans. Following this statement of her position, she pointed out that Americans *could* master the basic structure. This point did not support but contradicted her conclusion. From the Japanese perspective, to include a contradictory account is not to weaken one's argument; rather it shows one's holistic perspective. According to an example of Zen *mondoo*, "question and answer" between a Buddhist priest and a disciple, presented in Tsujimura (1987), the ability to integrate contradictions rather than choosing one point over the other is highly valued. A conclusion is expected to be inclusive rather than exclusive. The Japanese approach a question like the second topic in this study by asking, "In what way do I agree, and in what way do I disagree?" In order to make a conclusion as inclusive as possible, hence, perfect, from the Japanese standpoint, they include a contradictory account in advance. To exclude a contradictory account suggests that one is being neglectful of a weak point and one may be attacked on it. Thus, to be inclusive is, in a sense, a defensive way to present one's argument.

The American participants used "single-account" arguments, by which each participant presented one account and drew a conclusion per turn. Stan's presentation in the A-1 discussion illustrates the "single-account" argument, which will be shown in the following. When Stan's group, A-1, moved from the first topic ("Why are you studying Japanese?") to the second one ("Many people say that for Americans Japanese is difficult to learn compared to European languages. Do you agree?"), Stan acknowledged his turn and began.

[Excerpt 15]
(Stan)

> Okay.. I think it's harder than European languages, at
> least writing-wise, especially with the <u>kanji</u>.

Stan at first presented his position that the Japanese language is harder than European languages and then presented a qualification: "at least writing-wise, especially with the *kanji*." In addition, he mentioned that *kanji* are especially hard to learn. This is because there are about nineteen hundred Chinese characters and they are more complicated in terms of writing and reading than *hiragana* and *katakana,* the two Japanese syllabaries.

As Stan's presentation shows, in a typical "single-account" argument, a conclusion is drawn from one factor at a time. Other accounts may be presented by other discussants on different occasions. When a discussion is based on a "single-account" argument, it is very likely that a different conclusion can be drawn from another account, which creates a controversy or disagreement. In the A-2 group discussion, confrontation of opinions took place, and it took the form of "one-at-a-time argument." Let us look at an example of how a "single-account" argument developed into such a one-at-a-time argument. The following excerpt is a segment from the A-2 discussion in which Jill tried to claim that Japanese is hard because of its writing system and John disagreed.

[Excerpt 16]

1	Jill:	I think that what's hard about it is
2		learning a new alphabet. I think it's
3		hard.⌐
4	John:	└ But that's any language, though.
5	Jill:	No, well, no, no, no, not
6		⌐ a new alphabet.
7	Katy:	└ It depends. The Cyrillic
8		alphabet, you know, ⌐/there's ⌐ something→
9	John:	└ Uh, all the- └ Uh-
10	Jill:	└ Yeah.
11		like in/ Russian.

12	John:	Yeah, but, see, once you get that down,
13		it's, it's not as hard as-
14	Jill:	Once you get that down. Yeah, but in
15		Japanese and Chinese, you also, you have
16		to get the <u>kanji</u> down, not just the
17		<u>hiragana</u> and <u>katakana</u> /?/.

The first argument presented by Jill in (1) through (3) is that Japanese is hard because one must learn "a new alphabet." This was countered in (4) by John's argument that Japanese is not the only language in which one must learn a new alphabet. Furthermore, in (12) and (13), he claimed that Japanese is not hard once one has mastered *hiragana* and *katakana*: "Yeah, but, see, once you get that down, it's, it's not as hard as-."[12] At this point, he did not consider the fact that there are *kanji* that one must learn in order to be able to read a newspaper. Accordingly, Jill countered John by pointing out in (14)–(17) that one must also learn *kanji*.

As the above two excerpts show, the American participants tended to argue by giving a single account which supports a position that each had taken. From the American (and Western) perspective, a conclusion is expected to be exclusive. Americans, being asked the same question as the topic in this section, ask themselves, "Do I agree or disagree?" Logically, contradictions may not coexist. Thus, by giving only a supporting account, instead of both supporting and contradicting accounts, one can preserve logical consistency.

In addition to the differences in the way of giving an argument, the American and Japanese participants were different in terms of confrontation. As in the excerpt of the one-at-a-time argument between Jill and John, interaction in the American discussion groups tended to be confrontational. In contrast to the American group discussions, the Japanese ones were not confrontational because they presented arguments in a round-robin system in which very few interruptions occurred. Besides, their inclusive conclusion, which allows contradicting positions, does not explicitly allow an opportunity for confrontation to occur.

Conclusion

This study has demonstrated framing differences between the American and Japanese students as they interacted in group discussions. The analyses of the beginning and ending phases of the group discussions revealed that the American discussants entered and exited the discussion frame promptly while the Japanese discussants began and ended gradually and deliberately, because, in the beginning, they talked about how they would discuss, and in the end, they assured themselves that they had completed the discussion. The analysis of presenting reasons showed that the Japanese participants framed their reasons as "stories" as they tended to organize reasons according to chronological order and to give detailed contexts. In contrast, the

American discussants framed their giving of reasons as "briefing" or "reporting" by their use of flat intonation (which was completely different from the intonation used when telling stories) and their tendency to keep reasons to the point. The analysis of argumentation strategies demonstrated that the American participants used "single-account" arguments, which give a single account to support one conclusion/position at a time, while the Japanese participants used "multiple-account" arguments, which give more than one account, both supportive and contradictory, and draw a conclusion.

Each of the three analyses on the discourse level revealed cross-cultural differences on the framing level. The differences in the way Americans and Japanese began and ended suggest differences in their frames for group discussion. The Americans perceived the discussion as an activity which binds four individuals only in terms of the purpose of discussing, so they began their group discussions when they were told to do so and ended them when the purpose was fulfilled. In contrast, the Japanese perceived the activity as one they should carry out as a group rather than as co-present individuals. They perceived themselves as group members in a hierarchy established within a given group. Thus, they negotiated to establish the hierarchy when beginning discussion and punctuated the end of the activity in order to get out of the discussion frame as a group, all at once.

When discussing the first topic, which asked the participants to give reasons for a decision, the Americans framed the presenting of reasons as briefing or reporting while the Japanese framed the same act as storytelling. It should be pointed out again that the Americans chose to frame their presentations as briefing in spite of the fact that Americans, in general, often tell stories when asked the same type of question in a different situation such as casual conversation. I suggest that they framed the giving of reasons as briefing because they perceived that the speech event "group discussion" required them to get to the point without using too much time of the limited time available. For the Japanese, the time limit was not as important as sharing what one went through when deciding to study abroad.

The differences in ways of making an argument suggest another level of framing difference. The Japanese expected a conclusion to be inclusive, allowing both supportive and contradictory accounts at the same time, avoiding confrontation. The Americans' expectations about arguing were that one should take an exclusive position, not accepting any contradictory accounts, and that confrontation is accepted.

Founded on Goffman's (1986) notion of frame, that is, that people within a society (or a culture) share, to a certain extent, principles of organization that govern social events, this study investigated some governing principles of group discussion shared among American students, on the one hand, and among Japanese students, on the other. I found that, in the same kind of speech event, participants from different cultures interact differently, and this is partially due to differences in expectations about interaction, in general, or specific to the speech event.

I have shown, then, that some elements of frames are specific to a culture. This has significant implications for cross-cultural communication. For instance, the finding of the differences between the Americans and the Japanese in their expectations about how to argue enables us to predict that when Japanese and Americans are to discuss a controversial issue, the Japanese may experience frustration, being unable to participate in the argument because they find the one-at-a-time argumentation of the Americans too fast. At the same time, the Americans may perceive the Japanese as illogical and elusive because they give both supportive and contradictory accounts. In giving of a reason for a decision made in the past, Japanese, hearing Americans' brief reasons, may be unsatisfied, asking, "Is that all?" as they expect to hear personalized stories. In contrast, Americans may feel frustrated hearing Japanese give trivial, irrelevant details without reaching the main point immediately. Americans may perceive Japanese as overly cautious, prearranging the discussion manner and asking one another whether the discussion should be ended. In contrast, Japanese may perceive Americans as too individualistic, ignoring the importance of hierarchy within a group.

In conclusion, this chapter has shown cultural differences between Americans and Japanese in their expectations about interaction in group discussions. It also demonstrates that a frame analysis provides a strong foundation for explicating the mechanism of cross-cultural communication. Theories of frames help identify what is shared among interactants, while they can also be the basis for the identification of causes of miscommunication among those from different cultures. Finally, the notion of frames, along with discourse analysis, enables us to connect cultural knowledge at the macrolevel to individuals' communicative behaviors at the microlevel, in the sense that the former is considered a resource for interactants as they rely on it to come up with a plausible interpretation of what is going on at a particular moment and make a proper move.

Appendix A: Transcription Conventions

Transcription conventions follow those used in Tannen (1984).

.. noticeable pause or break in rhythm (less than 0.5 second)
... 0.5 second pause
.... 1.0 second pause

Highlight marks emphatic stress, but, in some cases where so indicated, it indicates a point of analysis
. marks sentence-final falling intonation
? marks yes/no question rising intonation
- marks a glottal stop or abrupt cutting off of sound
: marks elongated vowel sound
/?/ indicates transcription impossible
/Words/ in slashes indicate uncertain transcription

[Brackets] are used for comments on quality of speech and context

⌈ Brackets between lines indicate
⌊ overlapping speech

Brackets on two lines indicate second utterance
latched ⌐
                ⌐ onto first, without perceptible pause

→ left arrows indicate points of the analysis

An arrow at right indicates speaker's turn →
continues without interruption and a succeeding line is anticipated

Appendix B: Abbreviations Used in Japanese Transcription

TP for *wa* = topic particle marking the preceding noun phrase as a theme or a topic

SP for *ga* = subject particle marking the preceding noun phrase as a subject

Q for *ka* = question particle which marks the sentence as a question

QT for *to, toka*, and *-tte* = quotation particles which are equivalent to "that" for English verbs "think," "feel," "seem," "say," etc.

FP for *yo* (I tell you,) *ne* (isn't it (?)), *naa* (interjection) = sentence final particles which assign extra meaning to the preceding sentence

ONO. = onomatopoeic expressions

Appendix C: Ethnographic Profiles of the Participants

Group A-1

Name	Sex	Age	Grade	Ethnic Background
Kris	F	N/A	Senior	Anglo-Saxon
Joan	F	22	Senior	Korean
Stan	M	18	Freshman	Anglo-Saxon/Japanese
Ken	M	N/A	Junior	Anglo-Saxon

Group A-2

Name	Sex	Age	Grade	Ethnic Background
Katy	F	19	Freshman	Anglo-Saxon
Jill	F	N/A	Freshman	Anglo-Saxon
Mary	F	18	Freshman	Anglo-Saxon
John	M	18	Freshman	Anglo-Saxon

Group A-3

Name	Sex	Age	Grade	Ethnic Background
Beth	F	19	Sophomore	Anglo-Saxon
Jenny	F	19	Sophomore	Anglo-Saxon
Sean	M	21	Senior	Anglo-Saxon
Mark	M	20	Sophomore	Anglo-Saxon

Group A-4

Name	Sex	Age	Grade	Ethnic Background
Cindy	F	20	Sophomore	Anglo-Saxon
Linda	F	19	Freshman	Anglo-Saxon
Paul	M	19	Sophomore	Anglo-Saxon
Steve	M	20	Sophomore	Anglo-Saxon

Group J-1

Name	Sex	Age	Subject of Study	Length of Stay in the United States
Hiroko	F	23	EFL*	1 month+
Satoko	F	20	EFL	1 month+
Teruo	M	22	EFL	1 month+
Jiro	M	20	EFL	1 month+

*EFL is English as a Foreign Language.

Group J-2

Name	Sex	Age	Subject of Study	Length of Stay in the United States
Kazuko	F	23	linguistics	1 year+
Minako	F	22*	government	7 years+
Masao	M	26	linguistics	1 year+
Kiyoshi	M	32	linguistics	1 year+

*Minako was an undergraduate student, and the others were graduate students.

Group J-3

Name	Sex	Age	Subject of Study	Length of Stay in the United States
Keiko	F	28	linguistics	6 months+
Fumiko	F	23	linguistics	6 months+
Yasuo	M	29	linguistics	1 year+
Ikuo	M	N/A*	Foreign Service	6 months+

*Ikuo was an undergraduate student, and the others were graduate students.

Notes

1. The tape recorders that were used were SONY TC-2 and TC-11.

2. The A-1 and A-2 group discussions took place in a Japanese drill session in which I was a drill instructor. The other group discussions were set up in discussion rooms in the university library.

3. Since I used a portion of a Japanese drill session which was naturally going on, I could not control gender ratio of group A-2.

4. Ethnographic profiles of the participants are shown in Appendix C.

5. Although the predicate parts of the first topics are different, both were designed to ask discussants to give reasons for something that they chose to do. In

addition, analysis will focus on how discussants presented reasons rather than on the nature of the reasons. Thus, it was assumed that the two versions of the first topic can be treated as similar in terms of the objective of the questions.

6. A paradigm of polite forms is prescribed in the language. An appropriate form is selected according to whether the speaker wants to exalt a superior or lower an inferior (including oneself). If the speaker chooses not to exalt or lower the addressee, neutral forms are used. For instance, *imasu, irasshaimasu,* and *orimasu* all refer to an animate kind of existence. When I am talking to my teacher, I use *irasshaimasu* in reference to my addressee:

> *Irasshaimasu.*   S/he (the teacher) is (here/there).

On the other hand, when referring to myself, I use *orimasu.*

> *Orimasu.*   I am (here/there).

However, when I am talking to my colleague who is of equal status, I use *imasu* in reference to my colleague or myself.

> *Imasu.*   I am (here/there) *or* S/he is (here/there).

7. *Sensei* is a Japanese word for teacher. Because the members of group A-3 and A-4 were taking my Japanese course, they were accustomed to calling me "sensei."

8. Tannen (1980) also found that the intonational variation in the Greek narratives was significantly greater than that in the Americans' as the Greeks displayed dramatic shifts both in loudness and pitch while the Americans used relatively flat intonation. However, in her study, it was the Americans' narratives that were longer and more detailed, as they strove to recall as much as possible in accurate chronological order.

9. "My house" in this context means his parents' house in Japan.

10. Or it is also possible that Beth interpreted Mark's remark as a shallow comment and she teased him about it.

11. *Kanji* is a set of Chinese characters. The Japanese syllabary is called *kana,* which consists of two kinds, *hiragana* and *katakana. Hiragana* is the cursive form of *kana,* and *katakana* is the square form of *kana.* The latter is used mainly for writing loanwords while the former is for general use.

12. In (12) and (13), John did not use the terms "*hiragana* and *katakana*"; instead, he referred to "a new alphabet" as "that." It is ambiguous whether or not he meant to include *kanji* in "that" as well. However, I believe that he only meant *hiragana* and *katakana* at this point because previously he had said, "I mean, once you learn, you know, you get the *hiragana* and *katakana* down, it's not that hard to write, I mean. . . ." Moreover, Jill's counterargument immediately after (12) and (13) supports this interpretation.

References

Bateson, Gregory. 1972. Steps to an ecology of mind. New York: Ballantine.

Benedict, Ruth. 1946. The chrysanthemum and the sword. New York: New American Library.

Goffman, Erving. 1986. Frame analysis: An essay on the organization of experience. Reprint. Boston: Northeastern University Press.

Gumperz, John J. 1981. The linguistic bases of communicative competence. Analyzing discourse: Text and talk, ed. by Deborah Tannen, pp. 323–34. Washington, DC: Georgetown University Press.

Gumperz, John J. 1982. Discourse strategies. Cambridge: Cambridge University Press.

Harada, S. I. 1976. Honorifics. Syntax and semantics: Japanese generative grammar, ed. by Masayoshi Shibatani, 449–561. New York: Academic Press.

Hirokawa, Randy Y. 1987. Communication within the Japanese business organization. Communication theory: Eastern and western perspectives, ed. by D. Lawrence Kincaid, 137–49. San Diego, CA: Academic Press.

Nakane, Chie. 1972. Japanese society. Berkeley, CA: University of California Press.

Ouchi, William G. 1981. Theory Z. Reading, MA: Addison-Wesley.

Ramsey, Sheila. 1985. To hear one and understand ten: Nonverbal behavior in Japan. Intercultural communication: A reader, ed. by Larry A. Samovar and Richard E Porter, 307–21. Belmont, CA: Wadsworth.

Rohlen, Thomas P. 1974. For harmony and strength: Japanese white-collar organization in anthropological perspective. Berkeley, CA: University of California.

Stewart, Lea P. 1985. Japanese and American management: Participative decision making. Intercultural communication: A reader, ed. by Larry A. Samovar and Richard E. Porter, 186–89. Belmont, CA: Wadsworth Publishing Company.

Tannen, Deborah. 1980. A comparative analysis of oral narrative strategies: Athenian Greek and American English. The pear stories: Cognitive, cultural, and linguistic aspects of narrative production, ed. by Wallace L. Chafe, 51–87. Norwood, NJ: Ablex.

Tannen, Deborah. 1984. Conversational style: Analyzing talk among friends. Norwood, NJ: Ablex.

Tannen, Deborah. 1985. Frames and schemas in interaction. Quaderni di Semantica's round table discussion on frame/script semantics, ed. by Victor Raskin. Quaderni di Semantica 6:326–35.

Tannen, Deborah. 1986. Discourse in cross-cultural communication. Text 6(2):143–51.

Tsujimura, Akira. 1987. Some characteristics of the japanese way of communication. Communication theory: Eastern and western perspectives, ed. by D. Lawrence Kincaid, 115–26. San Diego, CA: Academic Press.

Yamada, Haru. 1992. American and Japanese business discourse: A comparison of interactional styles. Norwood, NJ: Ablex.

7

"Samuel?" "Yes, dear?" Teasing and Conversational Rapport

CAROLYN A. STRAEHLE

Georgetown University

Introduction

In this chapter, I offer a sociolinguistic analysis of teasing in everyday conversation among adults, in this case, a recorded casual conversation in which I participate with two friends, Samuel and Diana. Upon initially replaying the conversation, I was struck by the way teasing stood out as clearly "different" from the rest of the conversation. Most interestingly, the teasing appeared to create distinct alliances among the participants: two of us (Samuel and I) regularly teamed to tease the third member of our triad (Diana). In addition, the recurrence of certain teasing routines further suggested that two of the participants (Samuel and Diana) already shared a well-established "teasing relationship."

The purpose of this chapter is twofold: first, I present examples of teasing which appear in extended segments of the conversation and discuss specific linguistic features that characterize this discourse type. Using additional conversational evidence, I then draw on other studies of conversation to suggest that the alliances occurring in the teasing presented here are not arbitrary. Instead, I argue that they are inextricably linked to the types of relationships the participants have with one another. Because Samuel and I

*Adapted from Tannen (1984:xix).

I would like to thank Deborah Tannen for her comments on earlier versions of this paper and her encouragement throughout. I am also grateful to Diana and Samuel for their cooperation in this study and especially for their friendship and good humor.

are only recently acquainted, engaging in teasing that is aimed at each other is a potentially threatening game; however, by directing our teasing at Diana, we instead create a nonthreatening means for building rapport. In contrast, Samuel and Diana are close friends and partners in the early dance of an intimate relationship. For them, teasing evolves as verbal play, which both mirrors and contributes to their growing intimacy.

Teasing: Theoretical Background

In his discussion of play and fantasy, Bateson (1972:180) observes that "the playful nip denotes the bite, but it does not denote what would be denoted by the bite." According to Tannen (1986:61), language forms that rely on hidden meaning, for example, humor and irony, are "common and satisfying," because "the feat of sending and getting unstated meaning . . . is aesthetically pleasing." As a form of humor or play, teasing is a language "nip" that can signal and enhance speaker enjoyment and rapport. At the same time, however, teasing is thought to be closely bound to real antagonism: the playful nip may easily be mistaken for a hostile bite.

Anthropological research on teasing focuses more on the relationship between teasing and real hostility and builds on early twentieth century ethnographies of preliterate societies. Radcliffe-Brown (1952:91) used the term "joking relationship" in reference to certain kinship ties characterized by a high degree of "permitted disrespect" in the form of teasing, joking, horseplay, ridicule, and the like. These behaviors exhibit "a peculiar combination of friendliness and antagonism" (p. 91) and provide an outlet for conflict that might otherwise threaten social ties (p. 103). Although they will not be discussed here, many later anthropological and sociological studies conducted in Western industrial societies, as reviewed in Apte (1983, 1985) and Fine (1983), also emphasize the conflict and/or stress regulation functions of humorous behavior like teasing, particularly in non-kin social groups such as those found in the workplace.

Sociolinguistic studies on teasing that combine aspects of ethnographic study with discourse analysis have tended to focus on the socialization function of teasing in adult-child interaction. For example, Schieffelin (1986:165) reports that in Kaluli society, adults "prefer verbal manipulation through teasing and shaming" rather than direct "physical intervention" in order to influence others. Teasing is systematically used with children in order to "include them [in Kaluli society] rather than set them apart" (p. 179). In another study, Eisenberg (1986) describes teasing directed at children in two Mexicano families, both as a source of amusement as "just play" and as a "subtle form of criticism" to show disapproval without "threaten[ing] the adult's authority" (p. 189). At the same time, teasing fosters closeness: "That it is 'safe' to tease . . . indicates that a special relationship exists" (p. 193). Miller's (1986) study of mothers and children in a Baltimore white working class community supports the observation that teasing is a significant form of language socialization. She found that teasing in this community provides a means for children to learn the "essential survival skills" (p. 205) of "self-assertion and self-defense (p. 200)."

Whereas the studies cited above focus on adult-child interaction, relatively few sociolinguistic studies have considered teasing among adolescents or adults. In one study, Eder (1993) shows that among adolescent females, teasing serves functions similar to those revealed in adult-child interaction, including providing opportunities for social bonding and language play. Eder furthermore suggests that teasing may be used as a resource to mock, and explore alternatives to, traditional gender roles. In another study, Drew (1987) examines teasing among adults to show how it is occasioned in talk. He concludes that teasing can provide a "form of social control of minor conversational transgressions" such as "complaining, extolling, [and] bragging" (p. 219). Thus, like earlier researchers, both Eder and Drew find evidence for socially significant functions served by teasing.

Participants, Setting, and Data

The participants in this study, Diana, Samuel, and Carolyn (this author), share roughly similar social and educational backgrounds, but different cultural histories and personal ties. At the time of the recording, all three of us, who are similar in age, have recently resumed academic life after extended hiatuses spent working in the United States and abroad: Samuel (age 30) and Diana (age 28) are in their first year at a prominent East Coast business school after living for several years in California and Hawaii, respectively, and I (age 28) am in my first year of a graduate program in linguistics at Georgetown after a five-year residence in Berlin, Germany. Our conversation reflects the pains we experience, and to a large extent share, as we adjust to our new environments: we complain generously about endless workloads, diminished incomes, and our respective (new) home cities.

Though our lives at the time of the recording are similar, our ethnic backgrounds differ substantially. Samuel, of Polish-Jewish descent, was born and raised in a Jewish community in Monterrey, Mexico. Although a native speaker of Spanish, he has lived, worked, and studied in the United States for over ten years and is a fluent English speaker who identifies primarily with American/Eastern European Jewish, rather than Mexican, culture. While Samuel is a nonnative speaker of English and permanent resident in the United States, Diana and I are both bilingual, first-generation U.S. Americans. Diana is a Chinese-American who grew up in Wilmington, Delaware, and most recently lived in Hawaii, where her family has since moved; I am a German-American who was born in Quebec, Canada, grew up in Maine, went to college in Connecticut, and then moved to Europe for five years before returning to the United States.

Finally, like our life histories, our personal ties differ: Diana creates the link between Samuel and me. Diana and I have been "best friends" since we first met as freshman roommates almost a decade ago. Similarly, Diana and Samuel, despite having met only recently, regard themselves as "best friends" at business school, where they study and socialize together almost daily and are about to begin a more intimate relationship. Samuel and I, however, have only met for the second time on this occasion, and although each knows a great deal *about* the other through Diana, we do not yet "know" each other (summarized in Appendix).

The teasing examined in this paper appears in a sixteen-minute excerpt of talk that is part of a larger four-hour body of conversation recorded in March 1989. It is the first Sunday of Spring Break, and Diana and Samuel have driven to Washington for brunch at my home and a Sunday outing. Much of the talk therefore centers on possible destinations, a task which Samuel and I have assumed, since Samuel is driving and I am the hostess (and presumed expert on points of interest in the area). The conversation analyzed here begins just as we have finished eating. Throughout the conversation, Samuel and I stay seated at the table to talk, while Diana joins us only intermittently, between telephone calls in another corner of my apartment and trips to the bathroom. Diana's phone calls—one to a friend, Tracy, whom Diana will visit in Washington the following day, and two to Jane, another former college roommate, whom we will visit in Charlottesville should Samuel and I agree on that destination for our excursion—provide a source for teasing, in particular when Diana rejoins Samuel and me at the table. Although some joking occurs while Samuel and I plan the drive, talk associated with trip planning is relatively serious. The nonserious teasing occurs almost exclusively when Diana is not telephoning and is available to converse directly with Samuel and me, either from across the room or while seated with us.

Teasing Frames and the Metamessage of Play

In distinguishing teasing from surrounding talk, it is useful to consider Tannen and Wallat's (this volume) discussion of "interactive frames" and Bateson's (1972) account of play. Incorporating Goffman's (1981:128) notion of footing—the "alignments" among participants—Tannen and Wallat (this volume: xx) define interactive frame as "a sense of what activity is being engaged in, how speakers mean what they say." This definition also assumes that conversational "meaning" is not conveyed merely through the informational content or message of individual words, but through "metamessages," or the attitudes of participants toward one another and the talk in which they are engaged (Tannen 1986:15–16). Put simply, frames are like labels that we use to identify what we and our interlocutors are doing, and metamessages, conveyed through linguistic and nonlinguistic cues, determine how it is that we know which labels to choose. To return to Bateson (1972), then, "this is play" involves a paradox of message and metamessage: when a "hostile" phrase is cast with a metamessage that signals a frame as "play," the utterance doesn't mean what it would under other circumstances, but conveys participant rapport instead. Thus, though words may denote hostility, we can interpret them as play.

Speakers communicate and identify metamessages or frames through "contextualization cues." According to Gumperz (1982:131), these cues include features such as "prosodic phenomena," "lexical and syntactic options," and "formulaic expressions." In addition, certain features may cluster to mark culturally relevant activities, for instance, teasing, joking, lecturing, or praising. In connection with the notion of frame, it is important to note that while contextualization cues enable speakers to frame and interpret individual utterances as joking rather than serious, or teasing rather than hostile, these smaller frames are embedded in, and, in fact, construct, even larger ones. In Tannen's (1986) words, "these small, passing frames reflect and create the larger frames that identify the activities going on" (p. 75). One goal of this paper is to identify the features that enable speakers to frame talk—individual utterances as well as extended sequences—as playful teasing. In the conversation I analyze here, the more serious frames generally center on trip-planning activity, while less serious frames build on instances of joking and teasing.

Teasing Frames: An Overview of Linguistic Features

In the conversation under analysis, I identified at least seven extended segments as constituting "larger" conversational frames of generally nonserious talk which, in turn, contrast with equally, or even more, extended frames of relatively serious trip-planning talk. Within the larger nonserious frames, many utterances, or sequences thereof, can be analyzed more specifically as instances of teasing. In other words, although what speakers say may appear aggressive and hostile in form, they frame their words with a metamessage that signals "this is play." It is the framing of these utterances in particular which is a main focus of this chapter. Taking examples from the larger nonserious frames, I illustrate the primary discourse and linguistic features of smaller teasing frames that appear in the conversation.

Although the teasing is introduced by a substantial variety of cues (e.g., prosodic features such as exaggerated intonation, stress, and laughter; and other discourse features such as marked pronoun use, overlap, repetition, and detail), I focus my discussion on the linguistic features—prosody, laughter, pronouns, and formulae—that are most salient for my data. In the examples I discuss, various constellations of these features contribute somewhat differently to the teasing talk. Since many instances of teasing, especially those consisting of extended sequences of utterances, assume an "aggressive" form—disagreement, challenges, rebuttals, imperatives, swearing, and insults—prosody and laughter, as well as provocative use of pronouns, provide essential cues which interlocutors rely on to frame the utterances as nonserious. This is the topic of my first section of analysis.

In the second portion of my analysis, I focus on pronouns and formulae and show how they operate uniquely both to frame utterances as teasing and to reveal significant aspects of the participants' relationships. Samuel and I frequently succeed in teasing Diana by referring to her, in her presence, with the third-person pronoun "she." Consequently, in much of the teasing, Diana appears verbally relegated to the position of a child. At the same time, throughout the conversation, a distinct pattern of speaker alignment emerges. In most instances, Diana suffers the consequences of teasing, while Samuel and I collude as teasers; in other cases, Diana and Samuel tease each other in my presence, but teasing does not appear in talk involving Samuel and me alone. Although Samuel and I joke, we do not tease each other. What is most interesting, however, is the way in which certain formulae appear in the teasing talk between Samuel and Diana. While these cues help frame their utterances as teasing, they also frame the nature of their relationship.

Prosody, Laughter, and Pronouns: Framing Antagonistic Talk as Play

The first example illustrates how prosodic features such as intonation, stress, and vowel and voice quality can "trigger" a teasing frame. This excerpt opens as Diana returns from the bathroom to join Samuel and me. We have been joking about my earning potential as a linguist, when Diana, walking from the bathroom to the dining area, complains about my bathroom mirror, which is situated in an unusually high position above the sink. Although this construction poses no difficulty for persons of above average height, for Diana, who is just shy of five feet tall, the mirror is almost impossible to use and is thus a source of consternation.[1]

```
008   Samuel:   I meanhh- we are not talking herehh big fortunes,
009             here, we are talking-
010   Carolyn:               └Subsistence! [laughs].
011    Diana:   [calling from other end of apartment]
                Carolyn?
012   Samuel:   Subsistence level, ⌈and..
013    Diana:   [whiny voice]       └Your mirror is a:wfully ta::ll.
014             [laughs]
015   Carolyn:  Well, ⌈I- I'm not that shorthh.
016   Samuel:         └No, that's not a good description hh.
017    Diana:   ₐ𝒸𝒸I couldn't even see into your medicine cabinet [laughs].
018   Carolyn:  hh Oh, that's right.
```

In this segment, it is Diana's interjection (011–014 "Carolyn? Your mirror is a:wfully ta::ll. [laughs]"), with its marked prosodic features, accompanying laughter, and implied meaning, that invites a teasing frame: she lengthens the vowels in "awfully" and "tall" and uses a high-pitched, somewhat nasal tone of voice to complain about my mirror. Since my "too tall" mirror interferes with Diana's grooming, her statement seems to suggest "inhos-

pitality" on my part and acts as a demand for sympathy, which compels
Samuel and me to reply. That Samuel and I take Diana's comment as an
opportunity to tease is reflected in our nearly simultaneous responses. In
015 ("Well, I'm not that short hh"), I disagree with Diana's assessment and
suggest that the true problem is Diana's height rather than the mirror. The
implication of Samuel's response in 016 ("No, that's not a good descrip-
tionhh") is virtually identical to that of my own. Again, it is not the "too tall"
mirror that has created Diana's difficulty, but rather, her own "insufficient"
height.[2] However, both Samuel and I close our responses by chuckling,
which suggests that our "criticism" of her height—a relatively "inalienable"
quality—is not intended seriously. In response, Diana maintains her original claim by providing additional support in 017 ($_{acc}$"I couldn't even see
into your medicine cabinet [laughs]"). Shaded with laughter, her utterance
is issued rapidly, with emphatic stress on "couldn't" and "medicine cabinet,"
furthering the teasing frame. Thus, although this exchange involves disagreement in form, prosodic features identify it as nonserious play.

Another example of teasing involves an exchange of insults which is
rendered nonserious primarily through pervasive laughter. However, to
better understand how the insults arise as they do, it is necessary to first
present an earlier instance of teasing in which Samuel and I make remarks
about Diana while she is on the phone to Jane, the friend whom we will visit
if we drive to Charlottesville. Diana, who had spoken to Jane earlier in the
week to say that we might visit her on this particular weekend, is calling Jane
to give her an update on our plans. At this point, Samuel and I have, in fact,
decided on Charlottesville, as indicated by Sam's assessment in lines 373 and
374 of the trip as potentially "fun" and the Charlottesville area as "beautiful." To this I agree, and Samuel makes a motion for us to leave by saying
"Shall we?" in 376.

373   Samuel: No, it actually might be fun.
374   I've heard that it's really beautiful up there.
375   Carolyn: Yeh, I've heard that too.
376   Samuel: Shall we? (2.5)
377   She's talking with about five people there hhh.
378   Carolyn: I know.
379   ₍Diana!
380   Samuel: Diana, that's not your phon-.
381   Diana: It was Jane.

The 2.5 second pause following Samuel's utterance in 376 ("Shall we?")
suggests his realization that while he and I are now ready to leave, Diana,
who is still on the phone, is not. This situation occasions teasing, first
indicated in Samuel's comment in 377 ("She's talking with about five people
there hhh"). While Sam realizes that Diana has made no more than two
calls, he exaggerates in saying that she has been talking to more people. By
chuckling, however, he underscores the nonseriousness of his remark. Both
the exaggeration and laughter frame the utterance as teasing.

Once Samuel has framed his utterance as teasing, I join in, first by showing agreement with Samuel in 378 ("I know"), and then by saying "Diana!" in a loud and mock-scolding manner. Samuel further builds on the tone of my utterance by offering a "reason" for my "scolding": by reminding Diana that she does not own the telephone in 380 ("Diana, that's not your pho[ne]"), he hints that Diana has overstepped the bounds of telephone etiquette, either by telephoning too long or, perhaps, by making too many calls. Even though Diana interrupts her conversation at this point with the comment in 381 "It was Jane," she is momentarily unable to defend herself further against our teasing.

Upon finishing her call, however, Diana offers an excuse, shown at the beginning of the following segment, which, after a series of challenges by Samuel and me, ultimately leads to an exchange of insults.

441	Diana:	$_{acc}$Cal, I couldn't hang up
442		on someone / ? / -it was Janehh
443	Carolyn:	That's okay, Di.
444	Diana:	└Because we don't-
		we don't know what we're
445		doing yet anyway, so we have to tell her.
446	Samuel:	Oh, ⌈ we kno:ow=
447	Carolyn:	⌊ Yes, we do.
448	Samuel:	=We are going.
449	Diana:	We are going.
450	Samuel:	You're coming, too?

In 441–442, Diana repeats and elaborates on her earlier comment—"it was Jane"—and adds in 444–445 ("Because we don't- we don't know what we're doing yet anyway, so we have to tell her") an excuse for her lengthy conversation. Presumably, Diana's call was to inform Jane that we were not yet certain of our plans and that we would have to contact her again. Here Diana uses the pronoun "we" to attribute the state of "not knowing" to all three participants. At this point she truly is unaware that Samuel and I have decided on Charlottesville as the destination for our Sunday drive, making Diana's comment appropriate from her own standpoint, but not from Samuel's and mine.

Samuel and I take advantage of this information discrepancy by playing on the alternative interpretations of "we." Once again we seize the opportunity to tease Diana.

446	Samuel:	Oh, ⌈ we kno:ow=
447	Carolyn:	⌊ Yes, we do.
448	Samuel:	=We are going.
449	Diana:	We are going.
450	Samuel:	You're coming, too?

In Sam's and my comments in 446 and 447, we assert that we (Sam and I) *do* know that we are going to Charlottesville. These comments refute Diana's statement that we (the three of us) are still undecided and create a situation in which our use of "we" can be interpreted as excluding Diana. When Diana repeats, "We are going," in 449 to confirm her new understanding of our plans—which in her mind clearly include all three of us—Samuel makes another stab. By asking, as though surprised, "You're coming, too?" in 450, Samuel highlights the alternative interpretations of "we." In other words, to suggest that Samuel and I had planned to go without Diana, which is blatantly untrue, constitutes yet another instance of teasing.

I will reserve further discussion of pronominal use in teasing for the next section. My intention here has been to establish a context for an exchange, which under most circumstances would strike an observer as aggressive, but in this case, though agonistic in form, is clearly framed as play. As noted above, Samuel and I—and Samuel in particular—have created a situation in which we have deliberately, but not maliciously or seriously, "excluded" Diana from our plans. This culminates with Samuel's question in 450 ("You're coming, too?"), which is followed by an apparent attempt by Diana to respond in kind. Her invective against Samuel begins in 451 ("Asshole. Oh- [laughs]") with an expletive, followed by laughter upon realizing that she has been recorded.

450	Samuel:	You're coming, too?
451	Diana:	Asshole. Oh- [laughs]
452	Samuel:	You're being ⌈ recorded. [laughs]
453	Carolyn:	⌊ That's- [laughs]
454	Diana:	You're stupid.
455	Samuel:	Me stupid?
456		You're being ⌈ recorded!
457	Diana:	⌊ You're stupid.
458		Shut up [laughs]
459	Carolyn:	[laughs]

Samuel's comment in 452 ("You're being recorded") implies criticism of Diana's behavior, namely, her swearing while being recorded. Diana counters Samuel's statement with another insult in 454 ("You're stupid"), suggesting that he is somehow at fault for her faux pas, perhaps for teasing her in the first place. In other words, Diana implies that she is justified in calling Samuel names (a potentially threatening act), because he has excluded her from the group plans (if intended seriously, an equally threatening act). Diana then repeats her insult in 457 ("You're stupid"), followed by the imperative "Shut up" in 458 in response to Samuel's emphatic disagreement with Diana's contention that he is at fault (455/456: "Me stupid? You're being recorded!"). Under other circumstances, such as in a real dispute, claims of another's stupidity, use of expletives and the command to "shut up" would likely convey enmity. In this segment, however, hearty laughter by all participants underscores the nonseriousness of the otherwise disputatious exchange.

Pronouns and Formulae: Framing Roles and Relationships

Characteristic of the teasing frames identified in these data are the pronouns "we" and "she" used either (1) to exclude Diana from a particular frame of reference, or (2) to accord Diana less-than-adult status. As described in some detail in the previous section, the example involving insults was in part occasioned by contrasting pronominal use: the "we" referred to by Samuel and me included only ourselves and was therefore at odds with Diana's interpretation of "we" that included the three of us. It is this discrepancy which led to Diana's outburst and the ensuing exchange of nonserious insults. In short, verbal "exclusion" provides a resource for play.

While humor results from divergent interpretations of "we," another type of pronominal use emerges in the teasing episodes as well. In several instances, Samuel and I, and Samuel in particular, use the third person pronoun "she" to remark about Diana in her presence. In general, such reference is insulting, because it ignores or denies an individual's presence, which one might otherwise indicate with the pronoun "you." As noted by Tannen (personal communication), third person pronominal reference of this sort is often employed by adults in the company of children or otherwise unempowered individuals.

The "formulae" that I describe in this section refer to recurring patterns of dialogue found in the interaction between Samuel and Diana. These include Diana's repeated use of "shut up" in response to Samuel's teasing and a routine in which Diana addresses Samuel admonishingly by his first name, to which he affectionately responds, "Yes, dear?" That these patterns appear only in the context of teasing and as direct exchanges between Samuel and Diana suggests that the two share a relaxed teasing relationship. Drawing primarily on examples from the bathroom mirror segment, I examine how both pronouns and formulae frame the discourse as teasing.

In the bathroom mirror example, it is Diana's complaint regarding the height of my mirror which first triggers teasing. The result is an exchange of claims and counterclaims, in which Diana maintains that the mirror is too high and Samuel and I hint that Diana is too short. Part of my reaction to Diana is to point out two other mirrors in my apartment, both within her reach: a full-length mirror on the bathroom door and another in the hallway. In other words, by hinting to Diana that she could use either of the two additional mirrors, I imply that her initial complaint is largely unwarranted. My comment then leads to talk about how mirrors are not all equally flattering, the point at which the following dialogue opens.

047 Carolyn: So- so one miror is more
048   flattering than the other or something.
049   Diana: └Indeed, yes,
                    and the lighting.
050 Samuel: One mirror lies hh=

051   Carolyn: [laughs]
052   Samuel: $_p$=When it's very dark she looks a lot better.
053   Diana: Samuel,⌐   ⌐you wouldn't <u>know</u>, would you?
054   Samuel: └ Yes, dear?⌐
055   [Samuel and Diana laugh]

In response to Diana's agreement with my assessment of her behavior in 047, that is, that Diana does find some mirrors more flattering than others, Samuel makes a rather subdued comment in 052 ($_p$When it's very dark she looks a lot better), implying that Diana looks even better when she is not seen at all. Rather than addressing her directly, in this example, Samuel refers to Diana as "she." His message, in itself offensive if taken seriously, is even more insulting given his choice of pronoun. Not only does Samuel suggest that Diana looks better when she is not visible, but he effectively renders her absent by speaking about her as though she were not present. Despite the insults, however, Samuel and Diana's laughter in 055 reveals that the comments are not interpreted seriously.

At the same time, the utterances in 052 (Samuel: $_p$"When it's very dark she looks a lot better") and 053 (Diana: "Samuel, you wouldn't <u>know</u> would you?") are significant in another way, namely, with regard to what they reveal about the state of Samuel's and Diana's relationship. Both remarks could be interpreted as sexual innuendo, although, as Samuel and Diana later confirmed, only Diana's utterance was intended as double-entendre. By commenting as she does ("You wouldn't <u>know</u>, would you?"), Diana highlights the fact that she and Samuel have just reached the point in their relationship at which a shift from platonic to romantic involvement is imminent. Since Diana had been interested in changing the status of their relationship for quite some time before Samuel began to show similar interest, her remark has the effect of commenting on Samuel's hesitancy in a teasing way. In other words, had Samuel not shown reluctance about becoming lovers, rather than "just friends," presumably his state of "not knowing" would be irrelevant.

In addition to the use of pronouns in teasing, the repetition of Diana's telling Samuel to "shut up" and the "Samuel? Yes dear?" exchange also underscore important aspects of Samuel's and Diana's relationship. For ease of reference, I repeat a portion of the bathroom mirror segment here, but concentrate my discussion on the use of formulae.

040   Carolyn: You think you that look different in-
041   in different mirrors?
042   Diana: Well, you never ⌐ kno:ow. One hopes hh.
043   Samuel: └ Noo, no:a
044   you don't. ⌐ You actually-
045   Diana: $_f$└ Samuel, shu:t up [laughs].
046   Samuel: [laughs]

In 045 Diana tells Samuel to "shut up" after he has disagreed with her reasoning about the mirror in 043/044 ("Noo, no:a you don't. You actually-").

That Diana's command is not intended seriously is suggested by a combination of the prosodic features of her utterance—the elongation of the vowel in "shut" and her sudden loudness—and laughter by both participants.

Samuel's and Diana's exchange "Samuel? Yes, dear?" first appears in the extension of the same example.

```
053   Diana:    Samuel, ⌐              ⌐you wouldn't know, would you?
054   Samuel:            └ Yes, dear? ┘
055             [Samuel and Diana laugh]
```

What is interesting about the "Samuel? Yes, dear?" routine is that Samuel's "Yes, dear?" affords him the opportunity of feigning that he either has not heard or understood Diana's comment "you wouldn't know, would you?" However, their mutual laughter indicates that he has understood, if not the innuendo, at the very least, the playfulness of Diana's utterance. Indeed, the "Samuel? Yes, dear?" formula echoes a stereotype of conversation between long-married couples, which takes on special meaning since their relationship is new. Thus, both patterns, Diana's recurring use of "shut up" as a response to Samuel and the "Samuel? Yes, dear?" exchange, provide sources of fun, rather than anger, and suggest comfortable familiarity.

Another example involving "shut up" appears in a stretch of teasing in which Diana, who has just finished her second phone call to Jane (to report that we had finally decided to go to Charlottesville), makes an emotional exclamation in 583 ("Oh, no:o!"), for which she gives an unintelligible explanation in 586 ("I have the / ? /"). This utterance once more invites teasing by Samuel and me:

```
583   Diana:               Oh, no:o!
584   Carolyn:  What? Jane's not home?
585   Samuel:            └No?
586   Diana:    No, she's home. I have the / ? /
587             Okay ⌐              └shut up.
588   Samuel:         └ ⌐Oooh, ⌐oooh, oh ⌐wo-ow.
589   Carolyn:                    └That's terrible.
590   Diana:    ⌐Shut up!.
591             accYou're not making me lose my temper.
592             Okay.
```

Although it has not been possible to reconstruct Diana's entire utterance in 586 ("No, she's home. I have the / ? /"), it is clear that Samuel and I tease Diana in a way that trivializes her loud exclamation ("Oh, no!") in 583 and her unintelligible explanation in 586. Rather than showing empathy or concern (which would be our response if Diana's complaint were serious), we tease by showing mock concern for her predicament in 588 (Samuel: "⌐Oooh, ⌐ooh, oh ⌐wo-ow") and 589 (Carolyn: "That's terrible"). To this, Diana responds with "Shut up, Shut up!" in 587 and 590, which, said while laughing, indicates the nonseriousness of her remark. Nonseriousness is maintained as Samuel ignores her command in 591 "You're not making me lose my temper"—an indirect way of saying "Don't make me lose my temper"—and instead continues to tease, as described in the next example.

Teasing here begins as Samuel exploits the fact that Diana dozed while en route to Washington earlier the same morning:

```
593  Samuel:   Are you gonna sleep again?
594            It was really nice on the way down
595            because she was so quiet.
596            [Carolyn and Diana laugh]
```

By asking "Are you gonna sleep again?" in 593 and describing her in the third person in the next utterance (595 "She was so quiet"), Samuel talks about Diana just as one might in reference to a child. Not only is his choice of pronoun marked in the same way as was pointed out with respect to the bathroom mirror example, but it is also children who are often expected to sleep on long journeys.

The observation that Diana is in teasing often relegated a conversational role as child is supported by a comment that Diana herself makes near the end of the larger nonserious segment of discourse from which the previous examples were taken. At one point, Diana asks permission to use my bathroom (600 "May I use your bathroom? Cal?"). This appears to invite teasing both because of the inanity of the question (of course she can use my bathroom) and the tentative way in which she poses it, that is, with marked rising intonation on both the body of the question (603 "May I use your bathroom?") and on my name ("Cal?"). Moreover, at this point in the conversation, all three of us have been engaged in a fairly extended frame of nonserious talk, so our playful comments successfully extend the frame.

```
600  Diana:    May I use your bathroom? Cal?
601  Carolyn:  No, you may not. You- you have to pay a
               toll. ⌐
602  Samuel:        └ No, no, Diana, it's not-
603  Diana:    [laughs]
604  Samuel:   No, no, Di.
605            We're in a hurry.
606  Samuel:   Diana, we're in a hurry.
607            You cannot go to the bathroom.
608  Diana:    I cannot what?
609  Samuel:   Go to the bathroom.
610  Diana:    It's free, Samuel [laughs].
611  Carolyn:  Well, otherwise she's gonna bother us all
612            the way down so it's better t:o- to, ah,
               let her go.
613  Samuel:          └ Right, well she will anyway.
614  Diana:    [yelling from the bathroom] I'm not gonna be
               the kid again this time!
615  Samuel:   ꜰYes you will!
```

After initially being denied permission to go to the bathroom (601 "No you may not. You- you have to pay a toll"), Diana, who is finally in the bathroom, yells in 614 "I'm not gonna be the kid again this time!" in reference to the planned drive to Charlottesville. While this comment maintains the teasing frame, it essentially refers to Sam's earlier question in 593 in which he asks whether she, like a child, will sleep during the trip ("Are you gonna sleep again?"). To Diana's exclamation that she will not "be the kid again," Samuel responds loudly and emphatically "fYes you will!". The intonation in these two utterances emphasizes the childlike demeanor assumed by (and imposed on) Diana: while her exclamation in 614 ("I'm not gonna be the kid again this time!") is high-pitched and drawn out like a child's whine, Samuel's response in 615 ("fYes you will!") is fast and loud, much like a parent's scolding. In addition, in this segment further reference to Diana is made by using "she." I state in 611 that Samuel and I ought to grant Diana's request to use the bathroom, for otherwise "she's gonna bother us," to which Samuel in 612 agrees, "Right, well she will anyway." Thus, this lengthy exchange suggests that the use of certain features not only contributes to the participants' interpretation of a frame as play, but results in the framing of particular conversational roles as well.

Finally, despite the apparent productivity of strategies involving marked pronominal use, formulae, or routines in teasing between intimates, it is also important to note that sometimes a participant, in this case Diana, may attempt to "break" a particular frame.

593   Samuel: Are you gonna sleep again?
594   It was really nice on the way down
595   because she was so quiet.
596   [Carolyn and Diana laugh]
597   Diana: Samuel?
598   Samuel: Yes, dear?
599   Diana: ⌊Shut-up? ⌊please? ⌊Ok-ay?
600   May I use your bathroom? Cal?.

Although Diana laughs with me in response to Samuel's reference to her sleeping in the car (593 "Are you gonna sleep again?"), she addresses Samuel by his first name (597 "Samuel?"), in a more serious, admonishing tone of voice. At this point, the lowered pitch in Diana's utterance indicates that she is poised to break the teasing frame. Samuel does not appear to have picked up on this cue in his immediate "Yes, dear?" response in 598, forcing Diana, who appears slightly irritated (indeed perhaps also because Samuel did not adjust to her shift in frame), to utter in 599 " ⌊Shut up? ⌊please? ⌊Okay?" in rising intonation, but with emphatically lower pitch. In other words, I propose that precisely because the "Samuel? Yes, dear?" exchange is a routine that Samuel and Diana frequently employ in their playful teasing talk, Diana's shift to a more serious frame is unexpected. Although Diana is ultimately unsuccessful in breaking the larger teasing frame (as we go on to deny her permission to use the bathroom), the point is that although this example reflects the productivity of certain routinelike exchanges in teasing among intimates, it also highlights the fine line drawn between "the playful nip" of teasing and the "hostile bite" of real antagonism.

To summarize the discussion thus far, several features or contextualization cues serve to frame as teasing each of the examples analyzed in this section. These features are used strategically by speakers to signal that they are teasing, rather than speaking seriously, and by other participants in order to interpret the talk appropriately. First, prosodic features set off each frame, and often it is precisely an exaggeration of those features, for example Diana's high-pitched "whiny" voice, which first triggers a tease. In Diana's case, such features appear also to contribute to her frequently assuming (or being assigned) a childlike role in the conversation. Second, exploiting certain pronouns either to "exclude" individuals from talk or to emphasize particular conversational roles becomes an effective resource for teasing, in these data contributing to a sense of collusion by Samuel and Carolyn at Diana's expense. Finally, despite the frequent conversational alignment of Samuel and Carolyn, specific routines or formulae involving only Samuel and Diana arise repeatedly in the teasing frames. In the following section, I will consider what these patterns reveal about the participants' respective relationships.

Teasing Routines and Participant Alignment

In order to compare the participants' relationships and the form of their talk, it is helpful to transpose the transcript of one of the larger teasing frames into column form. The example presented below as Table 7.1 is the extended frame of talk in which Samuel and I tease Diana by mocking her emphatic exclamation as she gets off the phone and later by denying her permission to use my bathroom. Arrows drawn between the participants' utterances show how and to whom speakers direct their talk. Table 7.1 shows that most of the teasing talk is directed toward Diana. Furthermore, it is apparent that while I tease Diana with Samuel, most teasing occurs as direct banter between the two of them.

Table 7.2 shows the figures calculated for all of the teasing that appears in the sixteen-minute segment of data initially analyzed for this chapter. The columns are arranged to show the number of turns taken by each participant that can be interpreted as teasing, as well as the participant to whom each instance of teasing is directed.

The table reveals several striking patterns and confirms many of the observations made in this chapter. First, out of 65 instances of teasing, Samuel is responsible for the highest number of teases (31/65 or 48%), followed by Diana (23/65 or 35%) and Carolyn (11/65 or 17%). Second, both Samuel and I direct *all* of our teasing remarks at Diana. Not one instance of teasing occurs in conversation between Samuel and me alone. Finally, although Diana does direct some teasing remarks toward me (4/23 or 17%), the overwhelming majority of her teasing is directed at Samuel (19/23 or 83%). Why these consistent patterns?

Table 7.1 Speaker Alignment

Diana	Samuel	Carolyn
oh, no:o!		
	//no?]*	What? Jane's//not home?]*
no, she's home.		
I have the / ? /		
//okay]	oooh,//ooh, oh wo-ow!]:	//that's terrible]
₍f₎shut up. shut up!		
₍acc₎You're not making me		
lose my temper. okay.		
	are you gonna sleep again? it was really nice on the way down because she was so quiet.	
//laugh] Samuel?		//laugh]
	yes, dear?	
shut up? please?		
okay?		
may I use your bathroom? Cal?		
	//no, no, Diana it's not-	no, you may not. you- // you have to pay a toll]
laughs		
	we're in a hurry. Diana, we're in a hurry. you cannot go to the bathroom.	
I cannot what?		
	go to the bathroom.	
it's free, Samuel. [laughs]		
		well, otherwise she's gonna bother us all the way down
	//right, well she will anyway]	//so it's better to let her go]

*// ...] = overlapping speech.

Samuel, Diana, and Carolyn: On the whole, it is clear that all three participants engage in the teasing activity, suggesting some degree of familiarity in their relationships. Although the teasing builds on argumentative forms such as challenges and insults, the distinct prosodic features, laughter, marked pronoun use, and repetition of specific routines contribute to the

Table 7.2   Allocation of Teasing Turns

Name	No. Teasing Turns	No. Teasing @ Diana	No. Teasing @ Carolyn	No. Teasing @ Samuel
Samuel	31	31	0	—
Diana	23	—	4	19
Carolyn	11	11	—	0
Totals	65	42	4	19

speakers' understanding of the metamessage "this is play" (Bateson 1972). The fact that all participants join in the banter and that no one is forced to state explicitly, "I was only teasing" (see Tannen 1986:60), underscores their mutual understanding—and enjoyment—of the frames. As Tannen (1986:62) observes, understanding unstated meaning "sends a meta-message of rapport." In sum, "successful" or felicitous teasing suggests that the participants have relationships in which they already enjoy considerable rapport. Teasing also provides a conversational arena for further developing these ties.

Samuel and Carolyn versus Diana: As observed in my analysis, Samuel and I frequently "team" together to tease Diana, whereas we do not tease each other. In addition, Diana's rejoinders are primarily aimed at Samuel, rather than at me. To explain these patterns, it is useful to draw on Brown and Levinson's ([1978] 1987:61) notion of "face," or an individual's "public self-image." Since the friendships between Diana and me and between Diana and Samuel are already well established, the threat to Diana's "self-image" by either Samuel or me individually or by Samuel and me together is minimal. On the other hand, since Samuel and I have only met for the second time on this occasion, it is likely that a direct exchange of teasing—in which the interpretation of antagonistic discourse forms relies on the understanding of subtle linguistic cues—would run a greater risk of misinterpretation. By playfully aligning as we do against Diana, Samuel and I mitigate the risk of jeopardizing a beginning friendship and at the same time create an opportunity for developing mutual appreciation and rapport.

Samuel and Diana: The final issue which I address is Samuel's and Diana's apparently well-developed teasing relationship. Evidence for such a relationship includes the high concentration of utterances exchanged in the teasing frames by Samuel and Diana—despite my participation—and the repetition of teasing routines such as "Samuel? Yes, dear?" and Diana's telling Samuel to "shut up." Several explanations strike me as relevant.

First, it is likely that teasing between Samuel and Diana is a matter of conversational style. While not statistically significant, the figures presented in Table 7.2 showed that Samuel was responsible for 48 percent of the teasing appearing in the data, while Diana's contribution accounted for 35 percent of the teasing turns. In contrast, only 17 percent of those turns were taken by me. According to Tannen, (1984:130) "the use of humor" is "one of the most distinctive aspects of any person's style." As Diana reported to me, although she and I might tease each other, she would never admonish me to "shut up" or use expletives to "insult" me. When asked why such behavior is acceptable with Samuel, Diana responded that "Samuel asks for it." In other words, Samuel's conversational style is marked by his proclivity to tease. Diana noted further that in order to "defend" herself and to participate in Samuel's verbal game, she attempts to return in kind. Often when she cannot think of an appropriate sally to one of Samuel's playful barbs, she resorts to saying "shut up."

Second, the banter between Samuel and Diana may also be related to what Schiffrin (1984) has termed "sociable argument." In a study of a group of Jewish speakers in Philadelphia, Schiffrin found that many exchanges in her data assumed argumentive form "without the serious substance of argument" (p. 331). Instead, the arguments

> seem to show that the interactants' relationship is close enough to withstand what would be considered by outsiders to be verbal assaults. Sociable argument displays the tolerance of conflict through the playful enactment of such conflict—tolerance made possible by the taken-for-granted level of intimacy of the relationship. (p. 331)

Although Schiffrin's analysis does not focus on teasing as such, I maintain that teasing is similar to sociable argument in that it reflects familiarity and intimacy despite antagonistic form. In addition, it is worth noting that Samuel identifies primarily with his Jewish heritage. While the data presented in this chapter do not point to a definitive link between Samuel's teasing and his cultural background, they do point to the need for further study of the cultural conditioning of socially relevant "play."

Finally, although Samuel and Diana's teasing seems very much to grow out of their relationship, their ability to engage so deftly in teasing talk has probably contributed to their "becoming a couple" (Tannen, personal communication). As Tannen (1989:13) points out, "coherence and involvement" are the frequent result (and goal) of discourse meaning created by "familiar strategies." Teasing—and the "routines" employed within the teasing frames examined here—might be viewed as a type of "familiar strategy" that relies on and contributes to a speaker's sense of conversational involvement. In turn, such involvement "sends a metamessage of rapport between the communicators, who thereby experience that they share communicative conventions and inhabit the same world of discourse" (p. 13). Thus, while Samuel and Diana seem regularly to insult and argue with one another, their contentious banter displays and nurtures—rather than threatens—their closeness.[3]

Conclusions

In this chapter, I have used examples from adult conversation to highlight features that speakers use to create and identify teasing talk and argue that the emerging alignments can be understood only with regard to the participants' specific relationships. In the conversation analyzed here, teasing—to rely on Bateson's (1972) term—evolves as "play": in a paradoxical inversion of sense and form, antagonistic discourse structures carry a metamessage of rapport. Since a felicitous interpretation of the metamessage of play relies on the shared understanding of subtle linguistic cues, it is not surprising that the nature of teasing appears linked to the relative closeness of the individuals involved: whereas in a tentative relationship direct teasing might be cautiously avoided, in an intimate one, it may be vigorously pursued. Although the alliances created in teasing can reflect existing friendships, these same alliances enhance relationships by affording speakers "safe" opportunities for showing conversational involvement and rapport.

*Appendix A: Transcription Conventions**

___	emphatic stress
CAPS	very emphatic stress
⌈	high pitch on phrase, until punctuation
⌊	low pitch on phrase, until punctuation
.	sentence final falling intonation
?	rising intonation
-	glottal stop
:	lengthened vowel
→	point of analysis
=	to right or left of utterance indicates continuation
,	phrase final falling intonation
p	soft voice
f	loud voice
acc	noticeable increase in tempo
dec	noticeable decrease in tempo
/?/	impossible transcription
/words/	uncertain transcription
[ ]	overlapping speech
⌊	latching
[laugh]	extended laughter
[hh]	chuckle
∿∿∿	laughter while talking

Appendix B: Participants and Setting

Setting: Carolyn's studio apartment in upper Georgetown, Washington, D.C.

Time: The first Sunday of Georgetown's week-long Spring Break, March 1989.

Participants:

Diana, 28, Carolyn's "best friend" since they were undergraduate roommates almost ten years earlier; Chinese American, born and raised in Wilmington, Delaware; recently returned to the East Coast after several years in Honolulu, Hawaii; at the time of this recording, a first-year business school student.

Samuel, 30, of Polish Jewish descent; born and raised in a Jewish community in Monterrey, Mexico; first language is Spanish, but has lived, worked and studied in the United States for over ten years and is a fluent English speaker; primary identification not with Mexican but with American/Eastern European Jewish culture; also a first-year business student; Samuel and Diana live in the same apartment building and are about to begin a relationship.

Carolyn, 28, the hostess, born in Quebec, Canada, but grew up in a German-American household in Maine; recently returned from a five-year residence in Berlin, West Germany, where she worked as an English instructor; currently a graduate student in linguistics at Georgetown; although this occasion is only the second time that Carolyn and Samuel have met, they both know a great deal about one another through Diana.

Figure 7.1. Carolyn's apartment.

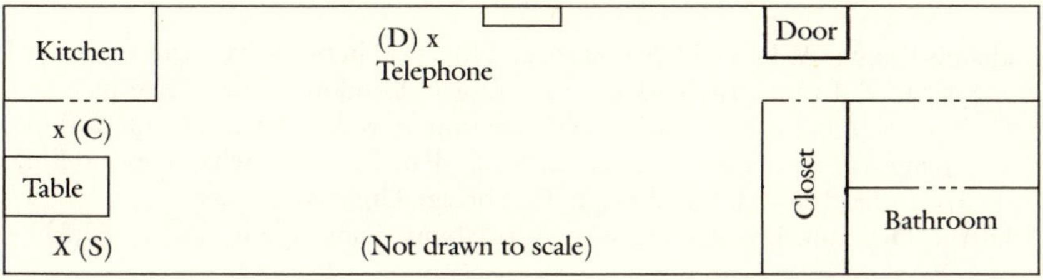

Notes

1. Line numbers in the examples presented in this chapter refer to those in the original transcript.

2. The fact that Samuel and I choose to "criticize" Diana's height is interesting, since it is a quality she cannot change. In general, in white middle-class culture, teasing that pokes fun at relatively "inalienable" characteristics—for instance, one's less than perfect build or the size of one's ears or nose—entails the risk of truly offending. However, in this case, the topic of our teasing appears sufficiently absurd, and Diana's height an innocuous enough target, so as not to risk offense.

3. I would like to add that as of this writing, Samuel and Diana are still together, with teasing embellishing as much, if not more, of their everyday conversation.

References

Apte, Mahadev. 1985. Humor and laughter: An anthropological approach. Ithaca: Cornell University Press.

Apte, Mahadev. 1983. Humor research, methodology and theory in anthropology.

Handbook of humor research, Vol. I, ed. by Paul E. McGhee and Jeffrey H. Goldstein, 183–212. New York: Springer Verlag.

Bateson, Gregory. 1972. Steps to an ecology of the mind. New York: Ballantine Books.

Brown, Penelope and Stephen Levinson. [1978] 1987. Politeness: Some universals in language usage. Cambridge: Cambridge University Press.

Drew, Paul. 1987. Po-faced receipts of teases. Linguistics 25:219–253.

Eder, Donna. 1993. "Go get ya a French!": Romantic and sexual teasing among adolescent girls. Gender and conversational interaction, ed. by Deborah Tannen. Oxford and New York: Oxford University Press.

Eisenberg, Ann. 1986. Teasing: Verbal play in two Mexicano homes. Language socialization across cultures, ed. by Bambi B. Schieffelin and Elinor Ochs, 182–97. Cambridge: Cambridge University Press.

Fine, Gary Alan. 1983. Sociological approaches to the study of humor. Handbook of humor research, Vol. I, ed. by Paul E. McGhee and Jeffrey H. Goldstein, 159–81. New York: Springer Verlag.

Goffman, Erving. 1981. Forms of talk. Philadelphia: University of Pennsylvania Press.

Gumperz, John J. 1982. Discourse strategies. Cambridge: Cambridge University Press.

Miller, Peggy. 1986. Teasing as language socialization and verbal play in a white working-class community. Language socialization across cultures, ed. by Bambi B. Schieffelin and Elinor Ochs, 199–212. Cambridge: Cambridge University Press.

Radcliffe-Brown, A. R. 1952. Structure and function in primitive society. Forward by E. E. Evans-Pritchard and Fred Eggan. London: Cohen & West.

Schieffelin, Bambi. 1986. Teasing and shaming in Kaluli children's interactions. Language socialization across cultures, ed. by Bambi B. Schieffelin and Elinor Ochs, 165–81. Cambridge: Cambridge University Press.

Schiffrin, Deborah. Jewish argument as sociability. Language in Society 13:311–55.

Tannen, Deborah. 1984. Conversational style: Analyzing talk among friends. Norwood, NJ: Ablex.

Tannen, Deborah. 1986. That's not what I meant!: How conversational style makes or breaks relationships. New York: Ballantine.

Tannen, Deborah. 1989. Talking voices: Repetition, dialogue, and imagery in conversational discourse. Cambridge: Cambridge University Press.

8

"Speaking for Another" in Sociolinguistic Interviews:

Alignments, Identities, and Frames

DEBORAH SCHIFFRIN

Georgetown University

Introduction

Our knowledge of linguistic variation within speech communities depends largely on speech produced by people during a social occasion that has come to be known as the "sociolinguistic interview." Although sociolinguistic interviews are similar in some ways to other types of interviews, i.e., asymmetrically structured speech events in which one person seeks to gain specific information from another, they are also quite different. One source of this difference is that both participants (interviewer and interviewee) are encouraged to introduce topics and to shift topics away from an already loosely structured agenda—in effect, to avoid the question/answer format and fixed topic structure typical of many institutional interviews (Labov 1984). Such shifts reduce the asymmetry underlying the participation structure of many interviews: not only can both interviewer and interviewee introduce topics, but both can ask and answer questions, tell stories, and so

My sociolinguistic fieldwork was carried out in Philadelphia with the support of a research grant from NSF (BNS75-00245) to William Labov (Principal Investigator) for analysis of linguistic change and variation. For fuller description of the data see Schiffrin (1987:41–47). More recent analyses have been facilitated by a research grant from NSF (BNS88-19845) for a sociolinguistic analysis of topic. I am grateful for these sources of support. I also thank Deborah Tannen for comments on an earlier draft.

on. What this means is that sociolinguistic interviews allow a variety of exchange types (including, but not limited to, question/answer sequences) and permit a number of different speech activities, such as stories, descriptions, and arguments. One result of this is that sociolinguistic interviews can provide data useful not just for those interested in phonological and grammatical variation, but also for those interested in the discovery and analysis of discourse patterns (for examples, see Schiffrin 1984a, 1984b, 1987, 1991).

Just as sociolinguistic interviews can benefit discourse analysis, so, too, can the insights of discourse analysis be fruitfully applied to sociolinguistic interviews. One application is methodological. The influence of discourse analysis is found in the way researchers design procedures to collect data. Building upon Bell's (1984) ideas about audience design, for example, recent studies of French Canadian (Paradis forthcoming) and African American speech communities (Rickford 1993) demonstrate that alterations in the identity of the interviewer (i.e., speaker/hearer relationship) have systematic effects on phonological and grammatical variation. Another methodological application concerns the coding of utterances as tokens of particular types, and the coding of informants as representative of certain social categories. In Schiffrin (forthcoming (a)), for example, I build upon conversation analytic views of social identity to suggest that informants' social identities (e.g., gender, race, age) during interviews are no less situated than those that emerge during other activities, and that coding a speaker as a white middle class female, for example, may misrepresent the situated nature of that identity.

I have suggested thus far that sociolinguistic interviews sit at a methodological juncture between variationist and interactional approaches in sociolinguistics. My goal in this chapter is to use several constructs and concepts from interactional approaches—frames, participant alignments, and identity displays—to analyze a particular interactive move (what I call "speaking for another") that I noticed in sociolinguistic interviews I conducted in Philadelphia. Such an analysis enhances our understanding of discourse in general (since speaking for another is an interactive move, not restricted to sociolinguistic interviews, that has not previously been described) and provides a way to view two constraints (identity and context) that are critical to analyses of linguistic variation.

After describing some general features of speaking for another (2.0), I analyze the way two participants in a sociolinguistic interview (a husband and wife, Henry and Zelda) speak for another (their younger female neighbor, Irene; (3.0)). I then show how speaking for another locates and relocates participants relative to an interview frame (4.0). My conclusion considers how participation frameworks and identity displays are related to interactive frames through which utterances are interpreted (5.1), and how such analyses can further develop a reciprocity between variationist and interactional approaches in sociolinguistics (5.2).

Before I begin, I want to clarify the key terms I will be using: frames, participant alignments, and identity displays. I use the term "frame" to refer primarily to what Tannen and Wallat (this volume) call "interactive frames": what people think they are doing when they talk to each other. Interactive frames are related to what they refer to as "knowledge schemas" (a structure of knowledge about situations, actions, and actors) simply because such schemas provide expectations not only about what can happen, but about how to interpret what is said and done (Goffman 1974, Gumperz 1982, Tannen and Wallat this volume). Participant alignments are related to the way interactants position themselves relative to one another, e.g., their relationships of power and solidarity, their affective stances, their footing (Goffman [1979] 1981b); they are part of the broader notion of participation structure (or framework), i.e., the way that speaker and hearer are related to their utterances and to one another (Goffman 1981a:3). I use the term "identity display" to refer to the way a particular utterance (or action) can display those social roles and statuses that are sometimes thought to be relatively stable and enduring properties of persons (e.g., one's gender, social class, ethnicity).

Speaking for Another

Among the many assumptions that we make when we engage in conversation is that the person who has something to say is the one who can and should say it. This assumption—the "speak for yourself" rule—may be seen as part of what Goffman (1967a:12) called the "traffic rules of social interaction." Such rules reflect a tacit agreement between self and other to protect the other in exchange for protection of oneself (Goffman 1967a, 1967b): more specifically, because the speak for yourself rule (when applied symmetrically) gives both parties a license to make their own contribution to talk, in exchange for a willingness to refrain from making another's contribution, we can also see this rule as an offer of mutual deference to negative face wants: i.e., it serves peoples' desire not to be intruded upon (Brown and Levinson 1987).

One indication of the strength of the speak for yourself rule is that if we *do* speak for another, e.g., if we report another's words as "constructed dialogue" (Tannen 1989:chapter 4), we are required to use a wide array of devices (grammatical and/or paralinguistic) to show displacement in person, space, and time from the "I," "here," and "now" of the current situation. Note, also, that the one for whom we are most likely to construct dialogue is probably not someone who is with us at the time, especially not one to whom we are directing our speech (i.e., an addressed recipient, Goffman 1981): indeed, reporting the words of an addressed recipient to that recipient (e.g., "You said . . . ") seems likely to be heard as a challenge to the veracity or appropriateness of what was said. And even when we make statements about another's internal state—something that only the other is in a position to know about (Labov and Fanshel's [1977:226–228] B-events)—they are heard as requests for confirmation from the one about whom the state is predicated: saying "You're hungry," for example, elicits (at the least) either a confirmation or a denial of the state about whom it is assumed to hold.

Another indication of the strength of the speak for yourself rule is that we have folk terms that evaluate violations of the rule. Before discussing these folk terms, let us examine an example of speaking for another.

(1) (a)   Henry: Y'want a piece of candy?
     (b)   Irene: No.
     (c)   Zelda: She's on a diet.

(1) is an interchange from the "setting up" phase of a sociolinguistic interview: it occurred after I had explained how we would start our interview (with word lists and minimal pair tests) and while I was setting up my tape recorder and arranging my papers at the kitchen table. In (1a), Henry is offering his neighbor Irene a piece of candy; in (1b), Irene turns down the offer. Zelda (Henry's wife) is an unaddressed recipient of the offer: not only was the offer not made to her, but she was not at the kitchen table when it was issued. In saying *She's on a diet,* Zelda speaks for Irene: not only does she say something about Irene (referring to her with the third person pronoun *she*), but her utterance is in a sequential position that Irene could have occupied herself (people often provide their own accounts when they reject an offer) and whose main relevance bears on the exchange between Irene and Henry (Irene has turned down Henry's offer).

One of the key insights of interactional sociolinguistics is that meaning is situated. As shown by Bennett (1978) and Tannen (1984, 1989), for example, the turn-taking structure during which one person's utterance (or part thereof) is simultaneous with another's can be labeled in two quite different ways: as "interruption" (with negative connotations) or as "overlap" (with neutral or even positive connotations). Which label it receives (i.e., which metamessage is conveyed) depends on how that turn-taking structure is contextualized by speech activity, participant, and so on.

Our folk terms for referring to contributions like *She's on a diet* suggest that like many other interactive moves, speaking for another has little inherent meaning in and of itself. Like simultaneous speech, then, speaking for another can be interpreted in either a negative or a positive way. Its negative sense, glossed perhaps as "butting in," is consistent with an interpretation of the act as a violation of negative politeness (Brown and Levinson 1987) and as a violation of an avoidance ritual (Goffman 1967b): one is so invasive of another that she does not allow her to maintain her own position in conversation (cf. "You're always putting words in my mouth"). Its positive sense, glossed perhaps as "chipping in," is consistent with an interpretation of the act as a display of positive politeness (Brown and Levinson 1987) and as a presentational ritual (Goffman 1967b): one shares so much with another that she is able to take her position in conversation (cf. "You know me so well you can read my mind!"). Thus, speaking for another can be seen as either deferential, or demeaning, to the one being spoken for.

Before we discuss the meaning of specific instances of speaking for another, it is helpful to note some of the more general contextual factors that figure in such decisions—factors having to do with social relationship, social identities, speech event, and activity. Although space prevents me from a full examination of the interactive meanings of this move, it seems to be interpreted depending upon how responsibility for speaking comes to be transferred (does the spokesperson "take" responsibility or is it "given" to her?) and on how that transfer is viewed by participants (as intrusion or as welcome participation). Sometimes the right to make such a transfer is institutionally allocated, such that its meanings can be partially derived from institutionally sanctioned roles that may either free one from the need to speak for oneself or force another to accede her own speaking rights (McDermott 1987). To take some simple examples, I recently received a phone call in which a secretary, referring to her boss in the third person, said "Professor Robinson is calling you. He'll be with you in a moment." Part of the secretary's institutionalized responsibility was thus to speak for another (the boss) who was freed from the need to speak for himself. In different circumstances, however, using a third party to initiate (or even sustain) a phone call for oneself can reflect quite differently upon the status of the spoken-for, as when, for example, parents arrange play dates for their children who do not yet have the communicative competence to do so themselves.

Even during institutionally based occasions of talk, however, the meanings of speaking for another can vary. Let us take a hypothetical example. Suppose that a person who has just immigrated to another country is filling out papers and answering questions during a gate-keeping encounter with authorities and cannot understand enough of the indigenous language to answer a particular question from an interviewer; another person (e.g., an official translator, an accompanying relative, or a passing stranger) may become a spokesperson. Participants' interpretations of this act can vary depending on how responsibility to speak for another was transferred: e.g., did the spokesperson offer to help or intervene, did the spokesperson agree to a request from another (either the interviewee or the interviewer), and so on. Participant point of view may also vary: e.g., the spokesperson may feel a sense of solidarity with the spoken-for person that is not at all shared. Thus, even a single act of speaking for another, performed by those in relatively institutionally allocated roles, can have a range of different meanings.

The range of interpretations that can hold for speaking for another expands during conversation—when acts are bound not only (or not even) to institutional status and role, but to more fluid an emergent interactional positions and participant footings. Because participant roles shift during conversation, the right either to take or to abdicate responsibility for one's words can also shift. What this means is that the interactional meaning of speaking for another depends on current perceptions of alignments—such that speaking for another during a conversation can just as easily be positively or negatively glossed (as noted above). Furthermore, since social relationships are also reinforced (if not even created) during conversation, speaking for another during conversation can have not only local interactive meaning, but broader implications about one's own (and the other's) rights, privileges, and responsibilities.

Although the interactional meanings of speaking for another are by no means stable or determinate, there are some stable (and identificatory) features of this act. A key feature is that three participant roles are required. We might label these roles with the relatively standard terms associated with a code model of communication (Schiffrin 1990, forthcoming,b:chapter 9): a source is responsible for the content of a message, a recipient is the intended target of the source's message, and a sender acts as a spokesperson mediating the transmission of the message from source to receiver. We can also use Goffman's analysis of participant structure to be even more specific about these roles: since one person (the sender/spokeperson) produces a message whose content is the responsibility of another (the source), we can say that one person is acting as animator for another person who is in a principal role. Although we may still speak of a spokesperson, and a spoken-for person, then, the ways in which the two parties can be said to be "speaking" involve very different notions of selfhood—the former, the mechanical aspects of an animator; the latter, the more moral aspects of a principal. Thus, when Zelda says *She's on a diet* in (1), for example, she is an animator for Irene's principal: Zelda is reporting something about Irene that Irene could have said herself (being on a diet is personal information) and to whose sentiments (or content) Irene is committed.

In the next section, I build upon these preliminary observations about speaking for another to discuss the way this interactive move alters the participation framework and displays gender identities, during sociolinguistic interviews. My examples include, but are not limited to, Zelda's specific utterance *She's on a diet*.

The Negotiation of Participation and Identity

I focus initially in this section on an excerpt from (1). I then present other instances in which one speaker (either Henry or Zelda) speaks for Irene.[1] For each instance, I describe in detail how this particular interactive move alters participant alignments and provides a potential display of identity.

Let us begin again with (1), presented here in more detail.

(1)   Henry: (a)   Y'want a piece of candy?
       Irene: (b)   No. ⌐   ⌐ I don't-=
       Zelda: (c)   └ She's on a diet. ⌐ |
       Debby: (d)   └ Who's └ NOT on a diet.
       Irene: (e)   =I'm on a diet
                 (f)   and my mother ⌐ buys-=
       Zelda: (g)   └ You're not!

Irene:	(h)	= my	mother buys these mints. =
Debby:	(i)		Oh yes I amhhh!
Zelda:	(j)		Oh yeh.

As I noted above, speaking for another is an act whose meaning is interactionally situated, such that we must depend upon contextual information to infer even a potential meaning. I believe that Zelda's *She's on a diet* is both intended and interpreted in a positive way—as the sort of "chipping in" noted above.

One source of evidence that *She's on a diet* has a supportive meaning is the way this move is interactively situated: it is located during a supportive interchange (Goffman 1971). Note, first, that after Zelda's *She's on a diet,* I generalize the applicability of 'diet' with a rhetorical question (*Who's not on a diet* (d)). Zelda's response (*You're not* (g)) remedies the negative self-assessment that being on a diet implies (i.e., being overweight), but I persist in generalizing 'diet' at least to myself (*Oh yes I amhhh!* (i)). Overlapping this exchange between me and Zelda, Irene shifts from her own utterance (*I don't-* in (b)) to repeat the account offered by Zelda (*I'm on a diet* (e)). Irene's repetition leads into a story—a story that shows that she is so serious about dieting that she deceives her mother, who has given her candy, by throwing the candy out the window (see Schiffrin, forthcoming,b:chapter 4). Thus, the remarks about diet all function to minimize potential insults to weight (and physical appearance) and to build solidarity: my generalization of 'diet' ((d), (i)) and Zelda's remark that I'm not on a diet (g) build solidarity through positive politeness.

Another source of evidence that *She's on a diet* is a move with supportive meaning is that it is enacted by someone who acts supportive in other contexts and is viewed (by Irene) as a supportive person. Zelda and Irene are two close friends and longtime next-door neighbors: although Zelda is about twenty years older than Irene, both are mothers with three children; furthermore, although two of Zelda's children are married and have their own children, Zelda's youngest daughter (a teenager) is a classmate of Irene's eldest son. Zelda and Irene have multiple opportunities for interaction, and multiple ways to relate to one another. One source of evidence for their relationship is what they say about one another. In (2), for example, Irene answered a question about her neighborhood by describing the advantages of having a neighbor like Zelda.

(2) Cause I- I like to know that in case I need something, like with Zelda, or: y'know she's been a big help to me like since I'm workin' the kids- kids always here or in an emergency she's here to get them or whatever until I can get there. So: I know I have a girlfriend that lives in Horsham, and she doesn't know her neighbor on either side. Y'know? And I'm not that kind of person. Like in the wintertime, when you're snowed in and this and that, at least you can run next door, talk to somebody if you feel like you're gonna get closed in with the walls.

These comments reveal not only Irene's closeness with, but dependence on, Zelda. Some of Zelda's comments about Irene (although not included here) also reveal that their bond is built not just on friendship, i.e., a form of solidarity, but on mutual need: e.g., Irene helps Zelda shop for clothes for her teenage daughter (since Irene is younger, Zelda believes that she knows more about adolescent taste in clothing). Thus, Zelda is viewed by Irene as someone who acts supportive in other contexts and can be counted on as a supportive person.

Applying what we know about Zelda and Irene's relationship to the interactional meaning of *She's on a diet* reveals an especially acute link between their social relationship and this particular speech activity. We saw above that the friendship between Zelda and Irene is based on their similarities (they are neighbors; they are both mothers of adolescents) and their dependencies (stemming partially from their differences in age and experience). In other words, Zelda and Irene are in a relationship of solidarity, but it is a solidarity that is based on both their similarities and their differences. The participation framework created when Zelda speaks for Irene exhibits the same shared responsibility and mutual dependence that typify their friendship. Recall that Irene has just turned down an offer of candy from Henry. By providing an account for Irene's rejection of Henry's offer—note, before Irene's own account (which repeats Zelda's)—Zelda is creating a participation framework that mirrors (on a small scale) the more general bond that she shares with Irene: just as Zelda "is there" to help Irene with her children or to provide company during snowstorms (see (2)), so too, Zelda "is there" to help Irene soften the potentially threatening meanings created by her rejection of Henry's offer. Another way of saying this is that when Zelda says *she's on a diet,* her utterance serves the same general function as when she provides *a big help . . . in an emergency.* The difference is that the former displays solidarity on a microinteractional level (of talk) relevant to an expressive domain of Irene's life (her relationship with Henry), and the latter displays solidarity on a macrointeractional level (of social action) relevant to an instrumental domain of Irene's life (her ability to manage both her career and her family).

Finally, it is important to note that Zelda's account is built upon the provision of information about Irene that is essentially private information: being on a diet is something that one either has to observe about another or has to be told by that other. Thus, Zelda's account works by revealing information about Irene that had to be gleaned from a prior interaction and prior relationship (cf. Schiffrin 1984a). Although the revelation of information about another may actually threaten—rather than build—solidarity, I do not think this is the case here. Indeed, because we know that Henry, Irene, and Zelda often use openly competitive forms of talk for positive ends (Schiffrin 1984b), even an overtly negative gloss to *She's on a diet* might be reframed yet again: the ability to violate an avoidance ritual (to bypass negative politeness) playfully can attest to the strength of a relationship. Consider, also, that the information revealed by Zelda is essentially positive information about Irene: as typified by sayings such as "You can't be too rich or too thin," being thin is valued in American culture.[2] Furthermore, since being overweight is commonly interpreted as a lack of self-control, Zelda's account for Irene's refusal of the candy (and of course Irene's refusal itself) also portrays Irene in a positive way as someone who is "in control." Interestingly, these flattering portraits of Irene provide an implicit contrast with Henry—who (despite being overweight) is eating the candy.

We have seen, thus far, that *She's on a diet* is an interactive move with a supportive meaning. Although space does not permit extensive discussion of how Zelda and Henry speak for Irene (and for me, as well as each other), we will see in a moment that Zelda often speaks for Irene, or guides her toward speaking for herself, in a way that supports Irene's presence in the interaction. Henry, on the other hand, speaks for Irene in a more controlling manner—in effect, "putting words in her mouth." (3) is a striking example of the different ways that Henry and Zelda speak for Irene. In (3), I am asking questions about neighborhood life and friendships in an effort to learn about communication networks, a factor significant for the analysis of sociolinguistic variation.

(3)   Debby: (a)   Well, Irene, is there anybody around here that you would call a best friend?

          Irene: (b)   Now?

         Debby: (c)   Yeh. ⌐   hhhh

         Henry: (d)   ⌐In front of us?

          Zelda: (e)   No, we're not her best friends, we're her ⌐ neighbors!

         Henry: (f)   No! She's got a best friend.=

          Irene: (g)   No, ⌐ I don't really think any *one person* I=

         Henry: (h)   =But she's ⌐more of a friend to a=

          Irene: ⌐ =could say.

         Henry: =person than a person is to her.

          Zelda: (i)   ⌐She's not-

         Henry: (j)   ⌐ Let's put it ⌐ that way.=

          Irene: (k)   Yeh. ⌐ T'be honest. ⌐

         Henry: (l)   =And it- ⌐ it ⌐   ⌐ Am I right or wrong?

          Irene: (m)   ⌐ I ⌐ think ⌐ I've-

                      I've been getting ⌐ hurt, too much ⌐ lately.⌐

          Zelda: (n)   ⌐ Are you Irene?! ⌐

         Debby: (o)   ⌐Yeh.

         Henry: (p)   No but am I right or wrong Irene?

               (q)   I could see ⌐ some ⌐ damage! ⌐ Yeh.=

          Irene: (r)   ⌐ Yeh. ⌐   ⌐ I feel I'm hurt.=

         Henry: (s)   =⌐ See? ⌐

          Irene: (t)   =⌐ I ⌐ don't know how the other people feel.

Note, first, that my question in (a) is typical of a sociolinguistic interview frame: participants in such an interview understand that there is a main agenda in which one person (here thought of as "the interviewer") asks questions and another (here thought of as an "interviewee") answers questions (see (4.0)). Since both Henry and Zelda (in (d) and (e)) comment on, rather than allow Irene to answer, my question, their interchange maintains the interview frame, but slightly alters the allocation of participants into its question/answer format. In (f), Henry then speaks for Irene in what sounds like a supportive manner: *She's got a best friend.* He immediately uses his own assertion, however, to project, an inequity between the way Irene treats others (positively) and the way she is treated by others (negatively): *But she's more of a friend to a person, than a person is to her* ((h)). Although Henry's comparison reveals more about Irene than she might otherwise prefer, Irene does agree with Henry (in (k), (m)). Note that once Irene herself reveals "trouble," Zelda immediately offers sympathy on a personal level with *Are you Irene?!* (n). But Henry uses Irene's revelation of *getting hurt* as a basis for the correctness of his own assessment: he uses it to pursue the validity of his own point (*No but am I right or wrong Irene?* (p)), to reaffirm what he himself has seen (*I could see some damage!* (q)), and to gain consensus about his point (*See?* (s)). Thus, whereas Zelda offers support based on the personal implications of what Irene has said, i.e., how the inequity affects Irene herself, Henry uses Irene's situation as a basis from which to buttress a more general assessment of her dilemma.

The different ways that Henry and Zelda use the same interactive move (speaking for another) are reminiscent of Gilligan's (1982) findings about gender differences: instead of focusing on abstract principles and the impartial application of rules of right and wrong (the moral path favored by men), women emphasize human connections, caring, and the needs and situations of those affected by a problem. It is not only the different paths followed in (3) that suggest a gender difference: it is also the talk about diet in (1). Recall in (1), that it was Zelda who created a topic shift that is picked up by the two other women in the conversation—but not by Henry. It might seem that this is a topic of more interest to the women: i.e., women are traditionally assumed to be more concerned than men with personal topics such as physical appearance (Aries 1976). And some studies have shown that women talk a great deal about food and diets: Deakins (1989), for example, found that the third most frequent topic of women executives at lunch was diets.[3] But there might still be another explanation for the way that Henry and Zelda use the same interactive move for different ends—one that centers around the way they display (and create) gender identities through the structuring of participation frameworks.

That the differential construction of participation frameworks is a realization and reflection of gender is suggested by a variety of studies. Jones (1972) and Kalčik (1975), for example, suggest that women pursue topics of talk more interactively than men—that what one person proposes as a topic is progressively built upon by another. Cooperative topic building can easily be seen in terms of participation framework: it requires a joint alignment toward a focus of talk in which both addressor and addressee share the roles of animator and principal (Goffman's terms). Consistent with these findings is my own observation that Henry builds topics in ways less dependent upon others' active contributions (i.e., the listener places a relatively passive, supportive role) than either Irene or Zelda. Many of my questions to Henry, for example, were answered with lectures (Tannen 1990: 123–148): not only were Henry's turns at talk long with very few interruptions, but he imparted information, using traditional rhetorical devices, such as syntactic parallelism, to make a point. Studies of gender and dispute management can also be seen in terms of participation framework. Goodwin (1990), for example, shows that young African American girls have remarkably different ways of managing group conflict than do boys: such differences revolve around the use of stories as a means by which to create and recreate participation rights both inside and outside the group. Returning to Zelda and Henry, findings such as these suggest that the way the *diet* topic is pursued by Zelda, Irene, and me—but not by Henry—is due not just to topic relevance or personal importance per se, but to women's conceptions of what interactional needs should be pursued at that moment in the conversation, and to the way that it is participation in talk itself that can meet those needs.

Thus far, I have suggested the following: although both Zelda and Henry speak for Irene, their actions propose participant alignments that are strikingly different and whose difference is related to gender. One way to check this gender difference further is to examine other participant realignments—comparing those created during same-gender talk to those created during cross-gender talk. In (4), for example, I have been asking Zelda, Irene, and Henry about their personal contacts in the neighborhood (again, this is part of my efforts to learn about communication networks).

Debby:	(a)	How 'bout you Irene?
Irene:	(b)	What?
Debby:	(c)	Who would you-= ⌐
Zelda:	(d)	└Who would you ⌐ discuss it with?
Debby:	(e)	= └ if you had a hard day
		who would you complain to?
Zelda:	(f)	Jayhhhhh

In (4), Zelda speaks for me and for Irene. My initial question (*How 'bout you Irene?* (a)) is the focus of a request for clarification from Irene (*What?* (b)). It is Zelda who provides the clarification that Irene had requested from me: *Who would you discuss it with?* (d). Zelda's contribution overlaps with my own expansion of the question (in (c), (e)); note, also, how we both repeat the WH portion (*who would you*) of the question. In addition to sharing my questioning role, Zelda shares Irene's answering role by naming *Jay* (Irene's husband) in (f) as a potential answer. Thus, Zelda speaks first for me and then for Irene—her adoption of the two roles reproducing the structure of the question/answer sequence.

(4) continues with Irene's answer building upon Zelda's answer:

Irene:	(g)	Uh:: I don't know.
	(h)	Depending on what- what the problem really was, I might ⌈ talk ⌉ to a friend easier.=
Debby:	(i)	⌊ Yeh. ⌋
Irene:		=Than to a:-

In (g) and (h), Irene states that she might *talk to a friend easier*. By mentioning "friend," Irene is actually disagreeing with Zelda (who offered *Jay* as a candidate answer), although the disagreement is clearly mitigated with *uh::*, *I don't know,* and a contingency (*depending on what- what the problem really was*). Irene further explains her divergence from Zelda's suggestion by comparing herself to Zelda and Henry in (j). It is here that Henry joins the talk:

Irene:	(j)	=what- I'm not that family orientated.
Debby:	(k)	Uhhuh.
Irene:	(l)	⌈ Like they are. ⌉
Henry:	(m)	⌊ She should be. ⌋ She's got a nice family.

We saw a moment ago that Zelda's remarks reproduced the structure of the ongoing discourse and allowed others to maintain their participant roles. Henry's assessment (*She should be* (m)) of Irene's claim (*I'm not that family orientated. Like they are.* (j) (l)), however, shifts the participant alignment and forces others to fit their utterances into that framework. Whereas Zelda's remark created a duality in the speaker role (a split between animator [the spokesperson] and principal [the spoken-for]), Henry's assessment creates a duality in the addressee role: by assessing what Irene has said in her presence, and addressing that assessment to me, Henry divides his audience into an addressed recipient (me) and an unaddressed recipient (Irene).

Henry's realignment of the audience has an outcome quite different from the inclusionary effect of Zelda's utterances. In one sense, Henry's remarks exclude Irene from the interaction; at the very least, from active participation in the dialogue that Zelda and I had initiated and maintained. Furthermore, since Henry's remarks offer a moral assessment of the content of Irene's answer, they open Irene to scrutiny from me—a relative outsider to their group (cf. (3)). Thus, in one sense, Henry's remarks create a participation framework that can potentially separate co-participants from one another. In another sense, however, Henry's assessment draws Irene into interaction with him: although she is not formally addressed by his remarks (note the third person pronoun reference to Irene as *she*), she is certainly expected to hear what has been said about her. We can consider the effects of this in terms of Goffman's (1963) notion of information preserve and Brown and Levinson's ideas about politeness. Offering unsolicited advice about what is considered another's domain (e.g., closeness to family), particularly when what is said concerns what that other should do, is a violation of negative face—the sort of violation commonly called "not minding your own business" or "butting in." Thus, Henry does draw Irene into the interaction, but he does so by intruding upon her affairs and by forcing her to defend the management of those affairs.[4]

Consider what happens next:

Zelda:	(m)	Well ⌈ she really- wait a minute she doesn't=
Henry:	(n)	⌊ She's got lovely children.
Zelda:	(o)	=have ⌈ sisters, ⌉
Irene:	(p)	⌊ I'm not ⌋ talkin' about my children.
Zelda:	(q)	Right.
Henry:	(r)	Well you should make it so, it's good.
Zelda:	(s)	Oh! C'mon!
Irene:	(t)	Hen, I'm not you, Henry!
	(u)	We've- we've had family problems where my husband and his brother were in business.
	(v)	And at one time we were *very* close.
	(w)	And now it's just hello, goodbye, how are you, and that's it.

Although Zelda's defense of Irene (*Well she really- wait a minute she doesn't have sisters* (m) (o)) continues the participation framework opened by Henry (note her third person reference to Irene), Zelda and Irene continue to collaborate. Irene responds to Henry (*I'm not talking about my children* (p)) along the same general lines as Zelda (both narrowing Henry's reference to *family*). Zelda agrees with Irene's own defense (*Right* in (q)) even though Irene has bypassed the specific content of Zelda's defense. Finally, although Henry redirects his criticism to Irene herself (*Well you should make it so, it's good* (r)), Zelda continues to defend Irene by discouraging Henry's continued participation (*Oh! C'mon!* (s)). Despite Irene's and Zelda's collaboration, Henry's shift of the participation framework becomes dominant: Irene defends herself to Henry (*Hen, I'm not you Hen!* (t)) but also orients that defense to me (her description of family problems in (u)–(w)). Thus, although Irene rejects the relatively passive role of the unaddressed recipient status, her defense still conforms to the participation framework created by Henry—simply because she defends herself relative to both her challenger (Henry) and the recipient of the words to whom the challenge was ostensibly addressed (me).

(3) and (4) have both illustrated a difference in participant realignments predictable from previous scholarship on gender and discourse. Although both Zelda and Henry alter the participation framework, they do so in different ways: Zelda's realignment was more supportive and integrative; Henry's stance was more judgmental and divisive; in (4), Henry drew Irene into interaction by challenging her (an act requiring a defensive response) and by treating her as an unaddressed recipient (a position of relatively low status).

If the alignment differences just described for (1), (3), and (4) really are related to gender we would expect them to reappear during other exchanges—even those that do not involve speaking for another. Suppose, for example, that instead of providing Irene's account by saying *She's on a diet*, Zelda had created a slot in which Irene would have to provide her own account, e.g., *Tell him why you don't want it* or *Henry doesn't know why you refused*. Fortunately, there were two interchanges in my data that contain this alternative means of reorienting the content of another's talk: one person (either Zelda or Henry) prompts another (Irene) to produce (animate) what the prompter (as principal) had in mind. As we see, there are some striking differences in the division of responsibility for those realignments that seem to be predicted by gender—differences similar to those already seen.

First is an example of a realignment in same-gender talk:

```
(5)   Debby:   (a)    Yeh, who d'y'go bowling with?
      Irene:   (b)    My next door neighbors.
               (c)    We have a team in the summer we bowl.
               (d)    Every summer ⌈ they- husband and wife-     ⌉
      Zelda:   (e)              ⌊ Tell her who you bowl with ⌋
      Irene:   (f)    Who we *bowl* with.
      Zelda:   (g)    D- y' know the teams.
      Irene:   (h)    Oh. Wha' d' y' mean ⌈ the kids?
      Zelda:   (i)                        ⌊ The kids.
      Irene:   (j)    ⌈ Oh yeh, this year the kids have=      ⌉
      Henry:   (k)    ⌊ Kids. They have a very good thing. ⌋
      Irene:          =their own team,
               (l)    ⌈ =and they're- ⌈ they're giving us a run=
      Henry:   (m)    ⌊             ⌊ They got a good thing going.
      Debby:   (n)    ⌊ Oh great!
      Irene:   (o)    =for our money cause we- we're in first
                      place and they're in second, and they're-
                      they cheer every time we lose a game.
```

The section to focus upon begins with Zelda's overlapping speech in (e): *Tell her who you bowl with*. This remark is an other-initiated repair (Schegloff, Jefferson, and Sacks 1977): by prompting Irene to provide a specific piece of information, Zelda is redefining something Irene has already said as "incomplete," i.e. as a repairable. By so doing, Zelda inserts herself into what has thus far been a question/answer exchange between me and Irene. Her role is somewhat like that of a monitor of the exchange: she is assessing the adequacy of the answer and prompting Irene to animate what she herself has "in mind" as a suitable answer to the question. In terms of participant alignments, then, Zelda is prompting Irene to animate the words for which she is principal.

Note, however, that Zelda repeats the content of my question *who d'y'go bowling with?* from (a). This may account for Irene's repetition (in (f)) of what Zelda has asked for and her contrastive stress on *bowl*: i.e., if I had already asked about 'bowling' why should Zelda also be asking about 'bowl'? Following Irene's repetition of the slot that requires completion (the identity of "who you bowl with"), Zelda continues to prompt Irene in (g): in addition to appealing to shared knowledge (with *y'know,* Schiffrin 1987:chapter 9), she broadens the reference to *the teams.* In (h), Irene shows recognition with *oh* (Schiffrin 1987:chapter 4) and becomes more explicit (she refers to *the kids*)—nevertheless maintaining Zelda's role as promptor of information (as one who has the "right" answer "in mind") by asking for Zelda's confirmation (*Wha'd'y'mean the kids?*). Zelda has already begun to provide her own explicit meaning: *The kids* in (i) latches onto Irene's *Wha'd'y' mean.* In (j), Irene repeats the information given by Zelda: *oh yeh* shows that she is inserting it into the slot created by Zelda's prompting. Irene not only incorporates that information into her own contribution (*this year the kids have their own team*), but expands it into a brief narrative ((j), (l), (o)).[5]

(5) thus illustrates an alternative to speaking for another: rather than saying *Irene bowls with her kids,* Zelda prompts Irene to say this herself. Although it is Zelda's idea for Irene to include "the kids" in her answer, Zelda allows Irene to share responsibility for that information. In addition, Zelda brings Irene into the prompting process itself, such that they gradually build the mention of 'the kids' together, each giving the other just enough to allow that other to maintain an active stance in the conversation. Thus, although Zelda prompts Irene to animate that for which she is principal, she also allows her to share responsibility for the words.

An effort to prompt another to speak is also illustrated in (6); again, Irene is being prompted to tell me something, but this time it is Henry who is doing the prompting. Prior to (6), I had been asking Irene who she is friendly with; Irene is telling me how infrequently she sees her childhood friends.

(6) Irene: (a) I keep in touch with them y'know I go to
                   their affairs, but I don't *see* them that
                   often. One lives in Jersey and one lives up
                   in the Northeast.

     Debby: (b) Umhmm.
     Henry: (c) Tell her about the ⌈ girl you were real=
     Irene: (d)   ⌊ But-
     Henry: (e) =close:, you were raised, and they got money,
                   and they don't know you.

     Irene: (f) Who? Barbara? Oh. Well...
     Henry: (g) Well she wants t'know!
     Zelda: (h) Yeh but she's friends with her.
     Irene: (i) I talk to her occasion ⌈ ally,=
     Henry: (j)   ⌊ Yeh but=
     Irene: (k) = ⌈ but eh: she: she: has moved to Brookside=
     Henry: = ⌊ tell the way it is.=
     Irene: (l) = ⌈ and they have a whole new circle of eh:=
     Henry: (m) = ⌊ She wants t'know. She wants t'know.
     Irene: =friends. Y'know.

Although it is important to consider how responsibility for information emerges interactively and sequentially, it is helpful to begin by comparing how Henry prompts Irene in (6) to how Zelda prompted Irene in (5):

Zelda Prompts Irene (5)

Imperative
  Tell her 'X' (e)

Expands 'X'
  Creates Shared Knowledge
  D- y'know the teams. (g)

States 'X'
  The kids.(i)

Henry Prompts Irene (6)

Imperative
  Tell her about 'X'

Expands 'X' (c) (e)
  Lists Critical Events
    (4 narrative clauses)

Externalizes Need to Tell 'X'
  Well she wants t'know! (g)

Imperative
  Yeh but tell the way it is. (j)

Externalizes Need to Tell 'X'
  She wants t'know. (repeated) (m)

Henry and Zelda both initiate their prompts with the imperative *tell her;* both make explicit what Irene is to say and to whom she is to say it. However, the ways they pursue those prompts differ dramatically. In part, this difference is related to what they are prompting Irene to say: Henry wants Irene to reveal what is potentially embarrassing information, i.e., an incident in her own history that ended "badly." (Recall that this was essentially the outcome of (4), in which Henry spoke for Irene concerning the importance of being close to family; recall also that that forced Irene to reveal her failed venture into a family business.) Following their imperatives, Henry and Zelda both expand what it is that Irene is to tell me. These follow-up strategies display differences that can be seen as gender related: by listing four events recapitulating the experience that he wants Irene to report, Henry is "telling" Irene the answer, i.e., transferring information to her; by prefacing the information with a marker of shared knowledge, Zelda is "helping" Irene with the answer, i.e., collaborating in the production of information. In effect, then, Henry allows Irene little more than a role as animator; Zelda, however, allows Irene to share in the principal role.[6]

The prompting strategies diverge even further after the failure of the expansions to elicit the desired information. As we saw above, Zelda gives Irene the information—*The kids.* But Henry brings in an external justification for his persistent prompting: he couples a renewed imperative (*Yeh but tell the way it is.* (j)) with repeated assertions that I want the information that he is after: *She wants t'know* (m). Note, then, that Henry begins to speak for me: he uses me as an external validation for his own actions. Henry thus brings me back into the conversation, but with an altered role—as an addressed recipient—and the way he reevokes this role alters the agenda from the one I had established to one that he is directing.

Let us compare Irene's responses to both Henry and Irene:

Irene's Responses to Zelda

Who we *bowl* with. (f)
Oh. Wha'd'y'mean the kids? (h)
Oh yeh, this year the kids have
their own team [conts] (j)

Irene's Responses to Henry

Who? Barbara? Oh. Well... (f)
I talk to her occasionally, but
eh: she: she: has moved
t'Brookside and they have a
whole new circle of friends,
y'know (i) (k)

Irene's responses to Henry's initial prompt show reluctance to provide what he is after. Note that her first response (in (f)) is formally similar to her response to Zelda: Irene asks *who* and then offers a candidate identity (to Henry it is *Barbara?*; to Zelda, it was *we bowl with*). But following her recognition (*oh*) that this is indeed the "story" that Henry wants, she displays what seems like reluctance to go on with *well.....*: it is here that Henry brings me into the prompting process with *Well she wants t'know!* Note, however, what happens when Irene presents her eventual story (filled with hesitation about how to formulate what happened):

Irene:	(i)	I talk to her occasion⌈ ally, =
Henry:	(j)	⌊ Yeh but=
Irene:	(k)	= ⌈ but eh: she: she: has moved to Brookside=
Henry:		= ⌊ tell the way it is. =
Irene:	(l)	= ⌈ and they have a whole new circle of eh: =
Henry:	(m)	= ⌊ She wants t'know. She wants t'know.
Irene:		=friends. Y'know.
Debby:	(n)	⌊ Yeh. Got snobbish.
Henry:	(o)	Money makes a difference. =
Debby:	(p)	Yeh.
Henry:	(q)	=Money's important to a lot of people.
	(r)	It's a status.

The information that Irene presents (*I talk to her occasionally, but eh: she: she: has moved to Brookside and they have a whole new circle of eh: friends* (i)–(l)) seems to be what Henry has been after, since it is after Irene's short story that Henry presents a more general theme (*Money makes a difference* (o); *Money's important to a lot of people* (q)) that he (a lower middle class blue collar worker living near an affluent white collar suburb) has reiterated numerous times during our interviews. Yet Henry continues to prompt Irene during Irene's story: it is only after I present the "point" of the story (*Got snobbish* (n)) that Henry states his own theme. Thus, Henry's prompting continues until he is sure not only that what he had in mind has been said (animated by Irene) but, also, that it has been heard in a way consistent with the general theme that he is putting forth.

Observe, then, that Henry has done more than alter his footing in relation to Irene: he has shifted the structure of the discourse from a question/answer dialogue to a discussion of a general moral issue of which he is "in control" and to which he can orient his interlocutors. The continuation of (6) suggests that Henry is after still further restructuring:

Henry:	(r)	⌈ It's a status.
Debby:	(s)	⌊ D'you- Yeh.
	(t)	Its: works in funny ways.
Zelda:	(u)	Umhmm. That's exactly it.
	(v)	It ⌈ works in funny ways.
Henry:	(w)	⌊ D'you take a person for face value,
	(x)	or: or if they live in a big fancy house, does that make any difference to you?
Debby:	(y)	No. None at all.
Henry:	(z)	Well that's the way it should be.
	(aa)	You're a nice girl!

During Henry's restatement of his point (*It's a status* (r)), I begin to ask Irene a question (*D'you-* (s)) to recreate the question/answer structure of the interview. I quickly adapt my remarks to Henry's theme, however, even building upon that theme with *Its: works in funny ways* in (t). Zelda supports my statement of the theme (in (u)) with agreement tokens (*Umhmm. That's exactly it.*) and repetition (*It works in funny ways*). Although this is certainly the moral theme that Henry has initiated, Henry's interruption of Zelda (to ask me whether my own experience conforms to his view of what is right, beginning in (w)) rejects the collaborative nature of what Zelda and I have said to shift the participant structure still further from its earlier form. Recall that the interchange began with my asking Irene questions; Henry then evaluated Irene's answers, prompted Irene to shift her answers, and finally, asked me questions and evaluated my answers. Thus, what the question (*D'you take a person for face value, or: or if they live in a big fancy house, does that make any difference to you?* (w) (x)), answer (*No. None at all.* (y)), evaluation (*Well that's the way it should be. You're a nice girl!* (z) (aa) does is complete the restructuring of the participation framework to one in which Henry is "in charge."

We have seen in (6) that Henry prompts Irene to reveal potentially embarrassing information—information that is not exactly what I had requested, but information that allows Henry to state a general theme. We commented earlier that Henry allows Irene little more than a role as animator, and that his persistent prompting uses me as an external validator for his own actions. These strategies shift the discourse structure from one that I had established to one that Henry is directing: Henry's prompting continues until he is sure that what he had in mind has been said and heard in a way consistent with the general theme that he is putting forth. He also shifts the structure from one in which I ask questions to one in which I answer questions (and have my answers evaluated). Interestingly, the point that Henry is making is one that unifies us—Henry, Zelda, Irene, me—in a joint moral stance "against" another group. But the solidarity that is built not only is defined in opposition to another group (i.e., "we" are different from those who have more money because they reject us), but is also interactively constructed in a way that differentiates participant roles from one another and allows one speaker (Henry) to manage the way that others present and interpret information.

We began this section by proposing that Zelda's *She's on a diet* speaks for Irene in a supportive manner. We then compared Henry's use of this interactive move and found that rather than a way of building solidarity through positive politeness, Henry's use of this move gained control of participants' next moves and reoriented the direction of talk. Put another way, Zelda's realignments were inclusive and reinforcing: they allowed participants to continue their prior, relatively active, roles. Not only were Henry's realignments more divisive, but he also pursued them more completely, and they created more radical shifts in participant structure. Although differences such as these are consistent with prior work on gender and discourse, we have also seen that such differences can be based in the organization of participant structures, and that the way participant alignments are created, maintained, and shifted is an interactive process that can be replicated at different times during the course of interaction.

Framing in Sociolinguistic Interviews

We saw above that one way that interactants can display attributes that are interpreted as female or male is through the use of a particular interactive move (speaking for another) through which they manipulate participant structure. Although variationist analyses of speech produced during sociolinguistic interviews do not typically consider either the interactive moves, or the identity displays, that emerge during the course of an interview, I suggest later that the variety of identities displayed during a sociolinguistic interview needs to be taken into account when we analyze speech from such interviews (5.2). In this section, I consider in more detail how the social occasion itself—the sociolinguistic interview—provides an interactive frame for the participant structures and identity displays just described. We see that the realignments and identity displays are located at particular junctures within the interview frame.

I noted at the outset of this paper that a sociolinguistic interview is a particular kind of social occasion: it is a naturally bracketed spate of activity in which particular kinds of actions and behavior are expected (Goffman 1963). Those expectations provide a framework for interpreting what is said, e.g., for interpreting a question as seeking a particular kind of information. Furthermore, the relationship of those expectations to the interpretive processes guiding all social interaction can be made more or less explicit within an utterance. It seems clear that what those being interviewed by a sociolinguist expect (at least initially) is an agenda in which one person (thought of as "the interviewer") asks questions that they are to answer. Awareness of this agenda provides a dominant frame within which what is said is understood, and specific utterances may display their relevance to this frame. To take some obvious examples, if an interviewee closes an answer to a question with "Is that what you wanted?" we might say that she is conveying the metamessage "I am participating in an interview." Just as some remarks may convey in-frame activity, however, others may mark a section as out-of-frame activity: Zelda once asked me, for example, to turn my tape recorder off before she asked Henry to tell me a particular joke, thus marking Henry's joke as out-of-frame. Still other utterances reveal an activity as between-frame (e.g., "we better get back to these questions"; see discussion below) or make explicit the salience (or temporary lack of salience) of the interview frame (e.g., "you mean that tape recorder has been on all this time?!"). It is the switching between in-frame and out-of-frame utterances that gives sociolinguistic interviews their status as a kind of mixed genre: those utterances that are in-frame are what make such occasions seem more typical of the broader class of speech events known as interviews, and those that are out-of-frame are what make such occasions seem more like conversations.

I begin again with (1), for it shows an especially clear transition from out-of-frame talk to interview talk. Recall that this segment was prior to the interview itself: I had just explained how we would start our interview and was setting up my tape recorder and papers at the kitchen table. Thus, Henry's offer of candy (and the refusal and accounts that follow) occurred while the occasion itself was being opened—what might be called a "setting up" phase. Ongoing with the physical activities of setting up was a discussion about the unexpected death of a teacher from the neighborhood school; in fact, this was the main topic of our talk before the interview. (7) is the entire "setting up" section of the interview.[7]

(7) Henry: (a) Y'want a piece of candy?
     Irene: (b) No. ⌐   ⌐ I don't-=
     Zelda: (c)   ⌐ She's on a diet.
     Debby: (d)   Who's ⌐ NOT on a diet.
     Irene: (e) =I'm on a diet
             (f) and my mother ⌐ buys-=
     Zelda: (g)   ⌐ You're not!
     Irene: (h) =my ⌐ mother buys these mints.=
     Debby: (i)   ⌐ Oh yes I amhhhh!
     Zelda: (j)   Oh yeh.
     Irene: (k) The Russell Stouffer mints.
             (l) I said, "I don't want any Mom."
             (m) "Well, I don't wanna eat the whole thing."
             (n) She gives me a little tiny piece,
             (o) I eat it.
             (p) Then she gives me an ⌐ other,=
     Henry   (q)   ⌐ Was =
     Irene   (r) =so I threw it out the window=

Henry		=there a lot of people?=
Irene	(s)	=I didn't ⌈tell her.= ⌉
Henry	(t)	⌊Was there=⌋
Irene	(u)	=She'd kill me.
Henry		=a lot of people at the house?
Zelda:	(v)	All: the teach⌈ers.
Irene:	(w)	⌊A lot of teachers will-

probably will all be there till late.

Henry:	(x)	Je:sus Christ.
Zelda:	(y)	All: the teachers.
Henry:	(z)	What a heartache.
Zelda:	(aa)	And that Miss DiPablo? She was d- she must be her very best friend. She was there. She said she was with her all: week. She must be stayin' at her house!
Irene:	(bb)	Probably.
Zelda:	(cc)	⌈With-⌉
Debby:	(dd)	⌊Did⌋ it happen today?
Irene:	(ee)	⌈Saturday.⌉
Zelda:	(ff)	⌊No:⌋
Debby:	(gg)	Oh, oh.
Henry:	(hh)	⌈Damn shame.⌉
Irene:	(ii)	⌊All right,⌋ let's go.
Henry:	(jj)	All right.
Debby:	(kk)	Okay, who wants to go first?
Zelda:	(ll)	Oh: I'll go first.
Debby:	(mm)	Okay.
Zelda:	(nn)	I better get my glasses.
Debby:	(oo)	Okay.
Irene:	(pp)	Well I'll go first, then.
Debby:	(qq)	Okay.
Irene:	(rr)	What am I su- just read-
Debby:	(ss)	Just read them. Umhmmm.

The interchange in (7) can be clearly divided into two sections: (a) to (ii), (ii) to (ss). The first section is out-of-frame: i.e., it is preliminary to the interview. The second section is between-frame: i.e., it leads into the interview. These two sections are characterized by radically different topic structures and participant orientations.

Let us take the out-of-frame section first. It is here that Henry offers Irene candy (*Y'want a piece of candy?* (a)), Irene refuses (*No* (b)), Zelda provides an account for the refusal (*She's on a diet* (c)), and Irene tells a story further accounting for her refusal ((c)–(u)). Henry's question in (q) *Was there a lot of people?* overlaps with Irene's story to initiate a return to the main topic (the teacher's death); Irene and Zelda jointly answer Henry's question (*All: the teachers. A lot of teachers will- probably will all be there till late* (v), (w), (y)), and Henry evaluates the situation (*Jesus Christ. What heartache.* (x), (z)). Thus, the talk outside the interview frame in (7) has a relatively fluid topic organization: three topics (candy, diets, the teacher) cross cut one another with none rigidly reinforced by participants. In addition, turn selection (who speaks when) is, for the most part, a matter of self-selection, such that the participant roles of speaker and hearer are relatively available to any party.

The topic structure and participant orientation of the between-frame section are in dramatic contrast to the out-of-frame section just discussed. Critical to the shift in frame is Irene's *All right, let's go* (in (ii)). Note, however, the role of my question (*Did it happen today?* (dd)) that overlaps Zelda's elaboration of the situation ((aa), (cc)). Because of the asymmetry in information that my question reflects (i.e., I am seeking information that I do not have), it reveals my status as an outsider to the topic, thus displaying a participation framework more typical of the interview frame than of out-of-frame talk. Although Henry then continues out-of-frame (*Damn shame* (hh)), Irene offers me an answer (*Saturday* in (ee)) that fits the interview frame simply because it does no more than provide the information that I had requested. It is after Irene answers my question that we find the utterance (*All right, let's go*) that is critical to the frame shift: Irene overlaps Henry's evaluation to insert a topic preclosing (*all right* in (ii), Schegloff and Sacks 1973) that is followed by a directive (*let's go*) that makes explicit not only that there is an agenda (we are gathered together for a purpose) but that it is time to start attending to that agenda. Thus, Irene's *all right, let's go* does open between-frame talk, but this relatively global transition in frame has itself been eased by the fact that our prior question/answer exchange is exactly what one would expect of an interview.

Going on to the between-frame section ((ii) to (ss)) itself, we see that topic and participation framework are explicitly directed toward starting our agenda; in fact, it is these features that allow us to characterize this section as between-frame talk. Following Irene's *let's go* is a series of short turns through which participants accept Irene's proposal and negotiate the specifics of who is to do what when (i.e., begin reading the words in the word list). The topic of each turn is narrowly constrained toward the goal of getting us started with the task: Henry agrees with the proposed transition (jj); I agree and offer others the opportunity to self-select the order in which they will do the task (kk). I continue to allow the others latitude in the way they plan to fulfill the task: my repeated *okay*'s ((mm), (oo), (qq)) transfer responsibility to the others to take the next action (Merritt 1976)—whether that action is Zelda's offering to go first (ll), Zelda's saying she needs her glasses (nn), or Irene's offering to go in Zelda's place (pp). Once it is decided that Irene goes first, responsibility for instructing the others in performance of the task is clearly transferred to me: note Irene's question about what she is supposed to do (rr). Thus, what gives this segment its status as between-frame talk is that both topic and participation are oriented toward making a transition to the main agenda: the topic is task-driven and participation rights are allocated and relatively circumscribed by the nature of the task.

As we have just seen, the interchange in (7) moves from being outside the interview frame to within the interview frame: speaking for another was part of out-of-frame talk, and it maintained the out-of-frame definition of the situation. Note, however, that the utterance which prompted Zelda to speak for Irene was a question from Henry: *Y'want a piece of candy?*[8] We see the importance of this in a moment.

We have just seen that *She's on a diet* was part of an interchange preliminary to the interview itself. When considered at this level of analysis, in relation to in-frame or out-of-frame talk, the examples of speaking for another considered in this paper seem to relate to the interview frame in a variety of ways. In (3), (4), and (5) Henry and Zelda both maintained the interview frame, but slightly altered the allocation of participants into the question/answer format (especially when they asked questions with me). In (3) and (6), Henry altered the interview from an in-frame question/answer exchange to an out-of-frame series of challenges and defenses (his evaluation of Irene's answer to one of my questions forced Irene to respond directly to him). Thus speaking for another can occur either within or outside the interview frame, and it can either change or maintain a current frame.

The variety of relationships within the interview frame per se, however, obscures a surprising constancy at a more micro level of analysis. Although speaking for another varied in terms of its relation to the overall interview frame, it was restricted at a local level of analysis to question/answer exchanges, an exchange type typically located at the crux of the interview frame itself. I present the key sections from earlier examples below, as (8).

(8) Realignments during Question/Answer Exchanges

(1)	Q	Henry:	(a)	Y'want a piece of candy?
	A	Irene:	(b)	No.
		Zelda:	(c)	She's on a diet.
(3)	Q	Debby:	(a)	Well, Irene, is there anybody around here that you would call a best friend?
	A	Zelda:	(e)	No, we're not her best friends, we're her neighbors!
(4)	Q	Debby:	(a)	How 'about you Irene?
	Q	Zelda:	(d)	Who would you discuss it with?
	A	Zelda:	(f)	Jayhhhhh
(5)	Q	Debby:	(a)	Yeh, who d'y'go bowling with?
	Q	Zelda:	(e)	Tell her who you bowl with.
		Zelda:	(g)	D- y'know the teams.
	A	Zelda:	(i)	The kids.
(6)	Q	Debby:		Do you still see your old friends?

A   Irene: (a)   I keep in touch with them y'know I go
                        to
                        their affairs, but I don't *see* them that
                        often. One lives in Jersey and one lives
                        up in the Northeast.
Q   Henry: (c)   Tell her about the girl you were real
                        close:, you were raised, and they got
                        money, and they don't know you.

Zelda and Henry either redo my question (as in (4) (5) and (6)) or provide
information bearing on Irene's answer (as in (1) (3) (4) and (5)). The
questions that I asked—the questions evoking others to speak for me or for
Irene—were all interview questions that were part of my agenda (but see
comment on (1) below). Thus, the realignments discussed in this paper
were initiated within an exchange type firmly situated within the interview
frame.

The fact that questions can trigger participant realignments should not
be surprising. Questions are often thought to be moves that seek to control
what happens next: they not only other-select the occupant of a next turn
(Sacks, Schegloff, and Jefferson 1974), but define the sequential relevance
of a next move (as a conditionally relevant answer (Schegloff 1972)) and
restrict its topic. It is precisely because questions provide so much information about what comes next that another speaker can step so easily into the
exchange to provide an answer or to comment on another's answer.

When Zelda and Henry speak for me and redo my questions, they are
entering the question/answer exchange from a more controlling position
within the exchange. I believe that what is responsible for these realignments is related to the identities and relationships that we brought to the
interview: I was interviewing people who were familiar with one another,
but not with me. Questions engage others in response: they create a mo-
mentary involvement in a topic in which one person reacts to what another
has said. When I asked Irene questions, then, I was, in effect, excluding
those who know her well from interacting with her. By redoing my questions, Zelda and Henry could not only bring speech from an outsider (me)
into a realm of the familiar (an interaction with their neighbor), but maintain and display their involvement with someone with whom their relationship would endure past the interview. And the strategy through which they
do so is one that they also use during out-of-frame talk (as we saw in
discussion of (1)): thus, they bring a strategy that can be outside the interview frame into the crux of the interview itself.

We have seen in this section that sociolinguistic interviews are occasions
in which particular utterances and exchanges can be in, out of, or between
the interview frame. Some acts of speaking for another stayed within the
interview frame, and still others altered that frame. But because speaking for
another was always initiated during a question/answer exchange, we also

saw that realignments could be proposed from within an exchange endemic to the interview frame itself.

Conclusion

I began this chapter by noting that speech from a particular social occasion provides data for sociolinguistic studies of the speech community and suggesting that discourse analysis can be used to enhance the methodological value of such data. I then analyzed how a particular interactive move could alter participant alignments and display identity within sociolinguistic interviews. We saw some of the different ways that interactants could position themselves relative to one another, and how such positionings helped to frame participants' sense of what was going on during the interview itself. In this concluding section, I want to consider in slightly more detail how participation frameworks and identity displays are related to the frames through which we interpret talk (5.1). I then briefly suggest how such analyses can further the methodological reciprocity between variationist and interactional approaches in sociolinguistics (5.2).

Participation Frameworks, Identity Displays, and Frames

The creation of a participation framework can evoke very local interpretive frames that can guide participants in their assignments of sequential relationships among utterances, and thus in their discovery of coherence. I support this proposal by first considering speaking for another in relation to other strategies for showing sequential coherence and as an act through which one person takes the role of another.

Frames and Sequential Coherence

Participants in a social interaction are both constrained by—and constructors of—the institutional and interactional orders (i.e., the contexts) in which they find themselves. Utterances (the use of language) have a critical role in this codependency between self and context simply because they provide information: a current utterance provides information that creates a range of potential contexts to which a next utterance can respond. Put another way, language evokes a number of potential frames (both institutional and interactional) within which a next utterance can be interpreted.

It is easiest to illustrate how language can locate utterances as part of a particular frame with an example of an institutional exchange. Consider, for example, the utterance *Drink?*. When said by a bartender to someone sitting at a bar, we understand *Drink?* as an offer to sell something (or as a directive to place an order) in a particular kind of service encounter; we also know that an appropriate response might be *Michelob*, but not *No thanks, I'm not thirsty.* Because *Drink?* would not be understood as an offer to sell a drink in other contexts (e.g., during a dinner party) or among different participants in the same setting (e.g., if said by one customer to another), *Drink?* reflects its institutional setting. It also helps to create an interpretation of the setting as one in which a service encounter is taking place in a way that other utterances might not, i.e., to evoke the frame of "service encounter."

Utterances can also reflect and create the particulars of different interactional frames. If we take Irene's refusal (*no*) of Henry's offer of candy (*Want a piece of candy?*) as a current utterance, we can imagine a number of different next utterances from Henry.

(9)   Henry: Want a piece of candy?
        Irene: No.   [current utterance]
        Henry: (a)   Oh c'mon.   [possible next utterances]
                (b)   There's nothing wrong with it!
                (c)   Suit yourself.
                (d)   Just testing you! I know you're on a diet.
                (e)   What?
                (f)   I didn't hear you.
                (g)   What time did the teachers leave?
                (h)   Y'know I bought this candy at that new place
                       in the mall, and when I was there [continue]

The utterances in (9) select different aspects of Irene's *No* as a basis for response, and in so doing, they provide an interpretive frame for the utterance pair. Some utterances in (10) are clearly linked to the prior offer/refusal sequence itself ((a)–(d)), whereas others are tied to more mechanical and general aspects of language production ((e)–(f)); still others provide the prior offer/refusal pair with an additional sequential identity, e.g., as a side sequence (g) or as a lead into a new topic (h). As I noted above, what is important about this range of responses (and certainly more could be added; see Goffman (1981:68–70), on which this example is modeled) is that each next utterance selects a slightly different aspect of the current utterance as a basis from which to respond, and in so doing, it provides an interpretive frame in which not only the next utterance, but the entire utterance pair, can be understood. Put another way, a next utterance is a slot in which a speaker can both respond to, and retroactively create, a prior frame.

The framing illustrated above has a general importance for discourse analysis because it provides another way of getting at the problem of sequential coherence. As I have been suggesting, the utterances in (9) reflect not just the variety of ways that a current utterance can be understood, but a variety of different frames for understanding talk—as action sequences ((a)–(d)), as language production ((e), (f)), as topic structures ((g), (h)). Thus, what makes all of the utterances in (9) interpretable as sequentially coherent is the availability of different interpretive frames for talk— different ways of contextualizing what is said. Each frame provides a different basis for understanding how one utterance follows another—a different resource for sequential coherence.

Taking the Role of the Other

Consider, now, that another resource in the repertoire of frames being described is the participants in talk themselves: self and other. That is, just as a next utterance can evoke a frame in which coherence is located through the interpretation of actions, the mechanics of language production, the development of topics, and so on, so too can a next utterance evoke a frame in which coherence rests upon attention to the participants in talk itself.

Let us take the self first; some different ways that the self can become a resource, again, for Henry's next utterance, are illustrated in (10):

(10)   Henry: Want a piece of candy?
       Irene: No.
       Henry: (a)   Yeh, I shouldn't have any either.
                (b)   Right, I forgot you're on a diet.
                (c)   Oh- I meant fruit.
                (d)   It annoys me when you don't take candy.
                (e)   I admire your will power.

As (10) illustrates, a next utterance can draw upon the self in a number of different ways: it can be a comment about one's own action ((a), (b)), a self-repair (c), or the expression of a personal sentiment ((d), (e)).

Just as the self can be a resource for response, so, too, can the other; (11) illustrates some ways—roughly parallel to those in (10)—that the other can be a basis for Henry's next utterance:

(11)   Henry: Want a piece of candy?
       Irene: No.
       Henry: (a)   You never accept my offers.
                (b)   You're on a diet again.
                (c)   Did you say no?
                (d)   You're stubborn about that diet.

Just as a response can focus upon the self in relation to an action, so too can it focus upon the other ((11a), (b)); similarly, a response can be either a self-repair or an other repair (11c); it can offer an assessment of the self or the other (11d). Thus, there are numerous ways that a next utterance can draw upon the other as a basis for response.

Speaking for another is an act that provides sequential coherence by drawing upon the other as a resource for a next utterance. It is different from the acts listed in (11) because it is an act confined to a three (or more) party interaction: i.e., a spokesperson animates the words of another (a principal) to an addressed recipient. But more critically, speaking for another displays an interpersonal stance in which a spokesperson not only uses the other as a basis for a next utterance, but enters into the other's perspective to issue a next utterance from that other's point of view. Thus, speaking for another is a way of "taking the role of the other."

Viewing speaking for another as a way of taking the role of the other helps to explain its interactional meanings. We have already conveyed these meanings in terms of Brown and Levinson's (1987) notion of face: speaking for another can be interpreted in a negative sense as "butting in" or a positive sense as "chipping in"—glosses that reveal interpretations of the act as either a violation of negative face (cf. "You're always putting words in my mouth") or a display of positive face (cf. "You know me so well you can read my mind!"). And as we saw in our earlier examples, the way an other-based next utterance is treated depends, in part, on what is said about the other: although negative assessments of the other (as in (4)) were violations, positive assessments (as in (5)) could actually reinforce self/other solidarity. Here I want to suggest even more: taking the role of the other is an act that reflects the process of interaction itself. Although not often mentioned in recent retrospectives of Goffman's work (e.g., Drew and Wootton 1988, Ditton 1980), the notion of taking the role of the other is critical to the foundations of his perspective precisely because it is critical to the interaction process. George Herbert Mead (1934), a social psychologist whose development of the perspective of symbolic interactionism influenced much of Goffman's early work, argued that neither the self nor language could fully emerge until children were able to anticipate others' responses to their own actions (not just particular others' responses, but also the "generalized" other of one's culture and community). Although anticipating another's response is critical to the emergence of conversational competence, this process by no means ends once we are socialized. Rather, taking the role of the other remains a critical part of interaction itself, but in a slightly broader guise. Not only is much of what we say explicitly oriented toward reception by a hearer, but speaking a language is itself a process that requires symbolically putting oneself in the other's place in order to know how to tailor one's information (syntactically, semantically, and pragmatically) so that it will be comprehensible to that other. Speaking for another thus represents the ritualization—the formal display—of a process that is at the very crux of social interaction: speaking for another can be seen as the linguistic submersion of the self in the interactive process.

Interactional Analyses of Sociolinguistic Interviews

I began this paper by noting that just as sociolinguistic interviews can benefit discourse analysis, so, too, can discourse analysis be methodologically useful for those analyzing speech collected during such interviews. I then analyzed a particular interactive move within sociolinguistic interviews with the help of the interactional concepts and constructs of frame, participant alignment, and identity display. In closing, I briefly note some methodological consequences of my analysis of speaking for another for sociolinguists whose data are drawn from interviews.

Many variationist analyses of speech produced during sociolinguistic interviews take as axiomatic Labov's (1972) demonstration that there are no single-style speakers: people's attention to speech varies (depending in part on topic, medium, and interlocutor) and such variation helps produce different styles. The way speaking for another alters participant alignments and reframes the question/answer structure of the interview can be related quite nicely to the distinctions upon which variationists depend when they code style differences. Labov (1972) suggests that answers to questions (at least the initial, most topic relevant part of an answer) are careful speech, but that informants' talk to one another is casual speech. Recall that Zelda and Henry spoke for Irene (and for me) during question/answer exchanges, and that the resulting realignments became group discussions in which Irene, Henry, and Zelda spoke to one another. In Labovian terms, then, we might say that speaking for another is a way in which informants themselves transform the interview frame and, by so doing, provide themselves with a route by which to shift styles.

My analysis also suggests that just as style changes during the course of an interview, so, too, does identity. Informants speak in a variety of voices during an interview (including, but not limited to, the voice of interviewee) and locate themselves not only inside the interview frame, but distinctly outside it as well. We have seen, for example, that the way people speak for one another during an interview allows them to locate themselves relative to the interview frame and to display a gender identity. What this suggests is that even identities thought to be relatively independent of particular occasions of talk are at least partially situated in particular social occasions. Variationists can build upon such insights to reconceptualize their notion not just of gender, but of other social categories, and on a very practical level, to rethink the way identity should be coded: just as variationist studies already build into coding procedures the belief that there are no single-style speakers, so, too, can they incorporate the idea that identity is dynamic and is mutually constitutive with the organization of talk.

In closing, it is important to note that there are many social occasions other than sociolinguistic interviews during which a person who represents a dominant social institution seeks to gain information about the lives, beliefs, and practices of people outside that institution. Briggs (1986:1), for example, notes:

> Interviewing has become a powerful force in modern society. Starting almost from birth, we are confronted by questions posed by educators, psychologists, pollsters, medical practicioners, and employers, and we listen to flamboyant interviewers on radio and television.

Thus, the interactive move described here may very well occur in other interviews: perhaps people create multiple voices and realign participant structures both inside and outside of the interview frame in other types of interviews as well.

Appendix: Transcription Conventions

.   falling intonation followed by noticeable pause (as at end of declarative sentence)

? rising intonation followed by noticeable pause (as at end of interrogative sentence)

, continuing intonation: may be slight rise or fall in contour (less than '.' or '?'); may be followed by a pause (shorter than '.' or '?')

! animated tone

... noticeable pause or break in rhythm without falling intonation (each half-second pause is marked as measured by stop watch)

- self interruption with glottal stop

: lengthened syllable

italics emphatic stress

CAPS very emphatic stress

When speech from A and B overlap, the starting point of the overlap is marked by a left-hand bracket, and the ending point of the overlap is marked by a right-hand bracket.

A: Do you know what time the party's supposed ⌈ to start? ⌉
B: ⌊ Six o'clock. ⌋

When lack of space prevents continuous speech from A from being presented on a single line of text, then '=' at end of first line and '=' at beginning of second line shows the continuity.

A: Do you know what time the party's supposed ⌈ to start?= ⌉
B: ⌊ Six o'clock. ⌋
A: =Because I have to work late tonight.

When a speech from B follows speech from A without perceptible pause, then ⌐ links the end of A with the beginning of B.   ⌐
                                                                                └

A: Do you know the time? ⌐
 ·   B: └ Six o'clock.

When speech from B occurs during what can be heard as a brief silence from A, then B's speech is under A's silence.

A: I can't wait to go to the party!   It'll be fun.
B: Oh yeh!

Notes

1. By speaking for Irene (and occasionally for me), Henry and Zelda are displaying the important interaction between age based status and speaking rights; parents, for example, speak for children more than the other way around. Although Henry and Zelda sometimes speak for each other, I have not found any instances where Irene speaks for either Zelda or Henry; Irene does, however, speak for her own 10-year-old daughter, who is briefly present during one interview, and she does engage in other kinds of realignments with both Zelda and Henry.

2. Note also the constant stream of new diet books and the prevalence in our culture of food-related neuroses. Interestingly, however, there are also opposing values, e.g., the association between weight and prosperity (I have heard portly men

described as prosperous looking) or the idea that we have "to fatten up" to be healthy.

3. As I noted earlier, Henry is overweight (more so than Irene), and elsewhere, he talks about how thin he was when he was young, and how he plans to lose weight when he eats more fish over the summer (since fish is lower in calories than meat). Thus, we might expect Henry to avoid the topic of diet precisely because he is overweight and he is the one who is eating candy.

4. Note that the role of *should* (a modal of obligation) is critical here, for it invokes Henry as an authority about Irene's own affairs. We can see the importance of *should* quite easily by imagining that, instead of saying *she's on a diet*, Zelda has said either *She should be on a diet* or *You shouldn't take it*. Regardless of whether reference to Irene is third person (as an unaddressed recipient) or second person (as an addressed recipient), we would interpret Zelda as invoking authority—and as being as intrusive as Henry. Similarly, if instead of saying *she should be*, Henry had just said *she used to be* and had then gone on with his description of Irene's family, we would be more likely to interpret Henry as building solidarity with Irene.

5. Although we are not focusing upon it here, note that Henry does some of the same interactional work in (5) seen earlier in (4)—although here, what he provides is a positive assessment of Irene's situation with her kids and kids in general. Because Henry's supportive endorsements of Irene's behavior are still forms of evaluation, however, it is still a stance based on status differentiation rather than inclusion.

6. These efforts to prompt another to provide information are similar to clarification requests: the difference is that instead of asking A for clarification about what A has said, B tries to get A to provide what B thinks should be a self-clarification (cf. Schegloff, Jefferson, and Sacks's 1977 other-initiated self-repair). Note, also, that both information prompts and clarification requests can vary in terms of who takes what part in reaching the target information; cf. Ochs's (1985) distinction between a minimal grasp strategy (B abdicates responsibility to A) and an expressed guess strategy (B offers to share responsibility with A).

7. Because the conversation about the teacher had been in progress before I turned the tape recorder on, I do not have a record of it and cannot include it in (7).

8. Earlier I spoke of *Y'want a piece of candy?* as an offer, and here I am calling it a question. In Schiffrin (forthcoming,b:chapter 4), I show that this utterance has multiple functions as question, request for information, and offer.

References

Bell, Allen. 1984. Language style as audience design. Language in Society 13:145–204.

Briggs, Charles. 1986. Learning how to ask. Cambridge: University Press.

Brown, Penelope, and Stephen Levinson. 1987. Politeness. Cambridge: University Press.

Bennett, Adrian. 1978. Interruptions and the interpretation of conversation. Proceedings of the 4th Annual Meeting of the Berkeley Linguistics Society, University of California, Berkeley.

Deakins, Alice. 1989. Talk at the top: Topics at lunch. Manuscript, William Patterson College.

Ditton, John. (ed.) 1980. The view from Goffman. New York: St. Martin's Press.

Drew, Paul, and Anthony Wootton (eds.) 1988. Erving Goffman: Explaining the interaction order. Cambridge: Polity Press.

Gilligan, Carol. 1982. In a different voice: Psychological theory and women's development. Cambridge: Harvard University Press.

Goffman, Erving. 1963. Behavior in public places. New York: Free Press.

Goffman, Erving. 1967a. On face-work: An analysis of ritual elements in social interaction. Interaction ritual, ed. by Erving Goffman, 1–49. New York: Anchor Books.

Goffman, Erving. 1967b. The nature of deference and demeanor. Interaction ritual, 49–95. New York: Anchor Books.

Goffman, Erving. 1971. Supportive interchanges. Relations in public, 62–94. New York: Basic Books.

Goffman, Erving. 1974. Frame analysis. New York: Harper and Row.

Goffman, Erving. 1981a. Introduction. Forms of talk, 1–4. Philadelphia: University of Pennsylvania Press.

Goffman, Erving. 1981b. Footing. Forms of talk, 124–59. Philadelphia: University of Pennsylvania Press.

Goffman, Erving. 1981c. Replies and responses. Forms of talk, 5–77. Philadelphia: University of Pennsylvania Press.

Goodwin, Marjorie Harness. 1990. Tactical uses of stories: Participation frameworks within girls' and boys' disputes. Discourse Processes 13:33–71.

Gumperz, John. 1982. Discourse strategies. Cambridge: University Press.

Labov, William. 1972. The isolation of contextual styles. Sociolinguistic patterns, 70–109. Philadelphia: University of Pennsylvania Press.

Labov, William. 1984. Field methods of the project on linguistic change and variation. Language in use, ed. by John Baugh and Joel Sherzer, 28–53. Englewood Cliffs, NJ: Prentice-Hall.

Labov, William, and David Fanshel. 1977. Therapeutic discourse. New York: Academic Press.

McDermott, Ray. 1988. Inarticulateness. Linguistics in context: Connecting observation and understanding, ed. by Deborah Tannen, 37–68. Norwood, NJ: Ablex Publishing.

Mead, George Herbert. 1934. Mind, self and society. Chicago: University of Chicago Press.

Ochs, Elinor. 1985. Clarification and culture. Meaning, form, and use: Linguistic applications, ed. by Deborah Schiffrin, 325–41. Washington, DC: Georgetown University Press.

Paradis, Claude. Forthcoming. Interactional conditioning of linguistic heterogeneity. Festschrift for William Labov, ed. by Gregory Guy, John Baugh, and Deborah Schiffrin.

Rickford, John. 1993. Addressee and topic controlled style shift: A quantitative sociolinguistic study. Perspectives on register, ed. by Edward Finegan and Doug Biber. Oxford: Oxford University Press.

Schegloff, Emanuel, Gail Jefferson, and Harvey Sacks. 1977. The preference for self-correction in the organization of repair in conversation. Language 53:361–382.

Schiffrin, Deborah. 1984a. Jewish argument as sociability. Language in Society 13:311–335.

Schiffrin, Deborah. 1984b. How a story says what it means and does. Text 4(4):313–346.

Schiffrin, Deborah. 1987. Discourse markers. Cambridge: University Press.

Schiffrin, Deborah. 1990. The principle of intersubjectivity in communication and conversation. Review of Talbot Taylor and Deborah Cameron, Analyzing conversation and Lauri Carlson, 'Well' in dialogue games. Semiotica 80:121–151.

Schiffrin, Deborah. 1991. The organization of lists in everyday discourse. Talk presented at Cognitive Science Colloquium, University of California, Berkeley.

Schiffrin, Deborah. forthcoming (a). The transformation of experience, identity, and context. Festschrift for William Labov, ed. by Gregory Guy, John Baugh, and Deborah Schiffrin.

Schiffrin, Deborah. forthcoming (b). Language as social interaction: Sociolinguistic approaches to discourse. Oxford: Basil Blackwell.

Tannen, Deborah. 1984. Conversational style: Analyzing talk among friends. Norwood, NJ: Ablex.

Tannen, Deborah. 1989. Talking voices: Repetition, dialogue, and imagery in conversational discourse. Cambridge: University Press.

Tannen, Deborah. 1990. You just don't understand: Women and men in conversation. New York: William Morrow.